COMPUTER SCIENCE, TECHNOLOGY AND APPLICATIONS

EXPERT SYSTEM SOFTWARE

ENGINEERING, ADVANTAGES AND APPLICATIONS

COMPUTER SCIENCE, TECHNOLOGY AND APPLICATIONS

Additional books in this series can be found on Nova's website
under the Series tab.

Additional E-books in this series can be found on Nova's website
under the E-book tab.

COMPUTER SCIENCE, TECHNOLOGY AND APPLICATIONS

EXPERT SYSTEM SOFTWARE

ENGINEERING, ADVANTAGES AND APPLICATIONS

JASON M. SEGURA

AND

ALBERT C. REITER

EDITORS

Nova Science Publishers, Inc.

New York

For permission to use material from this book please contact us:
Telephone 631-231-7269; Fax 631-231-8175
Web Site: http://www.novapublishers.com

NOTICE TO THE READER

The Publisher has taken reasonable care in the preparation of this book, but makes no expressed or implied warranty of any kind and assumes no responsibility for any errors or omissions. No liability is assumed for incidental or consequential damages in connection with or arising out of information contained in this book. The Publisher shall not be liable for any special, consequential, or exemplary damages resulting, in whole or in part, from the readers' use of, or reliance upon, this material. Any parts of this book based on government reports are so indicated and copyright is claimed for those parts to the extent applicable to compilations of such works.

Independent verification should be sought for any data, advice or recommendations contained in this book. In addition, no responsibility is assumed by the publisher for any injury and/or damage to persons or property arising from any methods, products, instructions, ideas or otherwise contained in this publication.

This publication is designed to provide accurate and authoritative information with regard to the subject matter covered herein. It is sold with the clear understanding that the Publisher is not engaged in rendering legal or any other professional services. If legal or any other expert assistance is required, the services of a competent person should be sought. FROM A DECLARATION OF PARTICIPANTS JOINTLY ADOPTED BY A COMMITTEE OF THE AMERICAN BAR ASSOCIATION AND A COMMITTEE OF PUBLISHERS.

Additional color graphics may be available in the e-book version of this book.

Library of Congress Cataloging-in-Publication Data

Expert system software : engineering, advantages, and application / editors, Jason M. Segura and Albert C. Reiter.
     p. cm.
 Includes index.
 ISBN 978-1-61209-114-3 (hardcover)
 1. Expert systems (Computer science) 2. System design. I. Segura, Jason M. II. Reiter, Albert C.
 QA76.9.E96E952 2010
 006.3'3--dc22
                            2010047019

Published by Nova Science Publishers, Inc. † New York

CONTENTS

PREFACE

This new book presents current research in the study of expert system software, including algorithms based on paraconsistent annotated logic in expert systems; expert flow systems in the agronomical, industrial, environmental, pharmaceutical and geological fields; expert systems in remote sensing; domain-wide expert system applications; modeling a parser as an expert system; embedded expert systems for flow control of delay sensitive real-time traffic in WLANs; expert systems in fund-raising management and algebraic approaches in the development of rule based expert systems.

Chapter 1 - In this chapter, the authors present functional algorithms based on the Paraconsistent Annotated logic for the treatment of information signals; and thus, able to perform as the main nucleus, analysis and decision within expert systems. The method presented is based on the fundamental concepts of Paraconsistent Annotated logic with annotation of two values (PAL2v). The PAL2v is a non-classic Logic that admits contradiction. In this chapter, a study using mathematical interpretation for a lattice representation is described, where algorithms and equations give an effective treatment on signal information that represent situations found in an uncertainty knowledge database. The authors present a logical-mathematical basis with the necessary visualization for obtaining these values for the degrees of evidence by illustrating degrees of certainty and degrees of contradiction in a PAL2v representative lattice. From these equations, algorithms are elaborated and utilized in computation models by Paraconsistent Systems for the treatment of uncertainties. It is then verified that these PAL2v algorithms possess easy implementation for a variety of computation languages. This therefore proves as a satisfactory method to view performance demands as a strong tool, capable of treating signals that generate uncertainties, as those originated from inconsistent and contradictory information. These algorithms were tested in small computational programs and are now being developed for great applications, mainly in the analysis of Overload Risk in Power Electric Systems. In this chapter, some significant application examples are presented in this area. The authors' results conclude that the paraconsistent reasoning system built according to the methodology extracted from the PAL2v notions reveals itself to be more efficient than the traditional ones, since it is able to work decisions on uncertainties in the information, with no interference from the appearance of conflict existing in the data that is received for analysis.

Chapter 2 - The flow analyzers are a powerful tool for large-scale analyses, and their potentialities are enhanced when computer-controlled discretely operated devices such as pumps, stream directing valves, injectors or commuters are used. This chapter is focused on the exploitation of these devices for accomplishing the different flow-based strategies required for the specific analysis, such as merging zones, zone sampling, stream splitting, flow reversals, sample stopping, etc. A discussion on multi-commutation is also included. Emphasis is not given to software flow charts but to the exploitation of the flow analyzer own software.

Expert flow systems relying on feedback mechanisms are dealt with too. These systems generally involve a preliminary assay and the analytical result is used to feed the software with information for real-time decisions. The need for in-line sample dilutions, sample replacement, activation of devices, as well as further optional sample handling is then real-time defined. The chapter ends up by highlighting applications in the agronomical, industrial, environmental, pharmaceutical and geological fields.

Chapter 3 - Expert systems have been an active research field in remote sensing. This chapter gives an overview about expert systems and reviews the current progress in applications of expert systems in remote sensing. Many expert systems have been implemented for remote sensing applications such as image classification, feature extraction, change detection. Remotely sensed data are the input to the expert systems i.e.mostely images, but also LIDAR data and synthetic Aperture Radar (SAR). The basic terminology of expert systems is given first, followed by a review of the major component of expert System, then the classification of expert systems methodologies has been stated, after that applications of expert systems in remote sensing have been reviewed. An overview of software that has been used for implementation of expert systems for remote sensing applications has been given. This chapter ends with discussion of some important issues and challenges as well as potential directions for further developments.

Chapter 4 - This chapter addresses the use of multiple expert systems and varieties of multiple expert systems are categorized. A special category is described of multiple expert systems that belong to the same problem domain and have certain characteristics. A notion of equivalent entities is developed that permits a linkage between the expert systems in such a way that they may be used in combination. A distinction is made between domain-level procedures (or queries) that may be applied to any individual expert system in the domain, and domain-wide procedures that are applied using all, or more than one expert system. Domain-wide procedures make use of domain-specific equivalence functions. Examples are drawn from two quite different areas – namely transport and academia, and equivalence in these areas is discussed. XML is used to define the problem domains and Prolog is used to implement knowledge bases, equivalence functions and procedures.

Chapter 5 - A parser is an essential component in all compilers. In many compilers, the parser acts as the main routine with all other components functioning in its hegemony. Parsers are used not only in compilers but also in other software tools like interpreters, query processors and natural language processors. The process of parsing is a complicated one. Therefore, a large number of studies both theoretical and experimental have been undertaken over the years to standardize the process. Nevertheless, the researchers still continue working on the advancement of the science and technology of parsing.

This chapter presents a parser modeled as an expert system. Modeling the parser as an expert system allows the use of different types of heuristics to facilitate the parsing process and makes it faster. The next section provides the details of the parser while the section after that discusses a compiler that uses the parser.

Chapter 6 - This chapter introduces an embedded expert system for flow control of delay sensitive real-time traffic inWireless Local Area Networks (WLANs). The expert system is based on the fuzzy set theory. It adjusts tranceivers' traffic flow(s) for prevailing network conditions to achieve maximum throughput in required application dependent delay limits. In wireless networks delay and throughput are very much dependent on the packet size, packet transmission interval, and the node connection density. Therefore, the expert system on the destination node monitors congestion by measuring an average one-way delay and a change of one-way delay of the incoming traffic. Thereafter it adjusts packet size and transmission interval of the source node by transmitting a control command to the source.

A linguistic decision making model of the expert system is described by linguistic relations. The linguistic relations form a rule base that is converted into numerical equations for tranceiver's computational efficiency. The developed congestion and flow control method does packet size definition by at most 56 computations. In the system level, the feedback control increases only lightly communicational load by transmitting application level acknowledgements after every 200 received packets.

The model was valitated by simulating User Datagram Protocol (UDP) traffic in OMNeT++ network simulator. The achieved results demonstrate that the developed expert system is able to regulate packet sizes and transmission intervals to the prevailing optimum level very fast, accurately and with minimal overshoot and to increase overall throughput of the network. Even if this work is mainly motivated by the congestion and flow control of WLAN systems and the simulations and results were performed for the IEEE 802.11b system, the approach and the techniques are not limited to these systems, but are easily applicable for other Packet Switched Access Networks (PSANs), too.

Chapter 7 - In social economy a great attention is devoted to nonprofit organizations, whose mission's fulfillment is strongly related to the success of fund raising strategies. Then a decision support system for optimizing them is very useful. Using associations donors database a fuzzy expert system has been developed, which is able to suggest the best strategies with respect to donors profiles. This system integrates the profiles with a model for historical information evaluation and operative rules suggested by experts in the field and related literature. There are however many little and medium size organizations which don't own or efficiently manage the donors database. In these cases another approach has been proposed, which is able to individuate the most promising raising strategies on the basis of the features of the association. The profile factors of a nonprofit association are widely explored and hierarchically organized in a decision tree, in order to effectively employ the Choquet integral methodology, which is recommended in these kind of multi-criteria decision problems.

In the present contribution, some extensions are developed in order to enhance the first approach. In particular an integration with the second methodology is proposed, by substituting some fuzzy components with a hierarchic organization of the knowledge, that allows to use also in this context the Choquet integral, with an improvement of the tuning process and of the computational effort required. Moreover a wide analysis of donors features is performed; the donors interests evolution is managed, allowing a more precise characterization of the donors profile; an *utility function* approach is developed as extension of the expected gift model; new elements in the management process are modeled. The results obtained in a real operational context show the effectiveness of the proposed improvements.

Chapter 8 - Based on previous mathematical results, questions related to consistence and tautological consequence in rule based expert systems can be translated into algebraic terms. Different algebraic approaches can be obtained depending the representation paradigm used. In this Chapter the authors will describe these algebraic approaches and show how to take advantage of them to implement easily different rule based expert systems. Mastering logic and computer algebra techniques is not required, as the Chapter should be suitable for unacquainted readers.

Chapter 9 - Expert systems are being applied with success in multiple fields like engineering, medicine, geology, chemistry, etc., for the realization of diverse tasks (interpretation, prediction, diagnosis, design, planning, instruction, control, etc.). Some of these applications in these fields include:

- Inside engineering: The management and design of Telecommunication Networks.
- Inside medicine: Disease Detection.
- Inside power supplies: Fraud Detection.

In this chapter, the authors will give an overview of the applications of Expert Systems in these fields. On the other hand, the author swill describe case studies of real problems solved in diverse projects carried out by the authors, explaining, from the experience of the authors, how to deal with such problems. The projects that will be described are the following ones:

- An expert system for the management of an ionospheric communication.
- An expert system for an efficient network management.
- An expert system for automatic routing of a HFC telecommunication network.
- An expert system for the diagnosis of stomach disorders.
- An expert system for the detection of frauds in a power supply.

All these expert systems have been developed by the group of authors in the Electronic Technology Department of the University of Seville (Spain).

Chapter 10 - This chapter examines Fuzzy Inference Systems (FIS) applications in mining industry using a recent literature review (2000-2010) in engineering and earth science oriented journals. Initially the basic principles of Fuzzy Logic and Fuzzy Inference Systems are presented and an illustrative example of a FIS application, for the evaluation of multiple-layer lignite deposits, is given. FIS applications from the literature review were classified into three main categories corresponding to the major activities of the mineral industry: mineral exploration, mine exploitation and mineral processing. Selected papers from each category are presented and finally, the advantages as well as the trends in future development are discussed.

In: Expert System Software
Editors: Jason M. Segura and Albert C. Reiter
ISBN: 978-1-61209-114-3
© 2012 Nova Science Publishers, Inc.

Chapter 1

ALGORITHMS BASED ON PARACONSISTENT ANNOTATED LOGIC FOR APPLICATIONS IN EXPERT SYSTEMS

*João Inácio da Silva Filho**

UNISANTA- Santa Cecília University,
GRAPL- Group of Research in Application of Paraconsistent Logic,
Santos-SP, Brazil

ABSTRACT

In this chapter, we present functional algorithms based on the Paraconsistent Annotated logic for the treatment of information signals; and thus, able to perform as the main nucleus, analysis and decision within expert systems. The method presented is based on the fundamental concepts of Paraconsistent Annotated logic with annotation of two values (PAL2v). The PAL2v is a non-classic Logic that admits contradiction. In this chapter, a study using mathematical interpretation for a lattice representation is described, where algorithms and equations give an effective treatment on signal information that represent situations found in an uncertainty knowledge database. We present a logical-mathematical basis with the necessary visualization for obtaining these values for the degrees of evidence by illustrating degrees of certainty and degrees of contradiction in a PAL2v representative lattice. From these equations, algorithms are elaborated and utilized in computation models by Paraconsistent Systems for the treatment of uncertainties. It is then verified that these PAL2v algorithms possess easy implementation for a variety of computation languages. This therefore proves as a satisfactory method to view performance demands as a strong tool, capable of treating signals that generate uncertainties, as those originated from inconsistent and contradictory information. These algorithms were tested in small computational programs and are now being developed for great applications, mainly in the analysis of Overload Risk in Power Electric Systems[1]. In this chapter, some significant application examples

---

* Oswaldo Cruz Street, 288 Santos-SP Brazil CEP- 11045-000. E-mail: *jinacsf@yahoo.com.br*.
[1] The algorithms of the Paraconsistent Logic are interlinked with Networks Analysis and are used for signal treatment originated by a Database (SCADA-Supervisory Control and data acquisition) and in the creation of Paraconsistent Expert Systems for support to the operation of Electric Power Systems. The first work

are presented in this area. Our results conclude that the paraconsistent reasoning system built according to the methodology extracted from the PAL2v notions reveals itself to be more efficient than the traditional ones, since it is able to work decisions on uncertainties in the information, with no interference from the appearance of conflict existing in the data that is received for analysis.

Keywords: expert systems, treatment of uncertainties, paraconsistent logics, Algorithms, Artificial Intelligence.

I. INTRODUCTION

The systems operating on data processing often face uncertainties and contradictions because, in most of the cases, the database which is to be worked is generally incomplete or it is not exact. Hence, the information treatment project must be ready to deal with these adverse situations. Data processing systems that deal with uncertainty knowledge must be able to represent, manipulate, and communicate data which is considered imperfect. Most of the time, the data we conventionally call imperfect are often those representing inaccurate, inconsistent, partially ignored, and incomplete information.

I.1. Treatment of Uncertainties

The presence of uncertainty in data for a system that is based on knowledge processing can occur from a variety of information sources. Among these information sources, we should mention some we know to have partial reliability; some present inaccuracy that stem from the representative language in which the information is shown; others may not show complete information as those that summarize or aggregate information from multiple sources. In the area of treatment where signals are extracted from non-exact knowledge there are many formal models available for the treatment of uncertainties, but in many cases these proceedings have been achieved through approaches based on combinations and representations of rules that are not supported by a well-established theory, or provide well-defined semantics. Among the more traditional approaches in use for the modeling and treatment of uncertainties one may find:

1. The Bayes rule.
2. The modified Bayes rule.
3. Certainty factor, based on confirmation theory
4. Dempster-Shafer theory.
5. Possibility theory or Fuzzy logic.
6. Default processing.
7. Theory of approximate groups.

developed was for the Electric Systems of Potency of AES Eletropaulo - Concessionary Company of Electric power in Brazil, in the area of the State of São Paulo - and in the Electric Power Systems of EDP – Escelsa - Concessionary Company of Electric power in Brazil, in the area of Espírito Santo State.

8. Rough Set Theory.

An intelligent system for decision making must be strong and well-established to meet certain theoretical criteria. It therefore needs to be supported by an adequate treatment of uncertainty theories that will allow for possibilities within certain limits, that provide some verification, independent from its application. Based on these considerations, a system for evaluating uncertainty measures must follow a certain number of criteria, and can be classified by the following:

1. *The system must be capable of generating results to present a satisfactory interpretation:* The uncertainty measure must be meaningful, clear and accurate enough to justify conclusions. Therefore the result must be presented clearly and accurately as possible so that the system is able to conclude and start its correspondence actions. Clearness and accuracy will permit rules to be established that will combine results and update values.
2. *The system must be capable of tackling non-exact information:* The uncertainty measure must be capable of modeling partial or incomplete ignorance of conflicting or limited information, as well as inaccurate displays of uncertainty.
3. *The system must be capable of permitting calculation for non-exact values:* In the processing of uncertainty values there must be rules to combine uncertainty measures, update them when there is new evidence of information and use them on the calculation of other uncertainties that allow conclusions which are capable of offering subsidies for decision-making.
4. *The system must be capable of presenting consist results:* For the treatment of uncertainties the system must supply methods to permit the verification for consist uncertainties to be displayed in all the default suppositions. The calculation rules must ensure that the conclusions are consist with all displays and suppositions supported by the method of treatment by the uncertainty utilized.
5. *The system must be able provide good computation for the involved data*: In uncertainty treatment the values must be computationally factual so it enables the system to set inference rules and obtain conclusions. In the treatment of data with non-exact values the system must allow for the combination of qualitative evaluations with quantitative non-exact values.

The methods presented for uncertainty treatment use the basic concepts and theoretical fundamentals of Paraconsistent logic that illustrate a quantitative evaluation through its representative Lattice. All manners of application and results are obtained through Paraconsistent Annotated Logic with annotation of two values (PAL2v) fundamentals.

II. PARACONSISTENT SYSTEMS FOR TREATMENT OF UNCERTAINTIES

Many possibilities within the non-classic family of logic has shown as its main purpose is the revocation of the third-excluded principle. This non-classic logic is called paraconsistent logic. Paraconsistent Logic therefore is a non-classic logic that repeals the principle of non-contradiction and takes the treatment of contradictory signals in its theoretical structure.

II.1. The Paraconsistent Logics

A summary of the theoretical principles that sustain paraconsistent logics may be seen as thus:

- It is common knowledge that the enunciations demonstrated as true in theory are called theorems. And if all sentences formulated in language are theorems, they are called trivial. We also know that a theory is consistent if among its theorems there are none that affirm something which is a negation of other theorems in the same theory. If this fact does occur then the theory would be called inconsistent.

A given theory (deductive) T, belonging to logics L, it is said to be consistent if among its theorems there are none which cause negation of the other. For a contrary hypothesis, T is said to be inconsistent. The T theory is called trivial if all sentences (closed formula) of its language are theorems; if that does not occur, T is non-trivial.

If L is one of the common logics, as classic, the T theory is trivial if and only if it is inconsistent.

The L logics is called Paraconsistent if it can work with inconsistent and non-trivial theories. This means that apart from particular circumstances that are not within our range, paraconsistent logic is capable of manipulating inconsistent systems with no danger of trivialization.

The pioneers of paraconsistent logics were the Polish logician *J. Lukasiewicz* and the Russian philosopher *N.A. Vasilév*, who simultaneously around 1910, independently suggested the possibility of a logic which would restrict the principle of contradiction.

The initial systems of Paraconsistent logics, that contain all logic levels, with propositionals, predicates, and descriptions, as well as superior order logics, are credited to N.C.A. Da Costa (1954 onwards). It happened in an independent manner, and there are, currently, paraconsistent systems of set theory, strictly stronger than the classic ones considered as paraconsistent subsystems.

The appearance of non-classical logics and, more specifically, the paraconsistent logics with new concepts closer to reality were considered and have contributed to obtaining models and tools capable of manipulating contradictions and ambiguities, thus enabling the development of new technologies.

II.2. The Paraconsistent Annotated Logic (PAL)

The Paraconsistent Annotated Logic (PAL) is a class of evidential logic that treats the signals represented by annotations. For each annotation there is a finite lattice that attributes a value for the corresponding proposition p. A Paraconsistent Annotated Logic can be represented as a finite lattice of "four states" (figure 1), where the propositional sentence will be followed by an Evidence degree. Therefore, an Annotated sentence associated to the Lattice of the Paraconsistent Annotated Logic can be read in the following way:

$P_{(T)}$ ==> the annotation or Evidence Degree T assigns a connotation of 'inconsistency' to the proposition P.

$P_{(t)}$ ==> the annotation or Evidence Degree t assigns a connotation of 'truth' to the proposition P.

$P_{(F)}$ ==> the annotation or Evidence Degree F assigns a connotation of 'falsehood' to the proposition P.

$P_{(\perp)}$ ==> the annotation or Evidence Degree $\perp$ assigns a connotation of 'indefinity' to the proposition P.

The annotation may be composed of 1, 2 or n values, depending on the paraconsistent logic utilized.

III. THE PARACONSISTENT ANNOTATED LOGIC WITH ANNOTATION OF TWO VALUES - PAL2v

The Paraconsistent Annotated Logic with annotation of two values (PAL2v) is an extension of PAL and it can be represented through a Lattice of four vertexes where we can determine some terminologies and conventions, as following:

Be $\tau = \; <|\tau|, \leq>$ a fixed finite lattice, where:

1. $|\tau| = [0, 1] \times [0, 1]$
2. $\leq = \{((\mu_1, \rho_1), (\mu_2, \rho_2)) \in ([0, 1] \times [0, 1])^2 \,|\, \mu_1 \leq \mu_2 \text{ e } \rho_1 \leq \rho_2\}$ (where $\leq$ indicates the usual order of the real numbers).

In this case, an operator $\sim$ is introduced:

$$|\tau| \rightarrow |\tau|.$$

where the operator $\sim$ constitutes the "meaning" of the logical symbol of negation $\neg$ of the system to be considered. Intuitively, the constants in the vertex of a lattice will show logical states extreme to the propositions.

- indicates the minimum of $\tau = (0.0, 0.0)$;
- T indicates the maximum of $\tau = (1.0, 1.0)$;
- *sup* indicates the operation de supreme.
- *inf* indicated the operation of ínfimo.

It is possible to obtain a representation on how accurate the annotations or evidences are on proposition P using a Lattice formed by ordained pairs, such as:

$$\tau = \{(\mu, \lambda) \,|\, \mu, \lambda \in [0, 1] \subset \Re\}.$$

This way, a four-vertex Lattice associated with the Paraconsistent Annotated logic with annotation of two values (PAL2v) may be presented as in figure 1.

The first element (μ) in the ordained pair is the degree in which the favorable evidences support the proposition P, and the second element (λ) represents the degree in which the unfavorable evidences, or contrary, deny or reject the proposition P. Thus, the intuitive idea of the association of a annotation (μ, λ) to a P proposition means that the Favorable Evidence Degree in P is μ, and the Unfavorable Evidence degree (or contrary evidence Degree) is λ.

In a intuitive manner, in such a Lattice we have the annotations:

$P_{(\mu, \lambda)}$ ==> $P_{(1, 0)}$ indicating existence of total favorable evidence (μ=1) and unfavorable evidence zero (λ=0), attaching a true connotation logical to proposition P. This Vertex represents the "True" logical state.

$P_{(\mu, \lambda)}$ ==> $P_{(0, 1)}$ indicating existence of favorable evidence zero (μ=0) and total unfavorable evidence (λ=1), attaching a connotation logical of falsity to proposition P. This Vertex represents the "False" logical state.

$P_{(\mu, \lambda)}$ ==> $P_{(1, 1)}$ indicating existence of total favorable evidence (μ=1) and total unfavorable evidence (λ=1), attaching an inconsistency connotation logical to proposition P. This Vertex represents the "Inconsistent" logical state.

$P_{(\mu, \lambda)}$ ==> $P_{(0, 0)}$ indicating existence of favorable evidence zero (μ=0) and unfavorable evidence zero (λ=0), attaching an indetermination connotation logical to proposition P. This Vertex represents the "Indeterminate" logical state.

Intuitively one can read the formula $P_{(\mu,\lambda)}$ as P is believed with favorable evidence until μ and unfavorable evidence until λ".

The formula ($\neg A$) is read "the negation, or weak negation, of A"; ($A \wedge B$), "the conjunction of A and B"; ($A \vee B$), "disjunction of A and B" and ($A \rightarrow B$), "the implication of B by A."

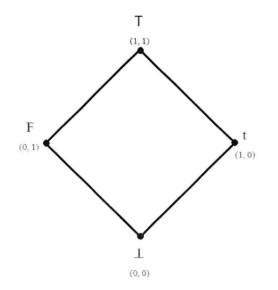

$$P_{(\mu, \lambda)}$$
T = Inconsistent = $P_{(1, 1)}$
F = False = $P_{(0, 1)}$
t = True = $P_{(1, 0)}$
$\perp$ = Indeterminate = $P_{(0, 0)}$

Figure 1. Four-vertex PAL2v Lattice τ.

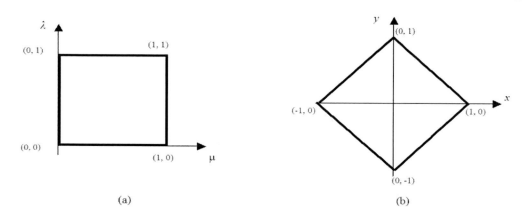

Figure 2. (a) Unitary Square on the Cartesian plane USCP. (b) τ Lattice supplied with a new system of coordinates.

In this way, the Lattice associated at Paraconsistent Annotated logic with two-values annotations is formed, where:

$$\tau = \{(\mu, \lambda) \mid \mu, \lambda \in [0, 1] \subset \Re\}$$

If P is a basic formula, the operator $\sim : |\tau| \rightarrow |\tau|$ is defined as $\sim [(\mu, \lambda)] = (\lambda, \mu)$ where, $\mu, \lambda \in [0, 1] \subset \Re$. And (μ, λ) is considered a P Annotation.

IV. ALGEBRAIC INTERPRETATIONS OF PAL2v IN A UNITARY SQUARE ON THE CARTESIAN PLANE

For a better representation of this annotation, and also for the practical uses of the τ Lattice in the treatment of uncertainties, some algebraic interpretations involving a Unitary Square on the Cartesian plane (USCP) and a Lattice of the PAL2v will be made. Initially a system of Cartesian coordinates is adopted for the plane, and the annotations of a given proposition P will be represented by points of the plane.

We call Unitary Square on the Cartesian plane - USCP the τ diagram with the system of coordinates, as proposed in figure 2(a). Therefore, there is an association of T to (1, 1), ⊥ to (0, 0), F to (0, 1) and t to (1, 0). In USCP the values of Favorable Evidence Degree μ are exposed in the axis x, and the values of Unfavorable Evidence Degree λ in the axis y. For each adopted system of coordinates, the annotations (Favorable Evidence degree μ, Unfavorable Evidence degree λ) of τ are identified by different points in the plane. In the system of figure 2(a) a given annotation (μ, λ) may be identified with the point of the plane in another system. As a system of coordinates may be fixed on τ, we then define transformations between USCP and $\mathcal{L}$, which will be the Lattice τ with another system of coordinates.

As it was done in USCP, in this $\mathcal{L}$ lattice we can associate T to (0, 1), ⊥ to (0, -1), F to (-1, 0) e t to (1, 0). This way, the intended $\mathcal{L}$ Lattice will be supplied with the following system of coordinates, as in figure 2(b).

For each adopted system of coordinates, the annotations (μ, λ) of τ are now identified with different points in the plane. We may, then, consider one more system of coordinates which can be fixed for τ. We have defined transformations between USCP and the $\mathcal{L}$ Lattice. Thus, $\mathcal{L}$ may be obtained from USCP through three phases; change in scale, rotation, and translation. For a better understanding, these three phases are now detailed:

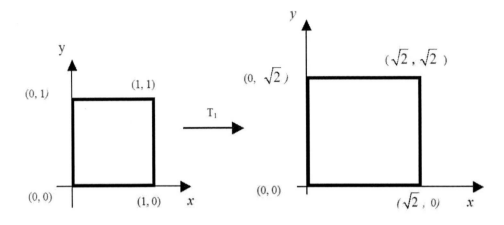

Figure 3. Increase in the USCP scale of $\sqrt{2}$.

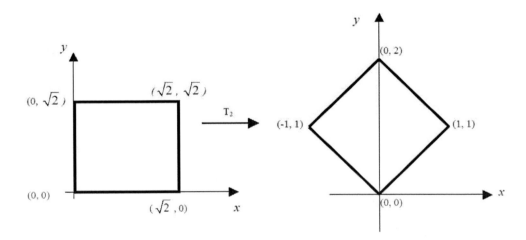

Figure 4. A 45° rotation in relation to the origin.

IV.a. Increase the Scale of $\sqrt{2}$ (as in figure 3)

The increase in the scale is given by the linear transformation:

$$T_1(x, y) = (\sqrt{2}x, \sqrt{2}y) \text{ ; whose matrix is: } \begin{bmatrix} \sqrt{2} & 0 \\ 0 & \sqrt{2} \end{bmatrix}$$

IV.b. A 45° Rotation in Relation to the Origin (as in figure 4)

This rotation in relation to the origin is given by the linear transformation:

$$T_2(x, y) = \left(\frac{\sqrt{2}}{2} x - \frac{\sqrt{2}}{2} y, \frac{\sqrt{2}}{2} x + \frac{\sqrt{2}}{2} y \right); \text{ whose matrix is: } \begin{bmatrix} \frac{\sqrt{2}}{2} & -\frac{\sqrt{2}}{2} \\ \frac{\sqrt{2}}{2} & \frac{\sqrt{2}}{2} \end{bmatrix}$$

IV.c. Translation (as in figure 5)

This translation is given by:

$$T_3(x, y) = (x, y - 1)$$

Through the composition $T_3 \circ T_2 \circ T_1$ we obtain the transformation represented by the equation:

$$T(x, y) = (x - y, \ x + y - 1) \tag{1}$$

The $\mathcal{L}$ Lattice will be the LPA2v Lattice τ with another system of coordinates.

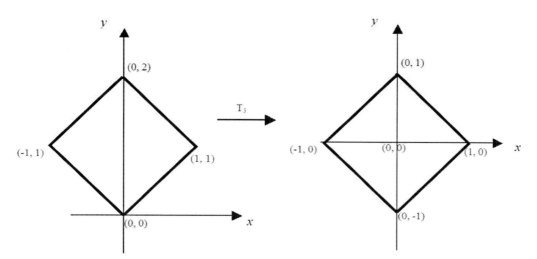

Figure 5. Translation of values between USCP and the PAL2v Lattice.

IV.1. The Certainty Degree D_C and the Contradiction Degree D_{ct}

In the transformation equation (1) we may convert points of USCP, that represent annotations of τ in points of $\mathcal{L}$, also represent annotations of τ. Combining the components of the transformation of the equation (1) as the usual elements of the PAL2v logic, we obtain:

$x = \mu$ Favorable Evidence Degree

$y = \lambda$ Unfavorable Evidence Degree

From the first term obtained from the ordered pair from the equation of the transformation (1), we have:

$x-y = \mu - \lambda$, is the denominated Certainty Degree D_C. Therefore, the Certainty Degree is obtained by:

$$D_C = \mu - \lambda \qquad\qquad (2)$$

These values belong to a set of Real numbers, $\Re$, that vary in the closed interval +1 and -1, and are in the horizontal axis of the Lattice, called "degrees of certainty axis."

When D_C is +1 it means that the logical state result from the paraconsistent analysis is True (t), and when D_C is -1 it means that the logical state result from the paraconsistent analysis is False (F).

From the second term obtained from the ordered pair in the transformation equation (1), we have:

$x+y-1 = \mu+\lambda - 1$, which is denominated Contradiction Degree D_{ct}. Therefore, the Contradiction Degree is obtained by:

$$D_{ct} = \mu + \lambda - 1 \qquad\qquad (3)$$

These values belong to the set of Real numbers, $\Re$, that vary in the closed interval +1 and -1, and are in the vertical axis of the Lattice, called "degrees of contradiction axis."

When D_{ct} is +1 it means that the logical state result from the paraconsistent analysis is Inconsistent ($\top$), and when D_{ct} is -1 it means that the logical state result from the paraconsistent analysis is Indeterminate ($\bot$).

IV.2. Obtain Evidence Degrees from the Values of the Certainty Degrees D_C and the Contradiction Degrees D_{ct}

When considering the values of the Certainty degrees D_C and of Contradiction degree D_{ct} we may obtain the values of the annotations represented by the Favorable μ and Unfavorable λ degrees of evidence.

For the linear transformations F_1, F_2 e F_3 the respective reverse of T_1, T_2 e T_3, the point $T(\mu, \lambda)$ obtained by the transformation T is represented by the Certainty degrees D_C and by the

Contradiction D_{ct}, obtained in $\mathcal{L}$, which may be considered a Lattice associated to PAL2v, as in the fundamentals of PAL2v previously seen. Changing x by μ and y by λ the inverse transformation $F(x, y)$ is:

$$F(\mu, \lambda) = \left(\frac{1}{2}D_C + \frac{1}{2}D_{ct} + \frac{1}{2}, \ -\frac{1}{2}D_C + \frac{1}{2}D_{ct} + \frac{1}{2} \right) \tag{4}$$

We then have in possession of T and F, it is indifferent working in the USCP or in the $\mathcal{L}$ Lattice, because we may find values that are interchangeable through T and F, as in figure 6.

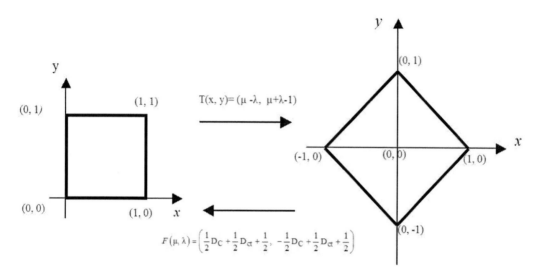

Figure 6. Conversion of values between USCP and the PAL2v Lattice.

IV.3. Logical Operations in a Unitary Square on the Cartesian Plane - USCP and in the PAL2v Lattice

In this analysis, PAL2v is a paraconsistent value and by definition represented by an atomic formula, in the form of:
$P_{(\mu, \lambda)}$ where in the annotation (μ, λ)

- μ represent the Favorable Evidence Degree to the proposition P;
- λ represent the Unfavorable Evidence Degree to the proposition P.

Together with these paraconsistent values, other operations in USCP are defined as thus:
Given two paraconsistent values P_1 and P_2 in USCP, with coordinates (μ_1, λ_1) and (μ_2, λ_2), respectively, we define $\neg P_1$ (logical negation) as the coordinates point: (λ_1, μ_1)
And $\neg P_2$ (logical negation) as the coordinates point: (λ_2, μ_2)

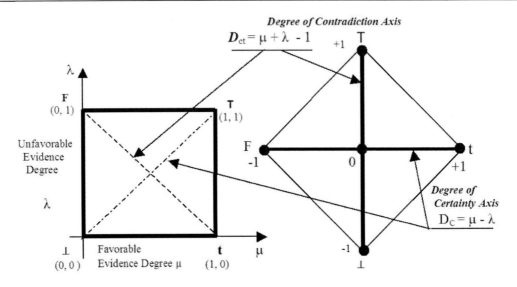

Figure 7. Representation of the *certainty* and *contradiction* axes of the PAL2v lattice with values.

We also define $P_1 \lor P_2$ (disjunction) as the paraconsistent value of the coordinates:
(min { x_1, x_2 }, max { y_1, y_2 })
and $P_1 \land P_2$ (conjunction) with the following coordinates: *(max { x_1, x_2 }, min { y_1, y_2 })*.

V. SYSTEM TREATMENT OF UNCERTAINTIES FOR DECISION-MAKING WITH PAL2v

In a paraconsistent decision-making system the Evidence degrees μ and λ are values contained in the closed interval between 0 and 1, and they belong to a set of Real numbers $\Re$. These two values come from two or more sources of information which look for favorable evidence, and are contrary in relation to the same proposition P.

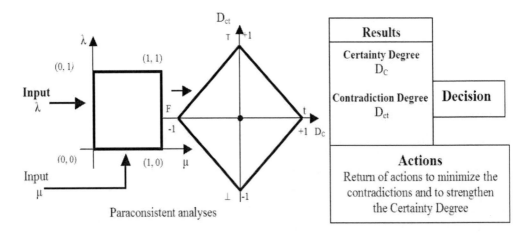

Figure 8. Typical system for paraconsistent analysis with two inputs.

Since the information originated from different sources, these may have equal values, representing a consistence; or different, representing a contradiction. As a variation between 0 and 1, as defined from different sources, the Certainty Degree D_C and the Contradiction Degree D_{ct}, result in values between +1 and -1 which quantify the certainty and the inconsistence, respectively.

The equations and analysis in the PAL2v representative Lattice give us these degrees on the values to express how close or near from the four vertexes of the associated PAL2v Lattice.

A typical treatment system for uncertainties using the Paraconsistent Logic with annotation with two values -PAL2v for analysis and decision-making may be seen in figure 8.

V.1. Study of the PAL2v Lattice for Treatment of Uncertainties

In the origination of PAL2v application, the degrees of evidence which feed the system for the treatment of uncertainties are the valued information obtained from a variety of sources, or from different specialists. Let us consider, then, two sources of information which send to the system evidence signals in relation to a certain proposition P_1, defined as such:

- μ_1 - signal sent by source of information 1.
- μ_2 - signal sent by source of information 2.

For the paraconsistent analysis, we should consider both sources of information as part of the annotation and gather them in a propositional formula. This incorporation results in a Logical Paraconsistent signal of the type $P_{(\mu, \lambda)}$, where:

- $\mu_1 = \mu$ Favorable Evidence Degree to the proposition P.
- $1-\mu_2 = \lambda$ Unfavorable Evidence Degree to the proposition P.

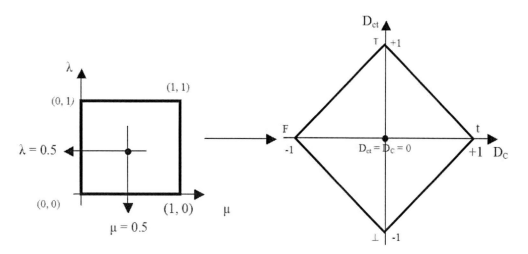

Figure 9. Zero degree of certainty and contradiction obtained from indefinite degrees of evidence.

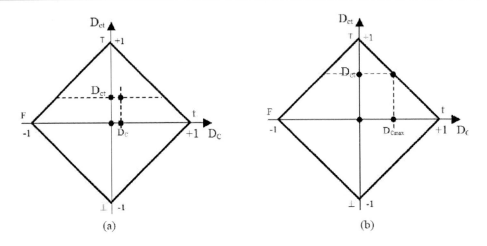

Figure 10. (a) Low intensity of evidence. (b) maximum Certainty Degree limited by the Contradiction Degree.

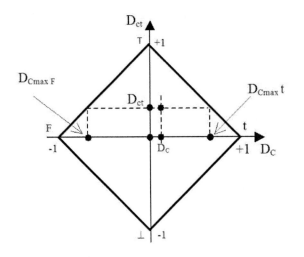

Figure 11. Representation in the Lattice shows the maximum values in the Degrees of Certainty with constant Contradiction Degree.

For example, if information source 1 presents to the system a valued signal representing a favorable evidence of $\mu_1=0.5$, and the information source 2 presents a valued signal representing a favorable evidence also of $\mu_1=0.5$; a defined correlation is then established.

As shown in Eqs. (2) and (3), the application of these two values in the USCP will result in a zero Certainty Degree ($D_C=0$), and also a zero Contradiction Degree ($D_{ct}=0$).

The zero degree of certainty means that the information sources do not show enough evidence to support an increase or a refutation of the P proposition.

So, each analyzed source of information sends to the system values for Indefinition valued as 0.5. That is, the input opinion is both 50% favorable evidence and 50% unfavorable evidence, defining the result of the analysis to a zero degree of certainty in relation to the proposition in question. However, whenever the paraconsistent analysis presents a low degree of certainty as a result, two situations must be taken in consideration:

1. The sources of the analysis has a low evidence intensity to allow the affirmation or to allow the denial of the proposition *P*.

In this case, the sources or specialists supplying this evidence lack information to feed the system for analysis. That is why they present information signals with indefinite values, close to 0.5. This way, a source of information (specialist, sensor, etc...) whenever it is not active, will present as its value $\mu=0.5$, and the result from the interpolation point between the values of D_C and D_{ct} in the Lattice will be close to the origin of each axis.

This condition can be seen in figure 10.a.

2. The sources of the analysis shows high evidence intensity with high contradiction.

In this case, the sources of information are sending values strong enough for the system to evaluate and present results affirming or denying the proposition. But, in spite of all the existing information for analysis, there is a contradiction among the sources that carries the results for a low degree and it limits the Certainty Degree of the analysis. In this case, the interpolation point between the values of D_C and D_{ct} will fall on the limit line of the Lattice.

From this point, it can be seen that the Certainty degree D_C will only advance to one of the maximum certainty values if there is a decrease on the value of the Contradiction degree D_{ct}.

The value of D_C may move in the direction of logical state True or in the direction of logical state False. This condition can be seen in figure 9.b.

V.2. The Interval of Certainty φ

When the Certainty Degree is low due to insufficient information, and not because by a high Contradiction Degree, the system conditions strengthen the values for the degrees of evidence applied to the inputs. In this case, the evidence must be strengthened until the Certainty Degree reaches a maximum value appropriate for the decision making. We can see in the Lattice of figure 11 that when given two values D_C and D_{ct}, the value of the Contradiction Degree permits variation in the value of the Certainty Degree. There will be an axis of certainty values with a maximum value degree for the extreme condition when the vertex considers a logical state True. This value is named maximum Certainty Degree favorable to the true, $D_{Cmax}t$. In the Lattice of the same figure, we can see the axis of the values of certainty, the maximum value degree for the extreme condition when the vertex considers a logical state False. This value is named maximum Certainty Degree favorable to the False, D_{CmaxF}.

When using the paraconsistent analysis system for decision making, the treatment of uncertainties is done by considering all the information, be them incomplete, indefinite, or inconsistent. This way, there can be a representation of an interval in values of certainty where the Certainty Degree may vary without being limited by the Contradiction Degree. This Interval is represented by φ, and it will be calculated by:

$$\varphi = 1 - |D_{ct}| \qquad (5)$$

V.3. Representation of the Resulting Certainty Degree

By application of the PAL2v concepts, the analyse result for the Certainty Degree information as represented by the degrees of evidence, will provide indication of how much the system may be strengthened in its evidence to increase the certainty in relation to the proposition P.

The Certainty Degree will then be represented by its D_C calculated value, together with another value which will indicate the Interval of Certainty given by φ. Therefore, the analysis representation of the resulting signal obtained will be:

$$D_{Cr} = \begin{bmatrix} D_C \\ \varphi \end{bmatrix}$$

(6)

where:

D_{Cr} = resulting Certainty Degree
D_C = calculated Certainty Degree, obtained by: $D_C = \mu - \lambda$
φ = Interval of Certainty, obtained by: $\varphi = 1 - |D_{ct}|$

The calculated Certainty Degree D_C shows that the values of the degrees of evidence by the given inputs, determine how much certainty can be given to the proposition P.

The Interval of Certainty φ shows how possible, given the level of inconsistency among the information input signals, the introduction of new evidence that is able to vary the certainty in relation to the proposition P in question.

This indication, represented by the Interval of Certainty φ, is the maximum value, be it in the sense of affirmation as in the sense of refuting the proposition P. We consider, then, that the value of the interval of certainty shows which will be the maximum negative Certainty Degree obtained by decreasing the affirmation (favorable evidence) and increasing the denial (unfavorable evidence). In this case, the result is closer to the logical state considered *False*.

Conversely, the value of the Interval of Certainty shows which will be the maximum positive Certainty Degree obtained by increasing the affirmation (favorable evidence) and decreasing the denial (unfavorable evidence). In this case, the result is closer to the logical state considered *true*.

In these cases, variations indicated by the interval of certainty without alterations in the value of the Contradiction Degree, it being constant, are permitted.

In the representation of the Interval of Certainty φ, the positive (+) or negative (-) signs are added to the symbol. This sign will show if its absolute value was originated by a positive Degree of Contradiction, favoring to the logical state of Inconsistent, or if from a negative Contradiction Degree, favoring to the logical state of Indeterminate. This way, after the end of a paraconsistent analysis, the representation of the output result will be as such:

$$D_{Cr} = \begin{bmatrix} D_C \\ \varphi_{(\pm)} \end{bmatrix}$$

(7)

where:

D_{Cr} = resulting Certainty Degree
D_C = calculated Certainty Degree, obtained by: $D_C = \mu - \lambda$
φ = Signaled Interval of Certainty, obtained by: $\varphi = 1 - |D_{ct}|$
If $D_{ct} > 0$ $\varphi = \varphi_{(+)}$
If $D_{ct} < 0$ $\varphi = \varphi_{(-)}$

V.4. Estimated Degree of Certainty

We have shown the analysis result of PAL2v presents the calculated Certainty Degree D_C and the Interval of Certainty φ, obtained from valued signals representing the evidence in relation to the proposition P in question. Using these two values, it is possible to make decisions, because after the conclusion of the paraconsistent analysis, the value of the Interval of Certainty φ will inform the system the level of increasing or decreasing evidence to get the maximum value of certainty. Besides, with the value and the signalization of the Interval of Certainty, it is possible an estimation of the signals of evidence, if favorable or unfavorable, and which value should suffer variation to reach the desired Certainty Degree.

The Contradiction Degree is obtained by Eq. (2)., The Interval of Certainty is obtained by Eq. (4). Thus, the procedure of estimating the values is done this way:

- it is possible to see that, in case there is high inconsistency among the information, the value of the Contradiction Degree is high, and, as a consequence, the Interval of Certainty decreases. For a Contradiction Degree equivalent to 1 the value of φ is zero, and in these conditions, the value of the Certainty Degree is zero. This means that the contradiction among the evidence is so high that no affirmation or refutation can be achieved in relation to the proposition P in question.

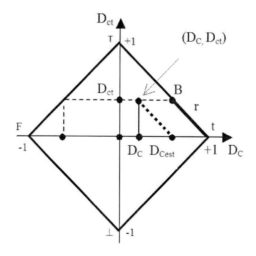

Figure 12. Representation of the Estimated Certainty Degree in the zero Contradiction Degree condition.

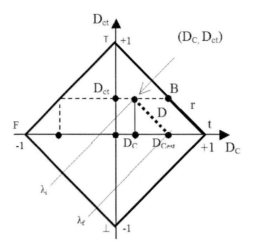

Figure 13. Representation of the variations of values of evidence in λ axis for obtaining the estimated Certainty Degree.

Let us consider, then, the situation where in a paraconsistent analysis the calculations of the Certainty Degree D_C and Contradiction Degree D_{ct}, when interpolated in the Lattice, result in an internal point (D_C, D_{ct}) as can be seen in figure 12.

Drawing a parallel line for the axis values of certainty, and crossing the point in the vertical axis with the value of D_{ct}, we have point B. The r arrow, which originates from the extreme point of the vertex represents the maximum value of certainty t (logical state True) to point B, is transferred to the maximum internal interpolation point (D_C, D_{ct}) meeting the axis values of certainty the $D_{Cest.}$ point – estimated Certainty Degree. By overlapping the axis values of the Favorable Evidence Degree µ and Unfavorable Evidence Degree λ in the given Lattice, we can see as in figure 13, that the point indicated as $D_{Cest.}$ is the value of the Certainty Degree obtained with zero Contradiction Degree. The value of $D_{Cest.}$ is obtained when the same value of Favorable Evidence Degree µ is kept.

In figure 13, it may be calculated in the r arrow, the distance between the B point to the maximum value of certainty t (logical state True) represented in the vertex of the Lattice by:

$$D^2 = (1 - \varphi)^2 + D_{ct}^2$$

$$D = \sqrt{(1 - \varphi)^2 + D_{ct}^2} \tag{8}$$

The value of the Certainty Degree with the addition of (D_{Cadded}) through the variation of the Unfavorable Evidence Degree λ will be:

$$D_{Cadded} = \sqrt{D^2 + D_{ct}^2}$$

$$(D_{Cadded})^2 = D^2 - D_{ct}^2$$

or: $(D_{Cadded})^2 = (1-\varphi)^2 + D_{ct}^2 - D_{ct}^2$

Resulting in:

$$D_{Cadded} = 1-\varphi \qquad (9)$$

The value of the estimated Certainty Degree is met by:

$$D_{Cest.} = D_C + D_{Cadded}$$

Therefore:

$$D_{C\,est.} = D_C + (1-\varphi) \qquad (10)$$

We can see that in this case, the calculated Certainty Degree is positive. As the Contradiction Degree is also positive, therefore favoring to logical state of Inconsistent, the Interval of Certainty will be represented by $\varphi_{(+)}$.

When the lattice values of D_C and D_{ct} both have positive signs, the variation for obtaining the value of the estimated Certainty Degree is made in the values of the Unfavorable Evidence Degree:

$$\Delta\lambda = \lambda_i - \lambda_f \qquad (11)$$

where: λ_i Initial Unfavorable Evidence Degree.

λ_f Final Unfavorable Evidence Degree.

To obtain the value of the final Unfavorable Evidence Degree, and meet the estimated Certainty Degree, we have:

$$\lambda_f = \lambda_i - D$$

$$\lambda_f = \lambda_i - \sqrt{(1-\varphi)^2 + D_{ct}{}^2} \qquad (12)$$

When the Certainty Degree D_C has a positive sign and the Contradiction degree D_{ct} has a negative sign, the internal point of interpolation $(D_C, -D_{ct})$ in the lattice will be to the right of the axis of contradiction and below the axis of certainty. In which case, the value of the estimated Certainty Degree is met by:

$$D_{Cest.} = D_C + D_{Cadded}$$

Therefore: $D_{Cest.} = D_C + (1-\varphi)$ equal the Eq. (10).

Being that D_C is positive and D_{ct} is negative, the logic state for the analysis favors for the logical state of Indetermination, and the Interval of Certainty will be represented by $\varphi_{(-)}$. For a zero Contradiction Degree the value of the Favorable Evidence Degree μ is the one that must be varied. Therefore:

$$\Delta\mu = \mu_i - \mu_f \qquad (13)$$

where : μ_i Initial Favorable Evidence Degree
μ_f final Favorable Evidence Degree

$$\mu_f = \mu_i + D$$

$$\mu_f = \mu_i + \sqrt{(1 - \varphi)^2 + D_{ct}^2} \qquad (14)$$

When the Certainty Degree D_C is a negative sign and the Contradiction Degree D_{ct} is a positive sign, the internal point of interpolation $(-D_C, D_{ct})$ will be located to the left of the axis of contradiction and above the axis of certainty.

The value for the degree of evidence is plus, (D_{Cadded}), due to the variation of the unfavorable evidences will be a negative sign, and can be calculated by:

$$D_{Cadded} = - \left(\sqrt{D^2 + D_{ct}^2} \right)$$

And yet by:

$$D_{Cadded} = \varphi - 1 \qquad (15)$$

The value of the estimated Certainty Degree is met by:

$$D_{C\ est.} = D_C + D_{Cadded}$$

Therefore:

$$D_{C\ est.} = D_C + (\varphi - 1) \qquad (16)$$

In this analysis, the Contradiction Degree is positive and the Interval of Certainty is represented by $\varphi_{(+)}$. For the Contradiction Degree to be zero, the value of the Favorable Evidence Degree μ may show some variation. Therefore:

$$\Delta\mu = \mu_f - \mu_i \qquad (17)$$

where: $\mu_f = \mu_i - D$
Or yet:

$$\mu_f = \mu_i - \sqrt{(1 - \varphi)^2 + D_{ct}^2} \qquad (18)$$

Being that the Certainty Degree D_C and the Contradiction Degree D_{ct} both have negative signs, the internal interpolation point $(D_C, -D_{ct})$ will be located to the left of the axis of contradiction and below the axis of certainty. The value of the degree of certainty plus (D_{Cadded}) by the variation of the unfavorable evidences will be of negative sign, and it can be calculated by:

$$D_{Cadded} = - \left(\sqrt{D^2 - D_{ct}^2} \right)$$

Or yet:

$D_{Cadded} = \varphi - 1$ equal the Eq. (15)

The value of the estimated Certainty Degree is met by:

$$D_{Cest.} = D_C + D_{Cadded}$$

Therefore: $D_{Cest.} = D_C + (\varphi - 1)$ equal the Eq. (16)

As in this analysis the Contradiction Degree is negative, and the Interval of Certainty is represented by $\varphi_{(-)}$. In this case, for the Contradiction Degree to be zero the value of the Unfavorable Evidence Degree λ is the one to suffer variation. Therefore:

$$\Delta\lambda = \lambda_f - \lambda_i \tag{19}$$

The final Unfavorable Evidence Degree is determined by:

$$\lambda_f = \lambda_i + \sqrt{(1 - \varphi)^2 + D_{ct}^2} \tag{20}$$

The analysis of the Lattice shows that for us to find the estimated values of the Certainty Degree through checking its values proximity to the extreme certainty states; where, *True*, for affirmation of the proposition and *False* for denying the proposition, variations were necessary for increasing or decreasing the evidence degrees. For decision making over each type of evidence, if favorable or unfavorable, must suffer variation for decreasing contradiction and reaching the estimated Certainty Degree. In the feedback of the paraconsistent analysis we can establish the following criteria:

If the Interval of Certainty has a positive sign:

For $\varphi = \varphi_{(+)}$

Decrease λ If $D_C > 0$

        or else   Decrease μ

If the Interval of Certainty has a negative sign:

For $\varphi = \varphi_{(-)}$

Increase μ If $D_C > 0$

        or else   Increase λ

V.5. The Real Certainty Degree

A decision system working with database information from uncertain knowledge will be stronger when, at the end of the analysis, it shows a certainty value which contains in its values the effect of the influence of the inconsistencies obtained from conflicting information.

The analysis in the lattice of the PAL2v allows us to, after the treatment of uncertain information; obtain a lower Certainty Degree value due to the effect caused by the contradictions. The value of the Certainty Degree to be considered apart from the effect caused by the contradictions is called Real Certainty Degree D_{CR}. We may calculate the value of the D_{CR} from the value of the Certainty Degree obtained by the analysis of the lattice of the PAL2v. It can be done as such:

_ Let us consider that in a given paraconsistent analysis, the calculations of the Certainty Degree D_C and the Contradiction Degree D_{ct} resulted in positive values and are interpolated in the Lattice in an internal point (D_C, D_{ct}), as in figure 14.

The distance d, between the point of the maximum degree of certainty **t** (logical state True) represented in the right vertex of the Lattice, and the interpolation point (D_C, D_{ct}) is calculated by:

$$d = \sqrt{(1-|D_C|)^2 + D_{ct}^2} \qquad (21)$$

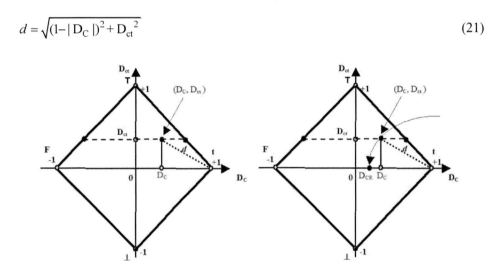

Figure 14. Determination of the Real Certainty Degree D_{CR} in the Lattice of the PAL2v with $(+D_C, +D_{ct})$.

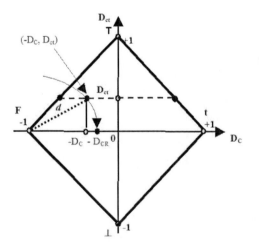

Figure 15. Determination of the Real Certainty Degree D_{CR} in the Lattice of the PAL2v with $(-D_C, +D_{ct})$.

Projecting the distance d in the axis of the values of certainty, we can have the point whose value will be considered the Real Certainty Degree D_{CR}.

$$D_{CR} = 1 - d$$

$$D_{CR} = 1 - \sqrt{(1 - |D_C|)^2 + D_{ct}^2} \qquad (22)$$

If the calculated Certainty Degree D_C result in negative value, the distance d will be obtained from the point of certainty **F** (logical state False) represented in the left vertex of the Lattice, to the point of internal interpolation ($-D_C$, D_{ct}).

And, in the same way, projecting the distance d in the axis of the certainty degrees, the value of the Real Certainty Degree is calculated by equation:

$$D_{CR} = d - 1$$

$$D_{CR} = \sqrt{(1 - |D_C|)^2 + D_{ct}^2} - 1 \qquad (23)$$

After the determination of the Real Certainty Degree the answer of a paraconsistent analysis should present a new value of the Interval of Certainty. As in this new condition the Contradiction Degree is zero, the representation of φ should be of unitary value. However, the same value of φ is kept in the representation, together with its signalization. This is done so that the system may retrieve the value of the calculated Certainty Degree and the Contradiction Degree, and establish which evidence may be varied, in case it is necessary. Therefore, the output signal of a paraconsistent system of treatment of uncertainties, when receiving the values of evidence in its inputs, will produce an output as such:

$$D_{Crr} = \begin{bmatrix} D_{CR} \\ \varphi_{(\pm)} \end{bmatrix}$$

where: D_{Crr} = Degree of Resultant Real Certainty

D_{CR} = Calculated Real Certainty Degree through Eqs. (22) and (23):

$$D_{CR} = 1 - \sqrt{(1 - |D_C|)^2 + D_{ct}^2} \qquad \text{If } D_C > 0$$

$$D_{CR} = \sqrt{(1 - |D_C|)^2 + D_{ct}^2} - 1 \qquad \text{If } D_C < 0$$

$\varphi_{(\pm)}$ = Signaled Interval of Certainty, obtained by: $\varphi = 1 - |D_{ct}|$

where: $\varphi = \varphi_{(+)}$ If $D_{ct} > 0$

        $\varphi = \varphi_{(-)}$ If $D_{ct} < 0$

In any internal interpolation point (D_C, D_{ct}) in the Lattice the value of the Real Certainty Degree D_{CR} can be calculated. However, for use in intelligent systems of decision-making, consider the points where the distance d is equal, or a smaller unit ($d \leq 1$). That is made because for larger distances than the unit ($d > 1$) the value of the Real Certainty Degree will be very close of the zero value. That happens because there exists a high contradiction between the signals of information (Favorable Evidence Degree μ, Unfavorable Evidence Degree λ) that are applied in the inputs of the paraconsistent analysis system.

V.6. Transformation of the Real Degree of Certainty into Resultant Degree of Evidence

Since a Paraconsistent Analysis produces values for a Real Degree of Certainty in the closed interval between -1 and +1, to transform a Resultant Degree of Certainty from the analysis of a proposition into Degree of Evidence for another proposition the normalization of the values is done in the following way:

As the Degree of Certainty is calculated through Eq. (2.2) where:

$D_C = \mu - \lambda$, then the Resultant Degree of Evidence may be obtained as:

$$\mu_E = \frac{D_C + 1}{2} \tag{24}$$

Or still:

$$\mu_E = \frac{(\mu - \lambda) + 1}{2} \tag{25}$$

where: μ_E = Resultant Degree of Evidence

μ = Favorable Degree of Evidence
λ = Unfavorable Degree of Evidence

The value of the Resultant Degree of Evidence obtained through equations will now have a variation in the closed real interval between 0 and 1.

V.6.1. Resultant Real Degree of Evidence

The values for the Resultant Real Degree of Evidence (μ_{ER}) will be obtained by calculating initially the value of Real Certainty Degree (D_{CR}) through Eqs. (22) and (23) reproduced here:

For $D_C > 0$

$$D_{CR} = 1 - \sqrt{(1 - |D_C|)^2 + D_{ct}^2}$$

For $D_C < 0$

$$D_{CR} = \sqrt{(1-|D_C|)^2 + D_{ct}^2} - 1$$

From these equations, we determine the resultant Real Evidence Degree by:

$$\mu_{ER} = \frac{D_{CR} + 1}{2} \tag{26}$$

The Real Evidence Degree (μ_{ER}) is important for interconnect of the LPA2v Algorithms allowing the formation of great Networks that make the analysis for paraconsistent signals.

V.7. Recovery of Data and Answers through Feedback Actions

As illustrated, a system of paraconsistent analysis presents in its output the value of the Real Certainty Degree D_{CR} with the signaled Interval of Certainty $\varphi_{(\pm)}$. For these two values, it is possible to recover the calculated Certainty Degree, the Contradiction Degree and it is possible to establish the Evidence Degree to be varied for decreasing the contradiction.

By the value of the signaled Interval of Certainty, the value of the Contradiction Degree can be recovered by:

$$D_{ctrec} = 1 - \varphi_{(\pm)} \tag{27}$$

The recovered Contradiction Degree D_{ctrec} has the same sign of the Interval of Certainty.

If the φ sign is positive $\varphi_{(+)}$, it means that the Contradiction Degree is above the axis of certainty; its values are positive and indicate a favorable logical state of the Inconsistency T.

If the φ sign is negative $\varphi_{(-)}$, it means that the Contradiction Degree is under the axis of certainty; its values are negative and indicate a favorable logical state of the Indetermination $\perp$.

From the value of the Real Certainty Degree D_{CR} and the retrieved Contradiction Degree D_{ctrec} we may calculate the value of the Certainty Degree D_C by:

If $D_{CR} > 0$

$$D_C = 1 - \sqrt{(1-D_{CR})^2 - D_{ctrec}^2} \tag{28}$$

If $D_{CR} < 0$

$$D_C = \sqrt{(D_{CR}+1)^2 - D_{ctrec}^2} - 1 \tag{29}$$

From the Eq. (4), the values of the evidence degrees (inputs) are met with the values of D_C e D_{ctrec} as in these equations:

$$\mu = \frac{D_C + D_{ctrec} + 1}{2} \tag{30}$$

$$\lambda = \frac{-D_C + D_{ctrec} + 1}{2} \tag{31}$$

This way, we can identify the evidence to be strengthened or weakened to result in the decrease in contradiction. For obtaining an answer by feedback actions within the system of decision, the variation in the values of the evidence must be done as such:

If the Interval of Certainty presented a positive sign: $\varphi = \varphi_{(+)}$
Decrease λ if and only if $D_C > 0$
Or else decrease μ
If the Interval of Certainty presented a negative sign: $\varphi = \varphi_{(-)}$
Increase μ if and only if $D_C > 0$
Or else increase λ

The process of Recovery of Data is important for the continuous verification and the control of the evidence degrees that are being applied in the inputs of Paraconsistent Analysis System.

VI. THE PAL2v ALGORITHMS FOR PARACONSISTENT ANALYSIS

The algorithms of paraconsistent analysis of the PAL2v that make up a system for treatment of uncertainties will be shown now.

VI.1. PAL2v Paraconsistent Analysis Algorithm with Resultant Certainty Degree Output

The algorithm of paraconsistent analysis to find the value of the Real Certainty Degree and the Interval of Certainty is as follows:

1.1. Enter the Input Values
  μ */ Favorable Evidence degree $0 \leq \mu \leq 1$
  λ */ Unfavorable Evidence degree $0 \leq \lambda \leq 1$

2.1. Calculate the Contradiction Degree
  $D_{ct} = \mu + \lambda - 1$

3.1. Calculate the Interval of Certainty
  $\varphi = 1 - |D_{ct}|$

4.1. Calculate the Certainty Degree
  $D_C = \mu - \lambda$

5.1. Calculate the d Distance

$$d = \sqrt{(1-|D_C|)^2 + D_{ct}^2}$$

6.1. Determine the Output Signal

If $d > 1$
Then have S1= 0.5 e S2= φ: Indefinition and go to item10.1
Else go to the next item

7.1. Determine the Real Certainty Degree

If $D_C > 0$ $D_{CR} = (1 - d)$
If $D_C < 0$ $D_{CR} = (d - 1)$

8.1. Determine the Sign for the Interval of Certainty

If $\mu + \lambda < 1$ negative signal $\varphi_{(\pm)} = \varphi_{(-)}$
If $\mu + \lambda > 1$ positive signal $\varphi_{(\pm)} = \varphi_{(+)}$
If $\mu + \lambda = 1$ zero signal $\varphi_{(\pm)} = \varphi_{(0)}$

9.1. Present the Outputs

Do S1 = D_{CR} and S2= $\varphi_{(\pm)}$

10.1. End

When in a network, the next lines are included in the Algorithm, in order to calculate the output Evidence Degree, as follows:

10.1.a. Calculate the Real Evidence Degree

$$\mu_{ER} = \frac{D_{CR} + 1}{2}$$

10.1.b. Present the Outputs

Do S1 = μ_{ER} and S2= $\varphi_{(\pm)}$

10.1.c. End

The Resultant Real Degree of Evidence μ_{ER} is the one considered when the calculated value of μ_E is attenuated, or free from the effects due to the existence of contradiction.

VI.2. Paraconsistent Analysis PAL2v Algorithm for the Estimation of Values

The paraconsistent analysis algorithm responsible for the estimation of the value of the Certainty Degree, thus to determine the variation of the evidence for getting zero contradiction, is as follows:

1.2. Enter the Input Values

μ */ Favorable Evidence degree $0 \leq \mu \leq 1$

λ */ Unfavorable Evidence degree $0 \leq \lambda \leq 1$

2.2. Calculate the Contradiction Degree

$D_{ct} = \mu + \lambda - 1$

3.2. Calculate the Interval of Certainty

$\varphi = 1 - |D_{ct}|$

4.2. Calculate the Certainty Degree

$D_C = \mu - \lambda$

5.2. Calculate the d Distance

$$d = \sqrt{(1 - |D_C|)^2 + D_{ct}^2}$$

6.2. Determine the Output Signal

If $\varphi \leq 0{,}25$ or $d > 1$

Then have $S1(D_{Crest}) = 0.5$ e $S2 = \varphi$: Indefinition and
$S3(\Delta\lambda) = 0.0$ e $S4(\Delta\mu) = 0.0$ go to item 10.2

If not, then go to the next item

7.2. Calculate the D Distance

$$D = \sqrt{(1 - \varphi)^2 + D_{ct}^2}$$

8.2. Determine the Value of the Estimated Certainty Degree for the Degree of Contradiction to be Zero

$$D_{Cadded} = \sqrt{D^2 - D_{ct}^2}$$

If $D_C > 0$ Calculate: $D_{Cest} = D_C + D_{Cadded}$

If $D_C < 0$ Calculate: $D_{Cest} = D_C - D_{Cadded}$

9.2. Determine the Value of the Estimated Evidence Degrees for Obtaining the Value of the Estimated Certainty Degree

For $D_C > 0$ *If* $D_{ct} > 0$ Calculate $\lambda_f = \lambda_i - D_{Cest}$

                Else   Calculate $\mu_f = \lambda_i + D_{Cest}$

For $D_C < 0$ *If* $D_{ct} > 0$ Calculate $\mu_f = \mu_i + D_{Cest}$

                Else   Calculate $\lambda_f = \mu_i - D_{Cest}$

Do $S1(D_{Cest}) = D_{Cest}$ and $S2 = \varphi_{(\pm)}$

$S3(\Delta\lambda) = \lambda_f$ and $S4(\Delta\mu) = \mu_f$

10.2. End

VI.3 Paraconsistent Analysis Algorithm of the PAL2v with Feedback

The paraconsistent analysis algorithm results defined the values for the Real Certainty Degree D_{CR} and the signaled Interval of Certainty $\varphi(\pm)$ recovers the calculated Certainty Degree D_C; the evidence values of input μ and λ indicate which of them must suffer variation for obtaining a zero Contradiction Degree, is as follows:

1.3. Check the Output Signals
D_{CR} */ Real Certainty Degree $\qquad$ $-1 \leq D_{CR} \leq +1$
$\varphi_{(+)}$ */ signaled Interval of Certainty $\quad 0 \leq \varphi_{(+)} \leq 1$

2.3. Calculate the Contradiction Degree
$D_{ct} = 1 - \varphi_{(\pm)}$

3.3. Calculate the Certainty Degree
$If\ D_{CR} > 0$ Do:
$$D_C = 1 - \sqrt{(1 - D_{CR})^2 - D_{ct}^{\ 2}}$$
Else:
$$D_C = \sqrt{(D_{CR} + 1)^2 - D_{ct}^{\ 2}} - 1$$

4.3. Calculate the Evidence Degrees of Inputs

$$\mu = \frac{D_C + D_{ct} + 1}{2} \quad \text{and} \quad \lambda = \frac{-D_C + D_{ct} + 1}{2}$$

5.3. Present the Output According to the Condition
For $\varphi = \varphi_{(+)}$	*If* $D_C > 0$	Decrease in λ
	Else	Decrease in μ
For $\varphi = \varphi_{(-)}$	*If* $D_C > 0$	Increase in μ
	Else	Increase in λ

6.3. Execute a New Paraconsistent Analysis (PAL2v Paraconsistent Analysis Algorithm VI.1) and Present the New Results
Do S1 = D_{CR} and S2= $\varphi_{(\pm)}$

7.3. End

VII. Application of Paraconsistent System for Treatment of Uncertainties with the PAL2v

We may compute values by utilizing the obtained equations, and this way, construct paraconsistent systems able to present satisfactory answers from the searched information within the database of uncertain knowledge.

The algorithm results define several values that give support to allow for efficient decision-making.

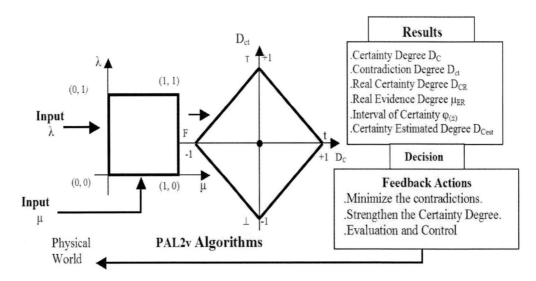

Figure 16. Typical Paraconsistent Expert system for treatment of uncertainties with the PAL2v Algorithms.

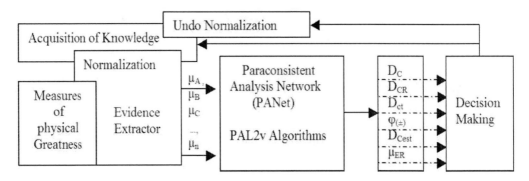

Figure 17. Typical system for Paraconsistent Analysis Network with the main procedures.

The paraconsistent system for treatment of uncertainties may be used in many fields of knowledge where incomplete or contradictory information will receive an adequate treatment through the PAL2v equations.

When considering a real application for the Paraconsistent Expert System some necessary procedures are required to correct the interpretation of the input signals, as well as analyzing the results obtained in the output.

A block diagram for the main procedures is shown in the figure 17.

VII.1. Acquisition of Knowledge and Paraconsistent Logical Value Modeling

Initially all of the signals that represent the evidence in relation to the proposition for analysis must be normalized and all the processing done in set of the real numbers for a closed interval between 0 and 1. Accordingly, as what was determined before, the information signals that feed a Paraconsistent Analysis Network are annotations. In Paraconsistent Annotated Logic with annotation of two values - PAL2v, an *annotation* is composed of two Degrees of Evidence:

Favorable Evidence Degree symbolized by the letter μ.

Unfavorable Evidence Degree symbolized by letter λ.

Thus, a *annotation* referring to a Proposition P in PAL2v is the ordered pair: (μ, λ)

A *Paraconsistent Logical Signal* is symbolized by a Proposition accompanied by its subscript annotation:

$P_{(\mu, \lambda)}$

Where: P is the Proposition to be analyzed.

(μ, λ) is the annotation

μ is the Paraconsistent Logical Value, or the Favorable Degree of Evidence to Proposition P.

λ is the Paraconsistent Logical Value, or the Unfavorable Degree of Evidence to Proposition P.

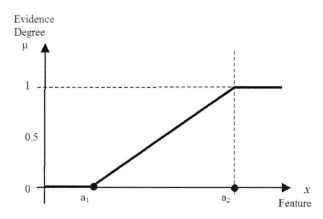

Figure 18. Valorization of the Evidence with linear variation and directly proportional to the measured feature.

VII.2. Normalization Process

The valorization of evidence is expressed by their Paraconsistent Logical Value or Degree; this is a number that belongs to the real numbers in the closed interval between 0 and 1. This number is determined from the original characteristics of the information sources, which establish their variation and behavior in a Universe of Discourse. If an information source is a human being, the Paraconsistent Logical Value is formed by their knowledge about the subject related to the Proposition. A human Expert may establish a value for a certain Proposition based on their professional experience knowledge. In this way, the first step to construct a Paraconsistent Analysis System, able to treat uncertainties, is by modeling or mining for source Knowledge from the various information sources.

VII.3. Linear Variation Modeling

By knowledge mining from several information sources, we can verify that the variation of the Evidences in respect to a certain Proposition is linear in a directly proportional fashion in the Universe of Discourse. In this case the valorization of the input Degrees of Evidence is done as follows:

We consider a Universe of Discourse that goes from inferior limit value of the feature measurement symbolized by a_1, up to the superior limit value of the feature measurement symbolized by a_2, whose Evidence varies in a linear form and directly proportional to the value of the feature.

Figure 18 shows a graph with the variation of the Degree of Evidence for this situation.

The Evidence Degree μ whose value varies from 0 to 1 in the Universe of Discourse, will be calculated by:

$$\mu_{(x)} = \begin{cases} \dfrac{x - a_1}{a_2 - a_1} & if \quad x \in [a_1, a_2] \\ 1 & if \quad x > a_2 \\ 0 & if \quad x < a_1 \end{cases} \tag{32}$$

Based on the Universe of Discourse, if the variation of evidence with respect to a certain Proposition is linear in an indirectly proportional fashion, the valorization of the input Degrees of Evidence is done as follows:

Consider a Universe of Discourse that goes from the inferior limit value of the feature measure symbolized by a_1, up to the superior limit value of the feature measure symbolized by a_2, whose variation is linear and indirectly proportional to value of the feature. The graph for the variation of this Degree of Evidence will be according to the one presented in figure 19.

The Degree of Evidence μ whose value varies from 0 to 1 in the Universe of Discourse, will be calculated by:

$$\mu_{(x)} = \begin{cases} \dfrac{x-a_2}{a_1-a_2} & if \quad x \in [a_1, a_2] \\[2mm] 1 & if \quad x < a_1 \\[2mm] 0 & if \quad x > a_2 \end{cases} \tag{33}$$

If the subject knowledge related to the Proposition we wish to analyze shows that the variations of evidence in the Universe of Discourse is non Linear, then the most adequate function must be chosen to treat the feature in question.

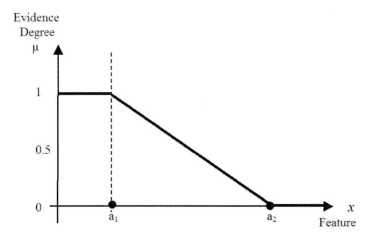

Figure 19. Valorization of the Degree of Evidence with linear variation and indirectly proportional to the measured feature.

We present here some of the functions when modeling input for the Degrees of Evidence. Nonetheless, the Paraconsistent logical signals may be modeled with other functions, as those commonly used in other types of Non-Classical Logics, for example *Fuzzy Logic* that uses Linguistic Variables. Linguistic Variables are words, clauses or statements in natural or artificial language. The Paraconsistent Logical Value may be constructed from a Linguistic Variable, such that typical values of these are heuristically assigned from the Universe of Discourse.

The undo normalization process is made through the same equations used in the normalization, or modeling of input signals.

VIII. EXAMPLE OF APPLICATION

The Paraconsistent Annotated Logic has become an object for research in several institutions, producing relevant research work for the implementation in Expert Systems and Robotics that use Paraconsistent Analysis Network (PANet) composed by interlinked PAL2v Algorithms. Good results were achieved in the application of the PAL2v Algorithms in the analysis for Risk of Overload in Electric Power Systems. Therefore, we will present in a simplified way, an application example for the LPA2v Algorithms in that specific area of electric engineering.

VIII.1. Application Example of the PAL2v Algorithms in the Analyses of Risk of Overload in Electric Power Systems

Consider that for 2 points in a net of electric power distribution it is critical to know the overload risk degree in real time. For this situation, the Paraconsistent Expert System has available for each point of interest the instantaneous measurements of two electric greatness: the electric tension E, in volts (v) and the electric Current I, in amperes (A).

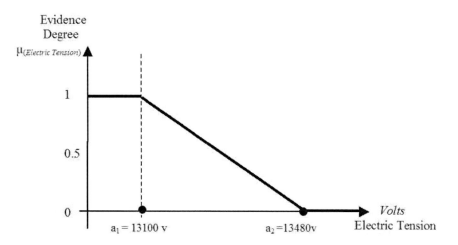

Figure 20. Evidence Degree of the Electric Tension - linear variation and indirectly proportional in the Universe of discourse.

Source of Information 1 - Electric Tension
In the process of knowledge acquisition, by use of this source information, the Paraconsistent Expert System defines the following values limits:

Electric Tension   Minimum Value limit V_{1min} = 13100 volts
                       Maximum Value limit V_{1max} = 13480 volts

These limit values will form the Universe of Discourse of Electric Tension of the Paraconsistent System of Analysis.

Considering that a low value of electric tension increases the Overload Risk Degree, then, the variation of the greatness Electric Tension inside of the Universe of Discourse will be linear and inversely proportional. Therefore, for the obtaining of the Degree of Evidence corresponding to the source of information electric tension, the Paraconsistent Expert System will consider the Proposition:

P_v = "The measure of the electric tension in the point of interest is low."

The source information for the analysis of overload risk will be represented in the graph as shown in figure 20. The instantaneous value for the measure of the electric Tension ($V_{meassure}v$), obtained in the point of interest in the net transmission of energy, the Eq. (33) that determines the value of the Degree of Evidence for the Proposition P_v is:

$$
\mu_{(Electric\ Tension)} = \begin{cases} \dfrac{V_{measuredV} - 13480v}{13100v - 13480v} & if\ V_{measuredV} \in [13100v, 13480v] \\ 1 & if\ V_{measuredV} < 13100v \\ 0 & if\ V_{measuredV} > 13480v \end{cases}
$$

Source of Information 2 - Electric Current

For that the second source of information, the Paraconsistent Expert System uses the following limit values:

Electric Current   Minimum Value limit I_{lmin} = 160 Amperes

                            Maximum Value limit I_{lmax} = 280 Amperes

These limit values will form the Universe of Discourse of the Electric Current of the Paraconsistent System of Analysis.

Considering that a low value of electric current decreases the Overload Risk Degree, then the variation of the greatness Electric Current inside the Universe of Discourse will be linear and directly proportional. Therefore, for the obtaining of the Degree of Evidence corresponding to the source of information electric current, the Paraconsistent Expert System will consider the Proposition:

P_I = "The measure of the electric current in the point of interest is high."

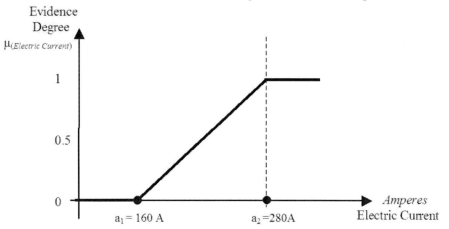

Figure 21. Evidence Degree of the Electric Current - linear variation and directly proportional in the Universe of Discourse.

The source of information for the analysis of overload risk will be represented in the graph of figure (21).

The instantaneous value for the measure of the electric Tension ($V_{meassureV}$), obtained in the point of interest by the net transmission of energy, the equation determines the value of the Degree of Evidence for the Proposition P_v is:

The instantaneous value for the measure of the electric Current ($I_{meassureA}$) obtained in each point of interest by the net transmission of energy, allows Eq. (32) to determine the value for the Degree of Evidence in the Proposition P_I :

$$\mu_{(Electric\ Current)} = \begin{cases} \dfrac{I_{measuredA} - 160A}{280A - 160A} & if \quad I_{measuredA} \in [160A, 280A] \\ 1 & if \quad I_{measuredA} > 280A \\ 0 & if \quad I_{measuredA} < 160A \end{cases}$$

Consider that some instantaneous values for Electric Tension and Electric Current measured in each point are given in an instant t :

.In the Point 1 $V_{meassureV}$ = 13,170 volts $I_{meassureA}$ = 270 Amperes
Then the Evidence Degree for the Proposition P_v is: $\mu_{(Electric\ Tension)}$ = 0.81579
Then the Evidence Degree for the Proposition P_I is: $\mu_{(Electric\ Current)}$ = 0.91666

.In the Point 2 $V_{meassureV}$ = 13,360 volts $I_{meassureA}$ = 230 Amperes
Then the Evidence Degree for the Proposition P_v is: $\mu_{(Electric\ Tension)}$ = 0.31579
Then the Evidence Degree for the Proposition P_I is: $\mu_{(Electric\ Current)}$ = 0.58333

In each point of interest, the net of electric power transmission for the proposition P_v and the Proposition P_I generate the Evidence Degrees that form the annotation of a logical Paraconsistent signal in relation to Objective Proposition of the analysis. For the analysis of overload risk, the Objective Proposition will be:

P_o = "The point of measurement of the net presents Risk of Overload."

. In the Point P1 we represent the annotation (μ, λ) as:

(0.81579, 0.08334)

The Paraconsistent Logical Signal is represented as follows:

$P_{0(\mu, \lambda)} = P_{0(\mu\ (Electric\ Tension),\ \lambda(Electric\ Current))} = P_{0(0.81579,\ 0.08334)}$

From Eq. (2) we determine the Certainty Degree D_C

$D_C = 0.81579 - 0.08334 \rightarrow D_C = 0.73245$

From Eq. (3) we determine the Degree of Contradiction D_{ct}

$D_{ct} = 0.81579 + 0.08334 - 1 \rightarrow D_{ct} = -0.10087$

The distance d from Eq. (21):

$d = \sqrt{(1-|0.73245|)^2 + 0.10087^2}$
$d = 0.285933136$

Since the Degree of Certainty D_C is positive, we determine the Real Certainty Degree from Eq. (22):

$D_{CR} = 1 - 0.285933136$

$D_{CR} = 0.7140668$

The Risk of Overload will be obtained through the calculation of the Real Evidence Degree, according to Eq. (26):

$\mu_{ER} = \dfrac{0.7140668 + 1}{2} = 0.8570334$

Therefore, for instant t, the Degree of Risk for the occurrence of an Overload in Point 1 of the net in electric power transmission is:

$\mu_{ER} = 0.8570334$

In these conditions, we have a positive Certainty Degree D_C and a negative Contradiction Degree D_{ct}; therefore, from Eq. (15) we calculate the Interval of Certainty:

$\varphi = 1 - |0.10087| \rightarrow \varphi = 0.89913$

As the Contradiction Degree is negative, then the signaling of the Interval of Certainty is negative.

$\varphi_{(-)} = 0.89913_{(-)}$

Through Eq. (16) we calculate the Estimated Degree of Certainty:

$D_{Cest} = 0.73245 + (1 - 0.89913)$

$D_{Cest} = 0.83332$

. In the Point P2 we represent the annotation (μ, λ) as:

(0.31579, 0.41667)

The Logical Paraconsistent Signal is represented as follows:

$P_{0(\mu, \lambda)} = P_{0(\mu \text{ (Electric Tension)}, \lambda(\text{Electric Current}))} = P_{0(0.31579, 0.41667)}$

From Eq. (2), we determine the Certainty Degree D_C

$D_C = 0.31579 - 0.41667 \rightarrow D_C = -0.10088$

From Eq. (3), we determine the Degree of Contradiction D_{ct}

$D_{ct} = 0.31579 + 0.41667 - 1 \rightarrow D_{ct} = -0.26754$

The distance d from Eq. (21):

$$d = \sqrt{(1-|0.10088|)^2 + 0.26754^2}$$
$$d = 0.93808018$$

Since the Degree of Certainty D_C is negative, we determine the Real Certainty Degree from Eq. (23):

$$D_{CR} = 0.93808018 - 1$$

$$D_{CR} = -0.061919819$$

The Risk of Overload will be obtained through the calculation of the Real Evidence Degree, according to Eq. (26):

$$\mu_{ER} = \frac{-0.061919819 + 1}{2} = 0.46904009$$

Therefore, for instant t, the Degree of Risk for the occurrence of an Overload in Point 2 of the net in electric power transmission is:

$$\mu_{ER} = 0.469036724$$

In these conditions, we have a negative Certainty Degree D_C and a negative Contradiction Degree D_{ct}; therefore, from Eq. (15) we calculate the Interval of Certainty:

$$\varphi = 1 - |0.26754| \rightarrow \varphi = 0.73245$$

As the Contradiction Degree is negative, then the sign of the Interval of Certainty is negative.

$\varphi_{(-)} = 0.73245_{(-)}$

Through Eq. (16) we calculate the Estimated Degree of Certainty:

$D_{Cest} = -0.10089 + (0.73245 - 1)$

$D_{Cest} = -0.36844$

CONCLUSION

The methodology presented in this chapter utilized the Paraconsistent Logic concepts to obtain the mathematical treatment of signals as generated through a database of uncertainty knowledge. The information considered as uncertain or contradictory was represented by annotations, whose values were put to analysis in a representative lattice of the Paraconsistent Annotated logic with annotation of two values (PAL2v). Through the lattice analysis, we obtained simple equations that made the construction of algorithms easier for the development of logical reasoning capable of working with the treatment of uncertainties. The obtained algorithms may be easily reproduced by means of any computer language or hardware tool, to provide conditions for application in several fields of Artificial Intelligence.

The three algorithms presented here are based on paraconsistent logics. That is to say, conceived to receive uncertain and contradictory information, equate their values and present results, with no restrictions regarding conflicts that may be present within the information. In this paraconsistent model, we may cross many nodes or information system analysis in the treatment of uncertainties. These configurations will constitute paraconsistent networks of decision, which unlike the known systems; the weight of the information conflicts will not bar the answers.Through this new approach of conflicting data treatments, we can produce information that will be relevant for decision-making.

The methodology of Paraconsistent Logic through the extended form of PAL2v, as presented in this chapter, is a most successful application. Furthermore, this methodology has application that can utilize the PAL2v algorithms with the potential to broaden its use in diverse fields of knowledge. This new method for the treatment of uncertainties differs from those previously known, exactly because it considers contradiction in the analysis. This is an important fact that opens up a vast field for application research and construction for innovative projects in Expert Systems for decision-making in the engineering area.

REFERENCES

Abe, J.M., and Da Silva Filho, J.I. (1998). Inconsistency and electronic circuits, *Proc. EIS'98 - ICSC Symposium on Engineering of Intelligent Systems*, Artificial Intelligence, E. Alpaydin, (Ed.), ICSC Academic Press International Computer Science Conventions Canada/Switzerland,, 3, 191-197.

Abe, J.M., and Da Silva Filho, J.I. (2002). Simulating inconsistencies in a paraconsistent logic controller, *Intl. J Computing Anticipatory Syst.*, 12, 315-323.

Anand, R., and Subrahmanian, V.S. (1987). A logic programming system based on a six-valued logic. *AAAI/Xerox Second Intl. Symp. on Knowledge Eng.* - Madri-Espanha,

Da Costa, N.C.A.; Henschen, L.J.; Lu, J. J., and Subrahmanian,V.S. (1990). Automatic theorem proving in Paraconsistent Logics: Theory and implementation (in Portuguese) *Estudos Avançados- Coleção Documentos-* IEA-USP, N°03,18p., São Paulo.

Da Costa, N.C.A.; Subrahmanian, V.S., and Vago, C., (1991). The Paraconsistent Logic, *PT Zeitschrift fur Mathematische Logik und Grundlagen der Mathematik, 37*, 139-148.

Da Silva Filho, J.I; Rocco, A.; Onuki, A.S.; Ferrara, L.F.P., and Camargo, J.M. (2007). Electric power systems contingencies analysis by Paraconsistent Logic Application, *Proc. ISAP2007*, Kaohsiung, Taiwan, pp. 112-117.

Da Silva Filho, J.I., and Rocco, A. (2008). Power systems outage possibilities analysis by paraconsistent logic. *Power and Energy Society General Meeting - Conversion and Delivery of Electrical Energy in the 21st Century, IEEE*, Pittsburgh, PA., pp. 1-6.

Da Silva Filho, J.I. (1999). Métodos de aplicações da Lógica Paraconsistente Anotada de anotação com dois valores LPA2v com construção de Algoritmo e Implementação de Circuitos Eletrônicos, PhD degree theses (in Portuguese) -EPUSP, São Paulo.

Da Silva Filho, J.I.; Rocco, A.; Mario, M.C., and Ferrara, L.F.P. (2007). PES - Paraconsistent Expert System: A Computational Program for Support in ReEstablishment of The Electric Transmission Systems, *Proc. LAPTEC2007 - VI Congress of Logic Applied to Technology*, Santos, SP, Brazil, p. 217.

Dempster, A. P. (1967). Upper and lower probabilities induced by a multivalued mapping. *Ann Math Statistics 38*, 325-339.

Duda, R. O.; Hart, P. E., and Nilsson, N. J. (1976). Subjective Bayesian methods for rule-based inference systems. *AFIPS Conference Proceedings*, N.Y., pp. 1075-1082.

Gordon, J., and Shortliffe, E. H. (1984). The Dempster-Shafer Theory of Evidence. *Rule-based Expert Systems*. New York, Addison-Wesley, pp.272-292.

Pawlak, Z. (1982). Rough sets. *Intl. J Computer & Info Sci, 11*(5), 341-356.

Reiter, R. A. (1980). Logic for default reasoning. *Artificial Intelligence 13*, 81-132.

Subrahmanian, V.S. (1987). On the semantics of quantitative logic programs, *Proc. Fourth IEEE Symposium on Logic Programming, Computer Society Press,*Washington D.C.

Zadeh, L. A. (1978). Fuzzy Sets as a Basis for a Theory of Possibility. *Fuzzy Sets & Systems 1*, 3-28.

In: Expert System Software
Editors: Jason M. Segura and Albert C. Reiter

ISBN: 978-1-61209-114-3
© 2012 Nova Science Publishers, Inc.

Chapter 2

EXPERT SYSTEMS IN FLOW ANALYSIS

Claudineia R. Silva, Mário A. Feres,
*Fábio R. P. Rocha and Elias A. G. Zagatto**

Center for Nuclear Energy in Agriculture,
University of São Paulo, Brazil

ABSTRACT

The flow analyzers are a powerful tool for large-scale analyses, and their potentialities are enhanced when computer-controlled discretely operated devices such as pumps, stream directing valves, injectors or commuters are used. This chapter is focused on the exploitation of these devices for accomplishing the different flow-based strategies required for the specific analysis, such as merging zones, zone sampling, stream splitting, flow reversals, sample stopping, etc. A discussion on multi-commutation is also included. Emphasis is not given to software flow charts but to the exploitation of the flow analyzer own software.

Expert flow systems relying on feedback mechanisms are dealt with too. These systems generally involve a preliminary assay and the analytical result is used to feed the software with information for real-time decisions. The need for in-line sample dilutions, sample replacement, activation of devices, as well as further optional sample handling is then real-time defined. The chapter ends up by highlighting applications in the agronomical, industrial, environmental, pharmaceutical and geological fields.

1. CHARACTERISTICS OF FLOW ANALYSIS

The demand for chemical analyses is worldwide increasingly. The requirements are becoming more specific, and include the need for precise and accurate determinations of lower analyte concentrations in volume-limited samples with minimum generation of toxic

---

* Corresponding author: Elias A. G. Zagatto, P.O. Box 96, Piracicaba SP 13400-970, Brazil. e-mail: ezagatto@cena.usp.br.

wastes. Usually, expedite results are needed in order to support decisions. Automation is a suitable way to accomplish these goals in modern chemical analysis.

Flow analysis [1] is a powerful approach to automation in analytical chemistry. A small volume of an aqueous sample (μL level) is introduced into the sample carrier stream flowing through a narrow-bored tube (Figure 1). During transport, the sample is subjected to different analytical steps such as *e.g.* dilution, reagent additions, pH adjustment and analyte separation / concentration. The handled sample reaches then the detector where is monitored under reproducible conditions. During sample passage of the handled sample through the detector a transient signal is measured and recorded as a peak proportional to the analyte concentration.

The consumption of reagents and waste generation are both minimized in flow-based procedures, allowing more environmentally-friendly chemical analysis [2]. Volume-limited samples (*e.g.* biological fluids, rain waters, blood serum) are easily run and *in situ* assays are efficiently performed.

The analytical path behaves as a closed environment; thus there is no contact of the sample with the external environment (and vice versa) during sample transport towards detection. Analyte losses or sample contamination, which might lead to unreliable results and/or environmental pollution are then avoided. Moreover, drawbacks related to the use of hazardous, carcinogenic or volatile chemicals are circumvented.

The sample residence time in the analytical path is usually short. Mechanization of analytical methods where chemical equilibrium is not reached, use of unstable reagents or quantification of unstable chemical species becomes then feasible, thus expanding the application range of these methods. Due to the short sample residence time, a high sampling rate (typically 20 - 400 h^{-1}) is inherent to flow-based procedures, and this aspect is more relevant for large scale analysis, including process monitoring.

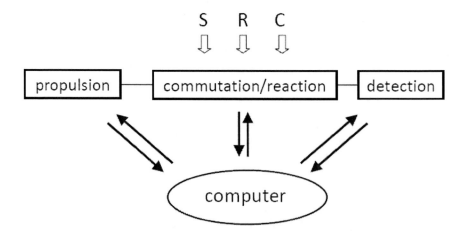

Figure 1. Block diagram of a typical expert flow analyzer. S, R, C = sample, reagents, carrier solutions (inlet represented by empty arrows); double arrows = computer / unit interaction. For details, see text.

The available time intervals for the analytical steps are strictly constant, and the sample and standard solutions are handled under reproducible conditions. As a consequence, reliable results are obtained.

The flow-through detector is positioned in a fixed manifold site, leading to an improved repeatability. In addition, monitoring the detector output in the presence (analytical signal) and absence (baseline) of the flowing sample constitutes itself in a useful diagnostic tool for assessing system operation.

The recorded peak refers to a number of measurements, each one associated with particular sample residence time, conditions for sample handling and analyte concentration. This aspect is worthwhile in relation to analytical procedures exploiting concentration gradients. To this end, algorithms for multi-parametric analysis are generally used.

The possibility of random errors due to operator intervention is significantly reduced through automation. Classical glassware (*e.g.* volumetric flasks, pipettes, funnels, burettes) designed a century ago are less intensively used.

In addition to the above-mentioned aspects, agreement to the present trend towards automation, miniaturization and *in situ* analysis reflects other attractive characteristics of flow analysis. The number of flow-based analytical procedures, commercially available instruments, users and publications in the field is increasingly, demonstrating the worldwide acceptance of flow analysis.

2. THE FLOW ANALYZERS

The flow analyzers present a distinct nature of flowing streams, versatility and degree of external control. In a broad context, they can be classified as segmented or unsegmented ones.

2.1. The Segmented-Flow Analyzer

This type of analyzer was proposed in the 1950's [3] and initially applied to clinical chemistry with the AutoAnalyzer® trade name. The availability of multi-channel analyzers yielding several peaks per sample - each for a different analyte - led to the appearance of the multiple analysis chart, a very important tool for clinical diagnosis [4]. The segmented-flow analyzer played a dominant role in automated chemical assays for several decades and is still in use, particularly in clinical and environmental laboratories.

Either sample or carrier stream is aspirated to merge with an air stream, resulting in a segmented flow formed by regularly distributed discrete aqueous plugs separated from each other by air bubbles. Segmentation minimizes sample dispersion, improves mixing conditions and scrubs the tubing inner wall. In general, the air bubbles are removed immediately before detection. Sample handling is however restricted due to the compression / expansion of the gaseous phase. As low sample dispersion is concerned, a steady state situation is approached at the central portion of the sample zone, leading to a flat recorded peak.

Several samples are simultaneously handled inside the analytical path, allowing long residence times (up to 10 min) to be achieved without impairing sampling rate. System miniaturization is however difficult, as the bubble pattern has to be preserved and a large sample volume is needed for getting the flat peak. Consequently, the reagent consumption is relatively high. The sample flowing through the pumping unit is also a drawback.

The system is very rugged and reliable, as its only moving elements are the sampler arm and the pump rollers. Hence, its operation is not very amenable to external control.

2.2. The Unsegmented-Flow Analyzer

In these systems, the sample is inserted into an unsegmented carrier stream, and the formed sample / carrier assembly behaves as an uncompressible and homogeneous liquid column that can be efficiently managed. The different strategies outlined in section 3 are then better accomplished. Versatility is enhanced, timing is more precisely controlled, system is easier miniaturized and hyphenation with other techniques is more efficiently carried out as compared with the segmented-flow systems. A high degree of external control can be exploited. These features are the main driving forces towards the rapid development and acceptance of unsegmented-flow analysis especially the flow injection and sequential injection modalities.

The flow injection analyzer, conceived in the 1970's, exploits the sample insertion into an unsegmented carrier stream [5,6] and is presently worldwide accepted. Without segmentation, commutation (see item 5) becomes an important feature for system design and enhances versatility. Although manual system operation is possible, computer control is usually used.

The sequential injection analyzer [7] utilizes a multi-position valve for selecting the sample and reagent aliquots to be sequentially aspirated towards a holding coil, generating a stack of well-defined zones. After a pre-set time interval, the flow is reversed and the zone stack is directed towards detection. During transport, the zones interact mutually yielding the species to be monitored. Each port of the selection valve is dedicated to an specific purpose; therefore combinations of sample, standards, reagents, sample treatment devices and detectors around the valve can be modified via keyboard to suit a particular analysis. Enhanced versatility is then attained, as the main parameters (*e.g.* solution volumes, timing, reactor lengths) can be modified through software control, thus avoiding physical modifications in the system architecture.

In view of the increasing use of computers in the laboratory, the need for enhanced system flexibility and the applications demanding *in situ* assays, novel modalities of analyzers have been proposed. The concepts of the above mentioned flow analyzers were expanded, leading to small, lightweight and portable systems. As a rule, a high degree of external control is inherent to these systems. Batch injection [8], bead injection [9], discontinuous flow [10], "lab-on-valve" [11], flow-batch [12], multi-syringe flow [13] and multi-commuted flow [14] analysis are examples of these modalities. Zone fluidics, *i.e.* control and manipulation of flowing zones [15], is the underlying principle of these flow analyzers.

All the above-mentioned flow analyzers, especially those involving unsegmented flows are amenable to act as expert systems, as outlined in Section 5).

3. FLOW MANIPULATIONS

Special strategies for accomplishing different flow manipulations such as merging zones, zone sampling, stream splitting, zone stopping etc. (Figure 2) have been exploited [16] and are outlined as follow. It is important to emphasize that their potentialities are expanded by exploiting feedback mechanisms.

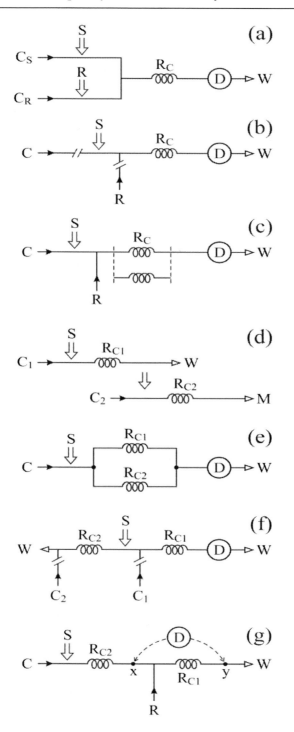

Figure 2. Flow diagrams of typical unsegmented flow systems with the merging zones (a), zone stopping (b), zone trapping (c), zone sampling (d), stream splitting (e), zone slicing (f) and multi-site detection (g) strategies. S, R, C = sample, reagent, carrier streams; R_C = coiled reactor; D = detector; M = towards manifold, W = recovery vessel for waste disposal; x, y = different monitoring sites; vectors = sites where pumping is applied; empty arrows = sample / reagent insertion; double lines = flow stopping. For details, see text.

3.1. Merging Zones

Sample and reagent aliquots are inserted into convergent carrier streams and interaction between the established zones occurs after stream merging (Figure 2a). In contrast to ordinary flow systems where the reagent solutions are always flowing, the reagent is consumed only in the presence of the sample and this leads to an amazing reduction in reagent consumption [17]. Possibility of simultaneous determinations, speciation and attainment of more stable baselines can be highlighted as other favorable characteristics of this strategy.

3.2. Zone Stopping

The sample is inserted into the flow system and, after receiving the required reagents, is halted inside either the flow-cell or the main reactor (Figure 2b). To this end, the pumping unit is programmed to stop for a pre-set time interval [18]. Alternatively, stream redirecting can be exploited [19]. The strategy has been sometimes referred to as stopped-flow and is worthwhile for analytical procedures relying on relatively slow chemical reactions. Another strategy to increase the residence time [20] involves the insertion of the sample into a carrier stream at a very low flow rate. After achievement of the analytical signal, a fast washing flow is added to flush the sample zone out.

3.3. Zone Trapping

When the sample zone is flowing inside the main reactor, it is moved outside the analytical path and the most concentrated central sample portion remains trapped during a pre-set time interval (Figure 2c). Thereafter, the sample is re-introduced into the main carrier stream, in order to be monitored [21]. The innovation is also worthwhile in relation to analytical procedures relying on relatively slow chemical reactions.

3.4. Zone Sampling

The sample zone is directed towards a re-sampling loop that selects an aliquot of the dispersed flowing zone and introduces it into another carrier stream for further handling (Figure 2d). Depending on the re-sampling instant, a different aliquot with a different concentration is selected [22]. The innovation has been exploited for attaining high and variable sample dilutions, simultaneous determinations, speciation, implementation of the standard addition method, etc.

3.5. Stream Splitting

The main stream into which the sample was introduced is split and the resulting streams carry different portions of the sample zone [23]. These emergent streams are further allowed to converge (Figure 2e) or otherwise are directed towards different detectors. The strategy involving further stream merging has been exploited for widen the dynamical concentration range and for differential kinetic analysis, whereas that without further merging is useful for attaining simultaneous determinations.

3.6. Zone Slicing

The sample is introduced into a carrier stream flowing backwards to waste. After a preset time interval, when most of the sample was discarded, the flow is reversed and the trailing portion of the sample zone is directed towards the manifold to be handled and monitored (Figure 2f). The strategy was originally named as split zone [24] and has been used mainly for attaining high degree of sample dispersion.

3.7. Addition / Removal of Manifold Components

Computer-controlled discretely operated commuting devices permit different components to be added or removed, in accordance to the analytical requirements. This potentiality has been often exploited in relation to stream re-directing, inclusion / removal of mini-columns in the analytical path, etc. In addition, it permits multi-site detection [25] involving positioning of the detector in two monitoring sites (Figure 2g).

4. MULTI-COMMUTATION

There is a clear link between the developments of flow analysis and commutation. This process involves discretely-operated devices such as rotary valves and sliding-bar commuters for sample introduction and other tasks such as *e.g.* multiple injections, stream splitting / redirecting and addition / removal of manifold components. Commutation is thus fundamental for flow manipulations, including the above mentioned strategies, as outlined in Section 3.

In spite of the large number of applications, flow systems designed with single commuters lack versatility, as these devices are operated in two resting positions (two states of commutation). The potential of flow systems are expanded by using an array of n independently controlled commuters, which yields 2^n states of commutation. Another possibility is the exploitation of sequential commutations of a single device in order to attain, *e.g.* a tandem stream [14]. These multi-commuted flow systems are highly versatile because the flow manifold can be re-configured through the control software. Indeed, they present potentialities to be used as general-purpose analyzers and examples of applications can be found in reviews articles [26,27].

Multi-commuted flow analyzers can be operated in a passive or an active manner. In the former, the steps of sample processing are defined previously to sample introduction into the analytical path. As the system present inherent timing, analytical features such as reagent consumption and sample throughput can be improved. Sequential determinations can be implemented due to the possibility of random access to different reagent solutions [28,29]. Other potential refer to the introduction of samples, reagents and diluents in a programmable fashion involving loop-based injection, time-based injection or binary sampling [14]. The performance of multi-commuted flow analyzers can be improved with active devices strategically positioned in the manifold. This permits the real-time modification of sample processing conditions, avoiding the need of re-processing outlier samples, such as those with analyte concentration outside the dynamic range. Other applications are discussed in Section 6.

5. EXPERT SYSTEMS

An automatic device is that *"able to operate independently of human control"* [30]. In chemical instrumentation, this idea was incorporated in the IUPAC[1] definition for automation: *"The use of combinations of mechanical and instrumental devices to replace, refine, extend, or supplement human effort and faculties in the performance of a given process, in which at least one major operation is controlled, without human intervention, by a feedback system"*[31]. The key point for an automatic system is then the indubitable actuation of a feedback system, which can be defined as the *"combination of a sensing and a commanding device that can modify the performance of a given act"* [31]. In other words, the response of a sensing device is used for in-line modifying the system operation. These definitions also hold for flow analysis. Automatic analyzers have been also named as expert, smart or intelligent systems.

The above-mentioned definitions are not always taken into account, and flow systems without feedback mechanisms have been erroneously named as automatic ones. In these systems, all steps involved in sample processing are defined previously to its introduction in the flow manifold.

Expert flow systems have lead to a paradigm shift in the practice of Analytical Chemistry by allowing response-oriented real-time decisions based on preliminary results (prior assays). In addition to the monitoring of the sensor response, automation requires computer interfacing and actuation of active devices (*e.g.* valves, pumps) in system hardware. The software in the expert system can modify the course of the analyses, for example, by altering pumping rate, solution volumes or reagents added to the sample. Other usual strategy is stream redirecting to submit the sample zone to different reaction conditions (*e.g.* heating and increasing dispersion or residence time). Commutation plays then a decisive role in expert flow systems and the potential can be expanded by exploiting multi-commutation (Section 4).

Expert systems are worthwhile for large-scale analysis, for controlling chemical assays, and for screening purposes aiming at real-time sample classification [32]. In view of the lower costs of installation and operation, inherent flexibility, ease of operation and control, as well as reduced consumption of reagents and analysis time, unsegmented flow systems have been often designed as expert systems. They also allow self-calibration and/or self-optimization [33-35].

---

[1] IUPAC = International Union of Pure and Applied Chemistry.

6. POTENTIALITIES

The main potentialities of the expert flow systems and examples of specific applications are mentioned as follows. For selected examples, see Table 1.

6.1. Screening Analysis

In flow analysis, the result of an in-line performed preliminary assay can be taken into account for modifying the steps of an analytical routine, aiming at to expand the capacity of the analytical laboratory. In this context, expert flow systems are important tools for screening analysis. The samples to be analyzed are selected by comparing the result of a preliminary assay with a pre-set threshold value specific for a given analytical problem. Thus, a binary answer such as yes/no, present / absent, high/low is obtained. A significant reduction in the total number of determinations is attained, thus expanding the analytical productivity of the laboratory.

The innovation was demonstrated in the determination of zinc and phosphate in soil extracts [36]. The number of determinations was reduced in about 30%, as zinc was determined only when phosphate was present in concentrations above a threshold level. Analogously, an expert flow system was proposed for the turbidimetric determination of chloride and sulfate in natural waters [37]. Both methods were implemented in the same manifold, and the need for sulfate determination was dependent on the in-line estimated chloride concentration.

Regarding industrial quality control, an expert system was designed for monitoring a bio-chemical process, involving the determinations of total acidity, reducing sugars, ethanol and pH during fermentation [38]. The system was able to decide when and which measurements should be carried out according to a pre-determined set of rules relying on in-line obtained analytical results. The expert system was also able to take decisions concerning eventual malfunctions.

6.2. Accuracy Assessment

Analytical procedures are often susceptible to systematic errors which are difficult to detect. In a lesser extent, this also holds for flow analysis. A typical situation refers to the partial overlap of sample and reagent zones in sequential injection and similar systems [39]. The samples and reagents are sequentially inserted into the same analytical channel, and the analytical signal corresponds to the interfacial region with optimized sample and reagent volumetric fractions. However, this region is not necessarily that yields the highest analytical accuracy, because interfering species may consume significant reagent amounts, modifying its concentration in that fluid element. The maximum response corresponds then to another fluid element with higher reagent amount but lower sample contribution. Inaccurate results can be also caused by differences in the kinetics of the chemical reactions involving samples and standard solutions (matrix effects) or lessening of the efficiency of a solid-phase reagent by continuous use. An expert flow system based on multi-commutation was effective for real-time characterizing and overcoming these sources of inaccuracy [39].

In addition to the detection and circumvention of specific sources of errors, expert flow systems are able to assess the accuracy of analytical procedures in a global manner. In this regard, the high sampling rate characteristic of flow analysis can be exploited for determination of a single analyte by two independent methods, eventually involving two detectors. Results are then checked by the control software and agreement between them is an indicative of accuracy. If discrepant results are obtained, in-line addition-recovery experiments can help to compensate for matrix effects, thus improving the accuracy.

This approach was originally applied to chloride determination in river water samples with high variability in matrix and acidity [40]. Spectrophotometric and turbidimetric procedures were implemented in the same manifold, and the analyte concentration was determined after considering the results obtained with both methods and the eventual correction of matrix effects. Methodological limitations due to variations in sample matrix were then circumvented. Other applications included analysis of pharmaceutical formulations by sequential injection [41,42] and single interface [43] flow systems.

6.3. System Optimization

Optimization is often a time-consuming step in the development of an analytical procedure, as it requires evaluation of the effects of the main involved variables, as well as the interactions among them to achieve the best analytical response. The optimum condition can however be altered in function of uncontrolled experimental parameters, such as temperature and composition of the sample matrix, thus requiring further optimizations. Automation of this process can then save time and yield more reliable analytical results.

Expert flow systems take advantage of iterative control devices which work in association and involve real-time alterations of the experimental parameters. They are designed to provide decisions leading to the real-time introduction of corrections and, eventually, manifold self-optimization. This feature also leads to an enhancement in the system versatility and flexibility.

Regarding self-optimization, a flow-injection system able to implement the real-time simplex algorithm was proposed [33]. The flow rate as well as the sample and reagent volumes were computer-controlled and permitted the in-line application of the algorithm relying on two experimental parameters (flow rate and sample-to-reagent volumetric ratio) and the detector responses. The feasibility of the approach was demonstrated by the chloride determination in natural waters with high variability in the analyte concentrations.

An analogous expert flow system was further designed, validated and applied to the sequential injection determinations of calcium and magnesium in natural waters with spectrophotometric detection and multivariate calibration [34]. As the system provided general information, sequential injection methodologies could be developed for other analytes and sample matrices [44].

6.4. Fault Detection

Detecting and circumventing eventual system failures such as those caused by inlet of air bubbles yielding spurious signals, system clogging and/or improper working of the system components (including the detection unit) is of utmost relevance. This is more critical during processing of large sample batches or process monitoring. In order to ensure reliable operation of the flow system, as well as to provide system diagnosis, automated supervision is worthwhile [45].

An expert system demonstrating this approach was designed for monitoring the total acidity and peroxide value in olive oils [46]. The feedback control allowed the remote control of the system, and in-line classification of the assayed samples. Results were valuable for estimating the overall quality of the oil, as well as for identifying adulteration, age, storage conditions and oxidation level.

Intelligent systems designed can also be exploited for diagnosis and validation. Regarding validation of the analytical procedure, an expert system was designed for amperometric flow injection determination of penicillin in pharmaceutical formulations [47]. Input data for validation were in-line obtained.

Another possibility for recognizing diagnosis faults and find their causes is to take advantage of artificial neural networks. The innovation was demonstrated in the sequential injection analysis of calcium and magnesium in natural waters [48]. The diagnosis was carried out by using real-time gathered information. The expert flow system was able to self-reconfiguration, recognized analytical signals through the neural network and provided network output interpretation. Thus, the system was able to detect faults, to assign failure causes, to classify samples and to manage them under different conditions. Depending on the sample classification (low or high concentration), the decision was to re-analyze the sample under different experimental conditions or not.

6.5. Localization of the Sample Zone

Analytical flow systems can be designed to permit the central portion of the sample zone to be re-sampled and inserted into a second carrier stream (V. Section 3.6). To this end, specific detectors are placed in strategic manifold sites to specify the instant position of a flowing sample.

The innovation was originally exploited in the determination of C_1-C_5 n-mercaptans in gasoline involving liquid-liquid extraction [49]. An aliquot of a NaOH solution (aqueous phase) was introduced into the flowing gasoline sample (organic phase) and the analyte was extracted by the aqueous phase. When passing through the second injection port, the aqueous phase was re-sampled and re-inserted into another NaOH solution. For real-time definition of the re-sampling instant, the conductivity of the solution flowing inside the re-sampling loop was monitored. A sudden increase triggered the injector, allowing only the central portion of the NaOH zone to be selected. With this intelligent flow system, cumbersome phase separation steps were avoided.

Another situation refers to the monosegmented flow systems which were proposed as an alternative for analytical procedures based on relatively slow reactions [50]. In these systems, samples are separated from the carrier stream by air bubbles at the front and tail portions, aiming at minimization of sample dispersion, and thus carryover. Several sample zones can be simultaneously processed, and this is another positive aspect towards improvement of sampling rate.

The air bubbles permit also the precise instant localization of the flowing sample into the analytical path. To this end, optical switches are used to sense the gas-liquid interfaces. Feedback mechanisms from changes in the logical level of the switches make feasible the reagent addition only to the sample zone, thus minimizing the reagent consumption. The strategy was demonstrated by the determination of glucose, creatinine and urea in blood plasma and serum [51], where enzymes and chromogenic reagents were sequentially added to the sample zone. Other applications involve liquid-liquid extractions and determination of gaseous species. For the former, aliquots of organic solvents were strategically added to the analytical path for single-phase [52] or dual-phase [53] separations. For the later, gaseous samples replaced the air bubbles in the mono-segmented pattern. For the analytical determinations, either volume contraction [54] or change of a physicochemical property in the flowing liquid sample [55] due to the selective analyte absorption was exploited.

6.6. Controlled Dilutions

Sample dilutions are often required in analytical procedures in order to match the expected analyte concentration with the dynamical range of the detector. This step is usually time-consuming, and may both affect precision and lead to systematic errors. Clinical analyses, where several parameters need to be routinely determined in thousands samples, can be mentioned as an example. In this field, extensive dilutions of biological fluids are usual in view of the high analyte concentration and also to minimize matrix effects.

The dispersion process typical of the unsegmented flow systems can be exploited for attaining the required degree of sample dilution. This process occurs under highly reproducible conditions and can be controlled by adjusting parameters such as *e.g.* sample volume, reactor dimensions and flow rates of confluent streams [56]. As a consequence, flow systems are a real alternative to circumvent the above mentioned drawbacks in routine works. On the other hand, difficulties may arise for sample batches with high variability in analyte concentration *i.e.*, when different samples need to be processed under different dispersion conditions.

Expert systems can be designed to achieve this goal, by comparing the analytical response with previously defined upper and lower threshold values. Samples with analyte concentrations within these values can be directly quantified, whereas excessively concentrated or diluted samples should be handled under modified dispersion conditions. To this end, trial measurements [57] can be exploited: different sample aliquots with decreasing dilution degrees are handled and the analytical signals are compared with a pre-set threshold. Quantification of the analyte is performed when this value is surpassed and the remainder portion of the sample zone is discarded. Otherwise, a larger sample aliquot is selected, analogously handled, and so on.

Matching the sample aliquot with the detector dynamical working range also minimizes the sample amount that reaches the detection unit, thus avoiding drawbacks such as clogging of the nebulizers of atomic spectrometers when processing highly saline samples. Feedback mechanisms were included in the control software for selection of degree of sample dilution for the determination of metallic ions by atomic absorption / emission spectrometry [58,59].

Controlled variation of the sample dispersion is a useful tool also for widen the linear concentration range, as demonstrated in the spectrophotometric determination of calcium [60]. As time-based sample slicing and zone sampling were involved, the software was developed to control all steps of sample processing, and to provide facilities to change the manifold configuration in accordance with the analytical response. The required sample dilution was attained with up to three trials, alloying direct analysis of samples with a large variability in analyte concentrations (natural waters, plant materials, milk, fertilizers and calcareous rocks), with a relative standard deviation of results estimated as 0.83% and a sampling rate of 60 h^{-1}.

Other approaches to widen the dynamic concentration range include: (i) automatic adjustment of the electronic gain of the detector, as demonstrated in the determination of mercury [61]; (ii) real-time decision on the need for analyte in-line concentration in the determination of iron [62] and (iii) selection of the detection mode (transmittance or reflectance) in the determination of sulfide [63].

6.7. Matrix Matching

There are situations where sample matrix modifies the analytical signal, and serious errors may result of improper calibration without considering these effects. Matrix matching is a requisite to achieve accurate results, but this approach requires information about the sample matrix, which is not always available. Variations in matrix composition within a sample lot are also a drawback and alternatives such as calibration by the standard additions method have been exploited. However, implementation of this strategy in batch procedures is laborious and time-consuming and flow-based procedures have been developed as alternatives [64]. In addition, expert systems have been proposed for analysis of samples with large variety in composition.

In a pioneer work, a feedback mechanism was exploited to minimize matrix effects on the determination of metals in seawater by ICP OES [65]. The sample salinity was roughly evaluated according to a prior determination of sodium, and the decision consisted in selecting the salinity of the standard solutions matching that of the sample. This was done by modifying the time delay in the zone sampling process, thus selecting a different amount of sodium chloride to be added to the samples. The software allowed the automatic choice of one of the three analytical curves obtained.

Another possibility is to take advantage of individual treatment of every sample, in contrast to ordinary flow analyzers where all the samples and standards are subjected to the same handling conditions. For sample lots with high variability in concentrations, pH or ionic strength, the required adjustments can be done in accordance to an in-line performed prior assay.

The approach was applied to the spectrophotometric determination of total nitrogen in Kjeldahl digests [66]. As the results were susceptible to variations in the sample acidity – rather different from sample to sample - an individual pH adjustment was needed. To this end, an alkaline solution was added to every sample and the amount was in-line defined according to a pH-oriented feedback mechanism. The results agreed with certified values of standard reference materials.

Individual sample conditioning was further applied to the spectrophotometric determination of aluminum in plant digests [67] and iron in estuarine waters [68], which are characterized by pronounced variations in acidity and salinity, respectively. For aluminum determination, feedback mechanisms based on the color changes provided by an acid-base indicator were exploited for the previous adjustment of the sample acidity. For iron determination, different amounts of a sodium chloride solution were added to every assayed sample in order to level off the salinity. Matrix effects in this catalytic method were then circumvented.

6.8. Flow Titrations

Titration is a classical analytical approach relying on reaction of the analyte (titrand) with another chemical species (titrant) with known concentration and nature. The determination is based on the measurement of the titrant volume (or mass) and reaction stoichiometry. Titrations can be classified as acid-base, precipitation, redox or complexation, and usually yield precise results. The process is often time-consuming, and this aspect is a drawback especially if several samples are to be handled. In order to circumvent this limitation, different automatic titrators operating in a batch-wise fashion have been placed in the market.

Another possibility to circumvent the above drawback is to take advantage of flow titrations, originally conceived by Blaedel and Laessig [69]. In this pioneer work, the sample and titrand streams were allowed to converge. The sample flow-rate was maintained while the titrant flow-rate was varied for searching the end point. Response curves for solutions of known concentrations were preliminarily obtained and thereafter the samples were run. As an analytical curve - unnecessary in conventional titrations – was required, the approach is regarded as a "pseudo-titration". The performance could be improved by automation as demonstrated in further works.

Titrations can also be accomplished in a flow injection system by inserting the sample into a chemically inert carrier stream, letting the sample zone to undergo high dispersion (usually inside a mixing chamber) and adding the titrant stream by confluence. Width of the recorded peak can be the measurement basis [70]. The innovation is characterized by a very high sampling rate and a low sample requirement and theoretical aspects are presented elsewhere [71]. As an analytical curve is needed, the approach is also considered as a pseudo-titration.

Automatic titrations can be implemented in expert flow systems by in-line modifying the volumetric fractions of sample and titrant in accordance with the involved algorithm. The analytical response is then evaluated to decide the next step of the titration.

An expert flow system exploiting the binary search strategy and spectrophotometric detection for end point search was proposed [72]. The system included solenoid valves for sample and titrant inlet: the volumes were simultaneously modified and total volume of the sample zone was maintained. After each measurement, the expert system decided if either the titrant or the sample volume should be increased according to a feedback mechanism. The accuracy level was previously set as a software parameter. Samples with concentrations ranging within two orders of magnitude could be titrated by making use of the same flow set-up. As an analytical curve was not involved, the approach can be regarded as a true titration. The feasibility of the proposal was demonstrated by the titration of hydrochloric acid with sodium hydroxide, and a 99.99% precision was attained. The strategy was further applied to the determination of total acidity in silage extracts [73], chloride in milk and wine [74] and total acidity in red wine [75].

Another strategy involves a prior assay for assisting the main titration. The analyte content is in-line roughly estimated and the titration steps are refined in accordance to the expected analyte concentration. The innovation was initially applied to the spectrophotometric titration of iron in ores [76].

The different types of both pseudo and true flow titrations are discussed elsewhere [77].

8. TRENDS

The increasingly need for reliable analytical results, improved detectability and short analysis time is a challenge for analytical chemists. Expert flow systems may play an important role to achieve these goals, improving the lab productivity by means of screening strategies and matching the analyte concentration to the detector response range. Accuracy assessment and sample conditioning for every assayed sample may become an essential requirement for accreditation of laboratories or specific procedures. For process monitoring, flow systems able to detect and circumvent fails during long-time working periods are also indispensable. Expert systems are then intrinsically more cost-effective and environmentally friendly.

Table 1. Selected analytical applications of expert flow systems

Application	Remarks	Ref.
Screening		
Phosphate and zinc in soil extracts	Phosphate determination as the basis for a concentration-oriented decision regarding to the need for zinc determination	36
Sulphate and chloride in natural waters	Real time decision on the need for next assay	37
Acidity, reducing sugars, ethanol and pH monitoring in fermentation process	System able to take decisions on possible malfunctions	78
Accuracy assessment		
Calcium and iron in natural waters	Detecting and circumventing inaccuracy sources	39
Chloride in river waters	Turbidimetric flow analysis with accuracy assessment	79
Lansoprazole in pharmaceutical formulations	Single interface flow system with two quasi-independent analytical methods	43
System optimization		
Chloride in natural waters	Real-time implementation of the simplex algorithm	33
Calcium and magnesium in natural waters	System able to real-time derive the parameters for system configuration	34
Several metals in synthetic and real samples	Automatic variation in pH or ligant concentration	35

Table 1. (Continued)

Application	Remarks	Ref.
Troubleshooting (fault detection)		
Glucose monitoring in bioprocess	Real-time knowledge-based mechanism for the supervision of flow system	45
Acidity and peroxide value in olive oils	Supervision of the system functioning, classification of the samples and evaluation of the oil quality	46
Penicillin in pharmaceutical formulations	Real-time evaluation of calibration procedure, system drift and matrix effects	47
Calcium and magnesium in natural waters	Artificial neural networks for fault detection and signal diagnosis in sequential injection analysis	48
Localization of the sample zone		
Glucose, creatinine and urea in blood plasma and serum	Reagent addition in a mono-segmented flow analyzer	51
Cadmium, copper and zinc in organic phase	Automated mono-segmented flow system for liquid-liquid extraction	80
Cholesterol in bood serum	Mono-segmented flow system for spectrophotometric assays	81
Controlled dilutions		
Calcium in different samples	Different dispersion degrees without modification of the manifold	60
Metallic cations in natural waters	Real-time controlled zone sampling	58
Iron in waters, vegetables and pharmaceutical formulations	Optional in-line concentration, speciation, monitoring without manifold reconfiguration	62
Potassium in soil extracts, parenteral solutions and wines	In-line dilutions for widen the dynamic concentration range in flame atomic absorption spectrometry	82
Sulfide in soil extracts with suspended particles	In-line dilution or concentration	63
Mercury in fish muscle	Instrumental gain real-time selected for every sample	61
Ammonium in natural waters	In-line concentration defined by a feedback mechanism	83
Iron in natural waters	System able to decide on the need for analyte in-line concentration	84
Matrix matching		
N-total in plant tissues	Automatic in-line pH adjustment	66
Heavy metals in saline waters	Four analytical curves with different salinities attained by zone sampling; in-line selection of the most suitable one for every assayed sample.	65
Detection of sources of inaccuracy		
Iron in environmental samples	Expert multi-commuted flow system for real-time characterization of sources of inaccuracy and for overcoming the problem for every assayed sample	39
Titrations		
Total acidity evaluation	True photometric flow titration involving binary search	72
Ascorbic acid in fruit juices and soft drinks	Automatic titration based on variation of volumetric fractions	85
Precipitation titration	Potentiometric precipitation titration in a multi-commuted flow system	86
Total acidity in silage extracts	Automatic flow titration in a multi-commuted flow system	73
Total acidity in red wines	Spectrophotometric flow titration in a multi-commuted flow system	75
Chloride in milk and wines	Potentiometric titration ion a monosegmented flow system	74

The literature overview presented here shows that feedback mechanisms have been limited to some smart systems devoted to specific applications. This situation tends to be modified by the incorporation of real-time decisions in commercially available systems. This depends mainly on software development, which may take into account the needs and expertise of analytical chemists aiming robust, effective and user-friendly tools.

REFERENCES

[1]   Zagatto, E.A.G.; Worsfold, P.J. Flow Analysis: Overview. In: Worsfold, P.J.; Townshend, A.; Poole, C.F. (Eds). Encyclopaedia of Analytical Science, 2nd Edn, Oxford: Elsevier, 2005; 3, 24-31.

[2]   Rocha, F.R.P., Nobrega, J.A., Fatibello-Filho, O. *Green Chem.* 2001, *3*, 216–220.

[3]   Skeggs Jr, L.T. *Am. J. Clin. Pathol.* 1957, *28,* 311-322.

[4]   Skeggs, L.T. *Clin. Chem.* 2000, *46,* 1425-1436.

[5]   Ruzicka, J.; Hansen, E.H. *Anal. Chim. Acta* 1975, *78,*145-157.

[6]   Stewart, K.K.; Beecher, G.R.; Hare, P.E. *Anal. Biochem.* 1976, *70,*167-173.

[7]   Ruzicka, J.; Marshall, G.D. *Anal. Chim. Acta* 1990, *237,* 329-343.

[8]   Wang, J.; Taha, Z. *Anal. Chem.* 1991, *63,* 1053-1056.

[9]   Ruzicka, J.; Scampavia, L. *Anal. Chem.* 1999, *71,* 257A-263A.

[10] Cardwell, T.J.; Cattrall, R.W.; Cross, G.J.; O'Cornell, J.R.; Petty, J.D.; Scollary, G.R. *Analyst* 1991, *116,* 1051-1054.

[11] Ruzicka, J. *Analyst* 2000, *125,* 1053-1060.

[12] Honorato, R.S.; Araujo, M.C.U.; Lima, R.A.C.; Zagatto, E.A.G.; Lapa, R.A.S.; Lima, J.L.F.C. *Anal. Chim. Acta* 1999, *396,* 91-97.

[13] Albertus, F.; Horstkotte, B.; Cladera, A.; Cerda, V. *Analyst* 1999, *124,* 1373-1381.

[14] Reis, B.F.; Gine, M.F.; Zagatto, E.A.G.; Lima, J.L.F.C.; Lapa, R.A.S.; *Anal. Chim. Acta* 1994, 293, 129-138.

[15] Marshall, G.D.; Wolcott, D.; Olson, D. *Anal. Chim. Acta* 2003, *499,* 29-40.

[16] Kolev, S.D.; McKelvie I.D. (Eds.), Advances in Flow Injection Analysis and Related Techniques, Wilson and Wilson's Comprehensive Analytical Chemistry Volume 54, Elsevier, Amsterdam, 2008.

[17] Bergamin-Filho, H.; Zagatto, E.A.G.; Krug, F.J.; Reis, B.F. *Anal. Chim. Acta* 1978, *101*, 17-23.

[18] Ruzicka, J.; Hansen, E.H. *Anal. Chim. Acta* 1979, *106,* 207-224.

[19] Feres, M.A.; Fortes, P.R.; Zagatto, E.A.G.; Santos, J.L.M.; Lima, J.L.F.C. *Anal. Chim. Acta* 2008, *618,* 1-17.

[20] Zagatto, E.A.G.; Jacintho, A.O.; Mortatti, J.; Bergamin-Filho, H. *Anal. Chim. Acta* 1980, *120,* 399-403.

[21] Krug, F.J.; Reis, B.F.; Gine, M.F.; Zagatto, E.A.G.; Ferreira, J.R.; Jacintho, A.O. *Anal. Chim. Acta* 1983, *151,* 39-48.

[22] Reis, B.F.; Jacintho, A.O.; Mortatti, J.; Krug, F.J.; Zagatto, E.A.G.; Bergamin-Filho, H.; Pessenda, L.C.R. *Anal. Chim. Acta* 1981, *123,* 221-228.

[23] Ruzicka, J.; Stewart, J.W.B.; Zagatto, E.A.G. *Anal. Chim. Acta* 1976, *81,* 387-398.

[24] Clark, G.D.; Ruzicka, J.; Christian, G.D. *Anal. Chem.* 1989, *61,* 1773-1778.

[25] Zagatto, E.A.G.; Bergamin-Filho, H.; Brienza, S.M.B.; Arruda, M.A.Z.; Nogueira, A.R.A.; Lima, J.L.F.C. *Anal. Chim. Acta* 1992, *261,* 59-65.

[26] Rocha, F.R.P.; Reis, B.F.; Zagatto, E.A.G.; Lima, J.L.F.C.; Lapa, R.A.S.; Santos, J.L.M. *Anal. Chim. Acta* 2002, *468*, 119–131.

[27] Feres, M.A.; Fortes, P.R.; Zagatto, E.A.G.; Santos, J.L.M.; Lima, J.L.F.C. *Anal. Chim. Acta* 2008, *618*, 1–17.

[28] Malcome-Lawes, D.J.; Pasquini, C. *J. Autom. Chem.* 1988, *10,* 192-197.

[29] Rocha, F.R.P.; Martelli, P.B.; Reis, B.F. *Talanta* 2001, *55*, 861–869.

[30] Cambridge international dictionary of English, Cambridge University Press, London, 1995.

[31] Kingston, H.M.; Kingston, M.L. *J. Autom. Chem.* 1994, *16,* 43-57.

[32] Valcarcel, M.; Cardenas, S.; Gallego, M. *Trends Anal. Chem.* 1999, *18,* 685-694.

[33] Gine, M.F.; Tuon, R.L.; Cesta, A.A.; Packer, A.P.; Reis, B.F. *Anal. Chim. Acta* 1998, *366,* 313-318.

[34] Rius, A.; Callao, M.P.; Rius, F.X. *Anal. Chim. Acta* 1995, *316,* 27-37.

[35] Marcos, J.; Rius, A.; Valcarcel, M. *Analyst* 1992, *117,* 1629-1633.

[36] Grassi, V.; Dias, A.C.B.; Zagatto, E.A.G. *Talanta* 2004, *64,* 1114-1118.

[37] Fortes, P.R.; Feres, M.A.; Zagatto, E.A.G. *Talanta* 2008, *77,* 571-575.

[38] Peris, M.; Maquieira, A.; Puchades, R.; Chirivella, V.; Ors, R.; Serrano, J. *Chem. Intell. Lab. Syst.* 1990, *234,* 207-212.

[39] Zagatto, E.A.G.; Rocha, F.R.P.; Martelli, P.B.; Reis, B.F. *Pure Appl. Chem.* 2001, *73,* 45-54.

[40] Oliveira, C.C.; Sartini, R.P.; Zagatto, E.A.G.; Lima, J.L.F.C. *Anal. Chim. Acta* 1997, *350*, 31-36.

[41] Pimenta, A.M.; Araujo, A.N.; Montenegro, M.C.B.S.M. *Anal. Chim. Acta* 2001, *438*, 31–38.

[42] Pimenta, A.M.; Araújo, A.N.; Montenegro, M.C.B.S.M. *Anal. Chim. Acta* 2002, *470*, 185–194.

[43] Silvestre, C.I.C.; Santos, J.L.M.; Lima, J.L.F.C.; Feres, M.A.; Zagatto, E.A.G. *Microchem. J.* 2010, *94,* 60–64.

[44] Valcarcel, M.; Luque de Castro, M.D. Automatic Methods of Analysis, In: Techniques and Instrumentation in Analytical Chemistry, Elsevier Sci. Pub., Amsterdam, 1988, Vol. 9, 560 pp.

[45] Brandt, J.; Hitzmann, B. *Anal. Chim. Acta* 1994, *291,* 29-40.

[46] Bonastre, A.; Ors, R.; Peris, M. *Anal. Chim. Acta* 2004, *506,* 189-195.

[47] Wolters, R.; van Opstal, M.A.J.; Kateman, G. *Anal. Chim. Acta* 1990, *233,* 65-76.

[48] Ruisanchez, I.; Lozano, J.; Larrechi, M.S.; Rius, F.X.; Zupan, J. *Anal. Chim. Acta* 1997, *348,* 113-127.

[49] Dasgupta, P.K.; Lei, W. *Anal. Chim. Acta* 1989, *226,* 255-269.

[50] Pasquini, C.; Oliveira, W.A. *Anal. Chem.* 1985, *57,* 2575-2579.

[51] Raimundo-Junior, I.M.; Pasquini, C. *Analyst* 1997, *122,* 1039-1044.

[52] Facchin, I.; Martins, J.W.; Zamora, P.G.P.; Pasquini, C. *Anal. Chim. Acta* 1994, *285,* 287-292.

[53] Facchin, I.; Pasquini, C. *Anal. Chim. Acta* 1995, *308,* 231-237.

[54] Silva, M.C.H.; Pasquini, C. *Anal. Chim. Acta* 1997, *349,* 377-384.

[55] Silva, M.C.H.; Rohwedder, J.J.R.; Pasquini, C. *Anal. Chim. Acta* 1998, *366,* 223-229.

[56] Ruzicka, J. and Hansen E.H. Flow Injection Analysis, 2nd Edn.; Wiley Interscience, N. York, 1988; pp 17-497.

[57] Reis, B.F.; Zagatto, E.A.G.; Martelli, P.B.; Brienza, S.M.B. *Analyst* 1993, 118, 719-722.

[58] Garrido, J.M.P.J.; Lapa, R.A.S.; Lima, J.L.F.C.; Delerue-Matos, C.; Santos, J.L.M. *J. Autom. Chem.* 1996, *18,* 17-21.

[59] Gine, M.F.; Packer, A.P.; Blanco, T.; Reis, B.F. *Anal. Chim. Acta* 1996, *323,* 47-53.

[60] Rocha, F.R.P.; Martelli, P.B.; Frizzarin, R.M.; Reis, B.F. *Anal. Chim. Acta* 1998, *366,* 45-53.

[61] Serra, A.M.; Estela, J.M.; Cerda, V. *Talanta* 2008, *77,* 556-560.

[62] Pons, C.; Miro, M.; Becerra, E.; Estela, J.M.; Cerda, V. *Talanta* 2004, *62,* 887-895.

[63] Ferrer, L.; Estela, J.M.; Cerda, V. *Anal. Chim. Acta* 2006, *573,* 391-398.

[64] Honorato, R.S.; Zagatto, E.A.G.; Lima, R.A.C.; Araujo, M.C.U. *Anal. Chim. Acta* 2000, *416,* 231-237.

[65] Gine, M.F.; Bergamin-Filho, H.; Reis, B.F.; Tuon, R.L. *Anal. Chim. Acta* 1990; *234,* 207-212.

[66] Carneiro, J.M.T.; Honorato, R.S.; Zagatto, E.A.G. *Fresenius J. Anal. Chem* 2000, *368,* 496-500.

[67] Honorato, R.S.; Carneiro, J.M.T.; Zagatto, E.A.G. *Anal. Chim. Acta* 2001, *441,* 309-315.

[68] Carneiro, J.M.T.; Dias, A.C.B.; Zagatto, E.A.G.; Honorato, R.S. *Anal. Chim. Acta* 2002, *455,* 327-333.

[69] Blaedel, W.J.; Laessig, R.H. *Anal. Chem.* 1964, *36,* 1617-1623.

[70] Ruzicka, J.; Hansen, E.H.; Mosbaek, H. *Anal. Chim. Acta* 1977, *92,* 235-249.

[71] Ramsing, A.U.; Ruzicka, J.; Hansen, E.H. *Anal. Chim. Acta* 1981, *129,* 1-17.

[72] Korn, M.; Gouveia, L.F.; Oliveira, E.; Reis, B.F. *Anal. Chim. Acta* 1995, *313,* 177-184.

[73] Tumang, C.A.; Paim, A.P.S.; Reis, B.F. *J. AOAC Int.* 2002; *85,* 328-332.

[74] Vieira, J.A.; Raimundo Jr, I.M.; Reis, B.F.; Montenegro, M.C.B.S.M.; Araujo, A.N. *J. Braz. Chem. Soc.* 2003, *14,* 259-264.

[75] Garcia, A.J.C.; Reis, B.F. *J. Autom. Methods Manage. Chem.* 2006, 1-8.

[76] Honorato, R.S.; Zagatto, E.A.G.; Lima R.A.C.; Araujo, M.C.U. *Anal. Chim. Acta* 2000, *416,* 231-237.

[77] Honorato, R.S.; Araujo, M.C.U.; Lima, R.A.C.; Zagatto, E.A.G.; Lapa, R.A.S.; Lima, J.L.F.C. *Anal. Chim. Acta* 1999, *396,* 91-97.

[78] Peris, M.; Maquieira, A.; Puchades, R.; Chirivella, V.; Ors, R.; Serrano, *Chemom. Intell. Lab.Syst.* 1993, *21,* 243-247.

[79] Oliveira, C.C.; Sartini, R.P.; Zagatto, E.A.G.; Lima, J.L.F.C. *Anal. Chim. Acta* 1997, *350,* 31-36.

[80] Facchin, I.; Rohwedder, J.J.R.; Pasquini, C. *J. Autom. Chem.* 1997, *19,* 33-38.

[81] Araujo, A.N.; Catita, J.A.M.; Lima, J.L.F.C. *Farmaco* 1999, *54,* 51-55.

[82] Almeida, M.I.G.S.; Segundo, M.S.; Lima, J.L.F.C.; Rangel, A.O.S.S. *J. Anal. At. Spectrom.* 2009; *24,* 340-346.

[83] Hong L.-C.; Sun, X.-Y.; Wang, L.-Q. *Anal. Lett.* 2009, *42,* 2364-2377.

[84] Pons, C.; Forteza, R.; Cerda, V. *Anal Chim. Acta* 2004; *524,* 79-88.

[85] Paim, A.P.S.; Reis, B.F. *Anal. Sci.* 2000; *16,* 487-491.

[86] Almeida, C.M.N.V.; Araujo, M.C.U.; Lapa, R.A.S.; Lima, J.L.F.C.; Reis, B.F.; Zagatto, E.A.G. *Analyst* 2000; *125,* 333-340.

In: Expert System Software
Editors: Jason M. Segura and Albert C. Reiter

ISBN: 978-1-61209-114-3
© 2012 Nova Science Publishers, Inc.

Chapter 3

THE POTENTIAL OF EXPERT SYSTEMS IN REMOTE SENSING APPLICATIONS DOMAIN

Lamyaa Gamal El-Deen Taha[*]

National Authority of Remote Sensing and Space Science(NARSS),
Aviation and Aerial Photography Division,
Digital Mapping Department, Egypt

ABSTRACT

Expert systems have been an active research field in remote sensing. This chapter gives an overview about expert systems and reviews the current progress in applications of expert systems in remote sensing. Many expert systems have been implemented for remote sensing applications such as image classification, feature extraction, change detection. Remotely sensed data are the input to the expert systems i.e.mostly images, but also LIDAR data and synthetic Aperture Radar (SAR). The basic terminology of expert systems is given first, followed by a review of the major component of expert System, then the classification of expert systems methodologies has been stated, after that applications of expert systems in remote sensing have been reviewed. An overview of software that has been used for implementation of expert systems for remote sensing applications has been given. This chapter ends with discussion of some important issues and challenges as well as potential directions for further developments.

Keywords: Expert systems - Expert system methodologies -Knowledge Base- Rule based expert systems- Case-based reasoning - Remote sensing.

---

[*] E-mail: Lamyaa@narss.sci.eg.

INTRODUCTION

Expert systems are computer programs that can perform some task, which typically requires the capabilities of a skilled human. These tasks are usually of a decision-making nature rather than physical actions. (Alexander et al.,1999)

Expert systems (ES) are a branch of applied artificial intelligence (AI).(Liao, 2005).Artificial intelligence (AI) emerged during the1950s and 1960s with one of its goals being to make machines more intelligent and therefore more useful. (Alexander et al.,1999)

Expert systems technology has two key qualities. One is that expert systems do things that cannot be done otherwise. Another is that expert systems do things faster, more reliably, less expensively, and with fewer highly trained people .(Quinlan,1987)

Careful choice of the domain in which to apply an expert system is important. Experiences gained in early expert system projects have established a number of criteria defining suitable domains: (i) an algorithmic solution should not exist; (ii) the task should be narrow and knowledge-intensive; (iii) cognitive skills only should be required; (iv) the task must be well understood; (v) genuine experts must exist; and (vi) the task should not be too difficult, or (vii) involve common-sense reasoning(Masson,1995)

The mid-1970s saw the emergence of the first expert systems for applications such as medical diagnosis, chemical data analysis, and mineral exploration. Since that time, thousands of expert systems across hundreds of different fields have been developed. (Alexander et al,1999)

Remote sensing domain is one of the major applications areas of expert systems.

This work has been made to produce a comprehensive summaries and reviews of expert systems applications in remote sensing.

BASIC TERMINOLOGY

Expert systems technologies have some complex terminology and unclear definitions. To establish a common base of understanding, some definitions are mentioned here

Artificial Intelligence: The sub-field of computer science concerned with understanding the concepts and methods of human reasoning, and the application of this understanding to the development of computer programs that exhibit intelligent behavior.

Expert System: A computer program that performs difficult, specialized tasks at the level of a human expert. Because of the reliance of these programs on varied types of knowledge, these programs are also known as Knowledge-Based Systems.

Heuristic Knowledge: Judgmental knowledge underlying expertise - often consisting of rules-of-thumb acquired through personal experience. This heuristic knowledge is usually implicit, not necessarily being explicit even to the expert.

Domain Knowledge: The term domain refers to the specific area of application, such as pump failure diagnosis, or chemical analysis, remote sensing . Domain knowledge is that knowledge, which is specific to the domain, rather than general knowledge, or common sense knowledge.

Knowledge Base: That part of the expert system (program) in which the domain knowledge is stored, using some method of representation, such as rules. (EIA,1997)

A knowledge base for remote sensing applications could be composed of user-defined variables and included raster imagery, vector coverage, spatial models, external programs, and simple scalars (Kahya et al., 2010)

Working memory: Part of an expert system that contains, the problem facts that are discovered during the session weather supplied by the user or inferred by the system. (Durkin, 1994)

Inference Mechanism: Also known as the "Inference Engine,"is the knowledge processor in an expert system that matches the fact contained in the working memory with the domain knowledge contained in the knowledge base in order to draw conclusions about the problem(Durkin,1994), it controls the reasoning operations of the expert system. This part of the expert system (program) deals with making assertions, hypotheses, and conclusions. It is through the inference mechanism that the reasoning strategy (or method of solution) is controlled. (Durkin,1994; EIA,1997)

MAJOR COMPONENT OF EXPERT SYSTEM

The expert system major components are knowledge base, working memory and inference engine and user inference. (Durkin,1994)

The general structure of an expert system can be described in terms of six main components:

1. The external data acquisition systems, which provide the input data for the specific application. These systems may be manual (that is, data must be collected and entered by hand) or automated (for example, remote sensing);
2. The knowledge base, which is a collection of domain specific knowledge usually represented as rules based on IF-THEN logic;
3. External application programs, with which the system exchanges information and data. For example, computer simulation models may provide quantitative estimates of air and water quality parameters or GIS may provide spatial data on the location and characteristics of key environmental components. Reports from expert systems may be exported to common word processing or database software programs;
4. The user, who controls the system, inputs information, selects options, and generates reports;
5. The user interface, which is the means by which the user communicates with other components. Most user interfaces are menu driven and have a number of display and reporting features; and
6. The inference engine, which is the reasoning mechanism that manipulates the rules in the knowledge base to provide conclusions. These specific conclusions depend on the information supplied by the user, external data acquisition systems, and external programs. (EIA,1997)

Figure 1 indicates the Architecture of an Expert System.

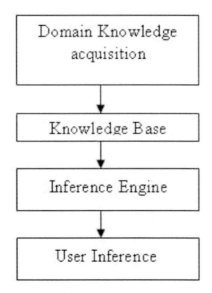

Figure 1. The Architecture of an Expert System.

HOW EXPERT SYSTEMS WORK

Typically Knowledge engineer (a user) interacts with an expert system in consultation dialog, much like one would converse with a human expert. The user explains the problem to be solved,

In the knowledge acquisition mode, Knowledge engineer obtain the knowledge from the expert and code it in the knowledge base using one of several techniques .One typical way of representing knowledge in an expert system are rules.

Through these two operational modes the expert system acts, in some sense, like an intermediary between the expert (acquisition mode) and the user (consultation mode). (Alexander et al.,1999)

The knowledge base contains the scientific knowledge and experience for the particular area of expertise. (Alexander et al.,1999)

During a consultation with an expert system, the user enters information on a current problem into the working memory. The system matches this information with knowledge contained in the knowledge base to infer new facts. The system then enters these new facts into the working memory and the matching process continuous. Eventually the system reaches some conclusions that it also enter into the working memory.

The inference engine works with both facts contained in the working memory and the domain knowledge contained in the knowledge base to derive new information. It searches the rules for a match between their premises and information contained in the working memory .When the inference engine find a match,it adds the rule's conclusion to the working memory and continues to scan rules looking for new matches. (Durkin,1994)

The term user interface refers to the physical and sensory interaction between computer and user.(Alexander et al.,1999)

Figure 2. indicates an expert system workflow for problem solving.

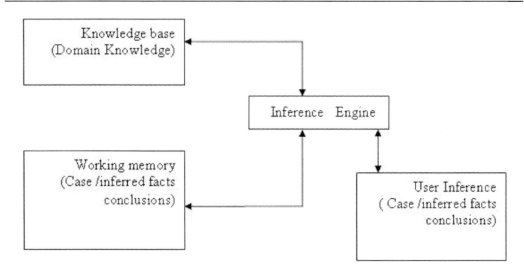

Figure 2. Expert system workflow for problem solving.

Developers of expert systems strive to provide systems with the ability to:

1. mimic the reasoning capability of human experts;
2. deal with incomplete and imprecise knowledge;
3. explain and provide a rationale for conclusions;
4. provide alternate options for consideration;
5. provide wider distribution and access to scarce expert knowledge; and
6. provide systematic and consistent application of knowledge.

The basic problems facing knowledge– based techniques today include:

– Acquisition of data that are relevant to the problem (dynamic and/or static);
– Data organization and storing in order to make it easily readable;
– Reasoning over it with the aid of knowledge– based techniques or predefined models.

DESIGN AND IMPLEMENTATION OF EXPERT SYSTEMS

Theoritical Steps

1. identify problem.
2. design a method for solving it.
3.

Engineering Steps

4. implement the method in a computer program.

5. Demonstrate the power of the problem and thus the method.

Analytical Steps

6. Analysis data collected for demonstration.
7. Generalize the results of the analysis to many pieces of research, to date stop after steps 2,3,or 4;the best experimental research involves all the six steps

Figure 3 shows software development life cycle model.

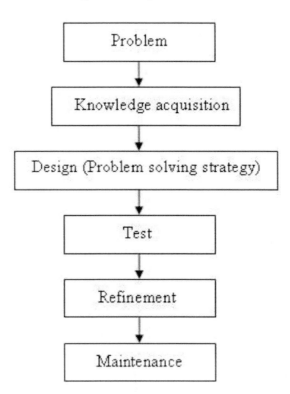

Figure 3. Software development life cycle model.

CLASSIFICATION OF METHODOLOGIES FOR BUILDING EXPERT SYSTEMS

ES methodologies are classified using the following eleven categories:

Rule-based systems, knowledge-based systems, neural networks, fuzzy ESs, object oriented methodology, case-based reasoning, system architecture, intelligent agent systems, database methodology, modeling, and ontology.(Liao,2005).

In this chapter the concentration will be upon building expert systems using two methods Rule-based systems and Case-based reasoning.

1. Rule-Based Systems

Commercial activity is not only focused on expert Systems, it is focused specifically on those expert Systems that are rule based.(Quinlan,1987)

A rule-based ES is defined as one, which contains information obtained from a human expert, and represents that information in the form of rules (Liao,2005), such as IF/THEN structure that logically relates information contained in the If part to other information in the Then part . (Durkin,1994). The rule can then be used to perform operations on data to inference in order to reach appropriate conclusion. These inferences are essentially a computer program that provides a methodology for reasoning about information in the rule base or knowledge base, and for formulating conclusions.(Liao,2005)

2. Case-Based Reasoning

Cases are the basic units in a CBR system. A case is a contextualized piece of knowledge representing an experience that can help a reasoner to achieve his goals.(Li and Yeh, 2004)The basic idea of CBR is to adapt solutions that were used to solve previous problems and use them to solve new problems. In CBR, descriptions of past experience of human specialists, represented as cases, are stored in a database (library) for later retrieval when the user encounters a new case with similar parameters. The system searches for stored cases with problem characteristics similar to the new one, finds the closest fit, and applies the solutions of the old case to the new case. Successful solutions are tagged to the new case and both are stored together with the other cases in the knowledge base. Unsuccessful solutions also are appended to the case base along with explanations as to why the solutions did not work.(Liao,2005)

EXPERT SYSTEMS IN REMOTE SENSING APPLICATIONS DOMAIN

Numerous studies using expert systems or knowledge-based systems have been reported in remote sensing applications

IMAGE CLASSIFICATION AND FEATURE EXTRACTION

Automated image interpretation of remotely sensed images has great interesting for many numbers of applications.

The objective of image classification is to assign all pixels in the remotely sensed satellite image to particular classes or themes (e.g. water, coniferous forest, deciduous forest, corn, wheat,roads,buildings, etc.). Knowledge-based systems (KBS) are considered as a good alternative to traditional classification methods with better performance. There is a need to develop such systems to facilitate the interpretation of remote sensing data in a more objective and efficient way. Supervised classification is a commonly used method, but it strongly depends upon users' skills and training procedures and often involves time-consuming analysis. KBS are useful when concrete knowledge about the application domain is available. It is expected that KBS can automatically classify remote sensing images without operator's intervention (Li and Yeh,2004)

Image classification knowledge-based systems can be defined as computer programs designated for matching a land cover type to a pixel in areas with high degree of complexity, which requires wide domain knowledge for achieving satisfactory recognition. In general, a knowledge-based system is composed of two main elements. Adjustments of these two elements for land cover classification are as follows:

1. A knowledge base: A set of simple facts composed of imagery and environmental data and information and a set of rules, which describe relations between facts and ways for reliable pixel labeling from them.(Cohen et al.,2000)Ancillary data, either in addition to or derived from remotely sensed data, has the potential for increasing classification accuracy. (Lawrence and Wrlght,2001)
2. A problem-solving mechanism: Finding a recognition path from a specific set of facts describing a pixel to one (or more) land cover through relevant production rules.(Cohen et al., 2000)

Expert systems allow for the integration of remote-sensed data with other sources of geo-referenced information such as land use data, spatial texture, and digital elevation model to obtain greater classification accuracy. Logical decision rules are used with the various datasets to assign class values for each pixel. Expert system is very suitable for the work of image interpretation as a powerful means of information integration. (Kahya et al.,2010)

Heyman (2000) proposed a rule-based expert system that implemented using ERDAS IMAGINE Expert Classifier for automatic extraction of natural objects. Aerial CIR photographs from the USGS National High Altitude Photography (NHAP) program has been used to identify hardwood stands in the semi-arid regions of the west. The developed system allows the utilization of various methods for segmentation and classification, and exploits the information concealed in the high spatial resolution remote sensing data available commercially worldwide since 1999.

Stefanov et al.(2001) applied an expert system approach based on logical decision rules with various data sets to the semiarid urban land cover of Maricopa County, AZ. In this study, expert systems have been used to classify land cover in temperate urban centers, but this is perhaps the first such application of the method to a semiarid–arid urban center. Initial classification of the Phoenix, AZ metropolitan study area was performed using VSWIR band reflectance of 1998 Landsat TM data and SAVI values derived from the same dataset. Spatial texture was also calculated from the TM data and combined with ancillary datasets in the expert system to perform post-classification sorting of the initial land cover classification. Overall classification accuracy obtained using the expert system was 85%. Individual class user's accuracy ranged from 73% to 99%, with the exception of the disturbed (commercial/industrial) class (49%). The poor performance of this class is due to confusion with other classes stemming from the similarity of sub-pixel components at the scale of a TM pixel. The generally high user accuracies for the individual land cover classes validate the use of the expert system model approach for semiarid–arid urban centers. The described methodology will be used to monitor future land cover changes in the CAP LTER study area using ETM+ and ASTER data.

Nangendo et al.(2007) compared four classification, i.e. Maximum Likelihood classifier (MLC), MLC combined with an Expert System (MaxExpert), Spectral Angle Mapper (SAM) and SAM combined with the same Expert System (SAM Expert). While MLC and SAM make use of the available spectral data (Landsat ETM+ image),the rule based Expert systems (MaxExpert and SAMExpert) make use additional data such as slope angle, elevation and terrain position. Each layer relating to a type of "evidence" for the existence of a certain class. For example, a GIS raster layer of slope gradient may comprise three different types of 'evidence' (flat being less than 5 degrees slope gradient, moderate being 5–15°, and steep being more than 15°).For this study, the layers used included output layers of a conventional classifier (MLC or SAM), DEM layers (slope, aspect, terrain position and elevation) and a percentage of canopy cover layer. In the expert system, the information from the conventional classifier is complemented by information from these layers. During the classification process, only those layers that can better differentiate a class from other classes were used. For example, a slope layer may be used if a vegetation cover class occurs only at a specific slope range. This expert knowledge supplements the classification information obtained from spectra using the conventional classifier. The implementation of these two expert systems has been performed using Standard commands of ENVI (the Environment for Visualizing Images) image-processing system to combine the pieces of evidence and create a single layer referred to as the "expert layer". In the expert layer, each piece of evidence is represented as an individual band. This layer is then used as the expert layer input into the expert system. The expert system algorithm, programmed using Interactive Data Language (IDL; Research Systems, Inc.), was used to combine the conventional classifier layer with the expert layer. They found that the combination of conventional classifiers with an expert System proved to be an effective approach for forest mapping. The classification accuracy has significantly improved by combining the conventional classifiers (MLC and SAM) with the expert system. The highest overall accuracy (94.6%) was obtained with SAMExpert. The MaxExpert approach yielded a map with an accuracy of 85.2%, which was also significantly higher than that obtained using the conventional MLC approach.

There is also a need to develop the methodology for classifying SAR images. Numerous studies have been carried out to classify land use types and detect land use changes from remote sensing. Dobson et al.(1995) made an experiments on developing knowledge based systems (KBS) that use rules to classify radar imagery. Although rule-based systems have a number of advantages for remote sensing classification,They have limitations in implementation because the identification and definition of rules are usually tedious, user-unfriendly, and time-consuming.

Li and Yeh (2004) proposed a new method for classifying remote sensing imagery applying case-based reasoning (CBR) techniques to the classification of SAR images to overcome the problems of rule based systems However, it still has the advantages inherited from KBS, such as artificial intelligence, reduction of repetitive tasks, and highly automated capability. The fast development of CBR is attributed to its capabilities of resolving some of the problems in knowledge acquisition and maintenance in rule-based KBS. It doesn't require users to elicit rules from training data and thus save much of the time in reasoning process. It is considered that much of human reasoning is case based rather than rule based.

CBR, which is a different type of knowledge- based systems (KBS), uses pervious cases to solve a new problem., the case library can be built by collecting data from remote sensing images, land use maps and field investigation. The attributes (features) of an input case (pixel) may include backscatters and ancillary GIS data. The information of texture and contexture can also be used as the inputs.

The proposed method has been tested in the Pearl River Delta in South China .The proposed method has better classification performance than supervised classification methods. Studies have also shown that the CBR method can even provide a much better accuracy of classification than traditional statistical methods.

Cole et al. (2005) classified land use/land cover change for a small region of New Delhi, India using an expert system approach with ASTER imagery. Their pilot area classified eight different land cover categories with a 72% overall accuracy based on 25 random points.

Stefanov and Netzband (2005) investigated the usefulness of MODIS NDVI data at scales of1 km/pixel, 500 m/pixel, and 250 m/pixel for characterization, monitoring, and modeling of biophysical change related to arid urban landscape structure (as defined by a suite of landscape metrics). For this, they compared gridded landscape metrics derived from expert system land cover classification of ASTER to corresponding MODIS NDVI data at scales of 250 m/pixel, 500 m/pixel, and 1 km/pixel in order to determine which of these scales is optimal for monitoring of urban biophysical processes and landscape structure change. Weak positive and negative correlations between NDVI and landscape structure were observed at all three spatial scales for the metrics class area, mean patch size, edge density, and interspersion/juxtaposition index. Landscape metrics of class area, mean patch size, edge density, and interspersion/juxtaposition index were calculated from 15 m/pixel-classified ASTER data and scaled up to the three MODIS data pixel resolutions. Correlation of the landscape metric results with the MODIS NDVI data suggests that, even at the 250-m/pixel scale, clear control of vegetation pattern by landscape structure is not clear.

Kim and Ku (2008) proposed a rule-based classification method for land cover classification.The proposed method was tested on Goyang-city for classification of a Landsat ETM+ multispectral image and GIS data layers including elevation, aspect, slope, distance to water bodies, distance to road network, and population density. Result shows that GIS data layers such as elevation, distance to water bodies and population density can be effectively integrated for rule-based image classification.

Kahya et al.(2010) applied an expert system to perform post classification sorting of the initial supervised maximum likelihood land cover classification of Landsat 7 (ETM+) imagery all spectral bands (except the thermal band(6)) were used in a part of Trabzon city using additional spatial datasets such as of geo-referenced information such as land use data, spatial texture, and digital elevation model. The overall accuracy of expert classification was 95.80%. Individual class accuracy ranged from 75% to 100% for each class.

BUILDING DETECTION ANDEXTRACTION

Loannidis et al.(2009) used Knowledge-based systems for building extraction, since they are probably the most popular method in this application. Knowledge-based systems can be very flexible, incorporating various kinds of methods and data in an intelligent way, they are more effective in extracting accurately buildings. The basic concept is to calculate the values of certain predefined criteria, referred to as cues, and from these to automatically decide if an object is a building and what are its exact properties (e.g., shape, size, etc.). The data used in these methods can be imagery, multi-spectral information, height data and even GIS information. In fact, the more diverse the base data, the easier it is to formulate robust cues. For situations where scene elements must be classified into several categories (e.g., "buildings", "water", "vegetation"), a hierarchical approach is usually implemented.By gradually eliminating all objects from unwanted classes, only the "buildings" class remains. The members of this class are then subjected to a refining stage where their exact geometric properties are defined.

Elshehaby and Taha(2009)compared Three approaches for building detection based on maximum likelihood classification. The first, building detection from classification of multispectral satellite image only. The second approach is building detection from classification of multispectral satellite image, while the height information from Light Detection and Ranging (LIDAR) data is applied as an additional channel together with spectral channel. The third approach is building detection based on classification of multispectral satellite image where normalized difference vegetation index (NDVI) and the height information from LIDAR data are applied as additional channels together with spectral channel. The contributions of the individual cues used in the classification have been evaluated .The third approach results have been improved by developing a rule based expert system for building detection based on integration of classified image, elevation data, and spectral information using knowledge engineer of ERDAS Imagine for post-classification refinement of initially classified output building mask. Each rule is a representation of each node in the tree that describes a building class or probability of presence of buildings pixel. Then, the building detection result has been evaluated. It has been found that the use of an expert system would further help in the discrimination of the classes and improve classification accuracy of buildings. The overall accuracy of expert classification was 96% and kappa coefficient was 0.95.

CLOUD AND SHADOW REDUCTION

Cloud-free remotely sensed images acquired from earth orbiting satellites are not always available, especially for areas of the earth characterized by tropical or humid climates.

Song and Civco (2002) developed a knowledge-based method to produce a cloud and cloud shadow-free multitemporal image composite of neo-contemporary images (e.g., within two to three months of one another) using ERDAS Imagine Spatial Modeler.

Two Landsat TM images were used for testing the developed expert system over Madagascar,the main image refers to the principal image to be used in subsequent analysis, such as land cover classification, and which possesses less cloud and shadow area than the secondary image, used to supplement the values for cloud and shadow areas in the main image .

CHANGE PREDICTION

Change detection is the process of identifying differences in the state of object or phenomena by observing it at different times.On the other hand change prediction is predicting change during a certain period of time.

Yunyan et al. (2010) proposed a three-component model ("problem", "geographic environment", and "outcome") to introduce the CBR approach for land use change study.

Three components were constructed for the cases. The first component, "problem", is to predict land use change during a certain period of time in the study area (Zhuhai area from 1995 to 2000). This change was quantitatively described by the variation in perimeter and area of land parcel polygon. The second component in the case is "Geographic environment" refers to the distribution of geographic features, including major rivers, reservoirs, city, highways, and light-duty roads. Previous study indicates that land use change is affected by a series of factors, including distance, surrounding land use types, and natural attributes.

Two topology indexes and six variables were used to describe the "geographic environment" component in Zhuhai area, including major surrounding land use types in 1995 (N1)and in 2000(N2), distance to the nearest town (D1), to the nearest built-up land(D2), to the nearest river (D3), to the nearest reservoir (D4), to the nearest highway (D5), and to the nearest light-duty road(D6). Land use change result is the "outcome" of the cases, i.e., predicting major land use types in 2000 based on land use types in1995. cases library has been created .The method was tested by examining the land use change between 1995 and 2000 in Pearl River Mouth area in China and yields a similar prediction accuracy of 80% as that derived by applying the Bayesian networks approach to Landsat TM images.The final component of the cases, "outcome", refers to the result of land use change during a certain period of time, for instance, from agricultural to built-up land during the past 5 years.

SOFTWARE FOR BUILDING EXPERT SYSTEMS FOR REMOTE SENSING APPLICATIONS

ERDAS IMAGINE Expert Classifier Image-Processing System

The IMAGINE Expert Classifier is composed of two parts: the Knowledge Engineer and the Knowledge Classifier. The Knowledge Engineer provides the interface for an expert with first hand knowledge of the data and the application (Kahya et al.,2010)

In Knowledge engineer: The fundamental building blocks of an expert system include hypotheses (problems), rules, and conditions. The rules and conditions operate on data (information). It is possible to address more than one hypothesis in an expert system. The best way to conceptualize an expert system is to use decision tree structure where rules and conditions are evaluated in order to test hypotheses (Jensen, 2005).

A rule-based expert system consists of essentially hypothesis (output;), and variables of a knowledge base

Hypotheses: The class to be tested (extracted) from the spatial data.

Rules: A human expert should develop the knowledge base (hypotheses, rules, and conditions). The rules and conditions were based on remote sensing multispectral reflectance and derivatives (e.g., NDVI), elevation data and derivatives (slope) and so on .

Conditions: The expert identifies very specific conditions that are associated with the remote sensing reflectance data, elevation data (Jensen,2005).

The expert classification software provides a rules-based approach to multi-spectral image classification, post-classification refinement, and GIS modeling. (Kahya et al.,2010)

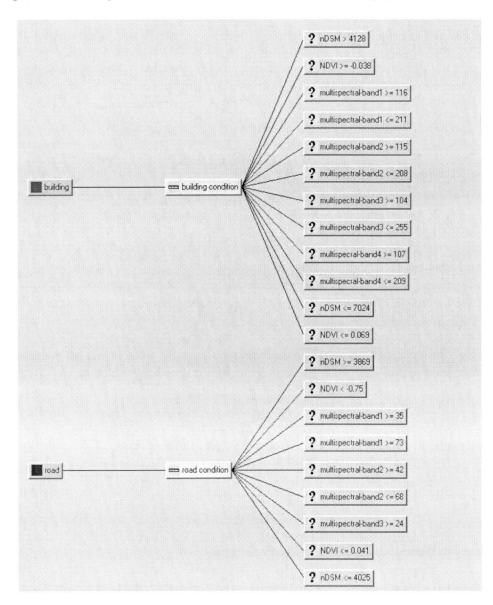

Figure 4. Rule based expert system for road and building extraction developed using ERDAS Imagine Knowledge engineer.

CONCLUSION

This chapter provides an overview about expert systems and gives novel developments of expert systems in remote sensing applications. In this research the core concepts of ES are briefly discussed and the categories of expert systems have outlined.

These chapter concentrated on two types of expert systems, Rule based expert systems and Case-based expert systems. Rule based expert systems are currently the most popular choice of knowledge engineering for building an expert systems in remote sensing domain.

Expert systems have been implemented in a variety of remote sensing applications, including image classification, automatic feature extraction,change detection, however, to date, only a few such systems have been developed fully operational. Most of these are in the prototype phase. Some of those systems developed are fully operational at a large number of sites. Data availability represents one of the challenges for generalization.

FUTURE DIRECTIONS

In this sense, future directions are always hard to precisely predict. Neverthless,the future developments in expert systems applications related to remote sensing may be towards

1. Analysis and Generalization

Future progress requires additional work in the analysis and generalization expert systems.

The prototype could be developed into full production expert systems.

Since developing an expert systems prototype may be done in a matter of weeks. However building full production expert systems from a promising prototype can take many years.

2. Entering other Expert Systems Methodologies in R.S Field

Till now not all expert systems methodologies have been entered R.S field .I expect other expert systems methodologies will be entered remotely sensed field.

3. Remotely Sensed Expert Systems Package

Remotely sensed applications based on expert systems could be collected in one package.As a starting point, remote sensing applications that could benefit from expert systems technology had to be identified.

4. More Open Source Based

Although the debate between open source and commercial solutions will continue,it is expected to see the increasing adoption of open source software for building expert systems for remote sensing applications.

REFERENCES

[1] Jensen, J.R. (2005) "Introductory digital image processing a remote sensing perspective", 3rd edn. Pearson Prentice Hall, Upper Saddle River

[2] Cohen, Y., Shoshany, M.(2000) Integration of remote sensing, GIS and expert knowledge in national knowledge-based crop recognition in Mediterranean environment" International Archives of Photogrammetry and Remote Sensing. Vol. XXXIII, Part B7. Amsterdam 2000.

[3] Jensen, L.M. (1997)"Classification of urban land cover based on expert systems, object models and texture" Comput., Environ. and Urban Systems, Vol. 21, No. 3/4, pp. 291-302, 1997 Elsevier Science Ltd.

[4] Alexander, D. E. and Fairbridge, R. W.(1999) "Encyclopedia Of environmental Science -Expert systems and the environment" 1999 Kluwer Academic Publishers ISBN 0-412-74050-8

[5] Masson,S. (1995)" Expert system- based design of close range photogrammetric networks *ISPRS journal of Photogrammetry and Remote Sensing* Vol .50,No.5,pp13-24

[6] Bandinia, S., Bogni, D., and Manzoni, S.(2002) "Knowledge Based Environmental Data Validation" http://www.iemss.org/iemss2002/proceedings/pdf/volume%20tre/260 _bandini.pdf

[7] Lawrence, R. L. and Wrlght, A.(2001) "Rule-Based classification systems using classification and regression tree (cart) analysis" *Photogrammetric Engineering and Remote Sensing* Vol. 67, No. 10, October 2001, pp. 1137-1142.

[8] EIA for Developing Countries (1997)Chapter 8: Application of Expert Systems December 1997

[9] Kahya,O., Bayram, B. and Reis, S. (2010)"Land cover classification with an expert system approach using Landsat ETM imagery: a case study of Trabzon" *Environ. Monit. Assess.* (2010) 160:431–438

[10] Stefanov, W. L., Ramsey, M. S., and Christensen, P. R. (2001). Monitoring urban land cover change: An expert system approach to land cover classification of semiarid to arid urban centers. *Remote Sensing of Environment*,Vol . 77,No.2, pp. 173–185.

[11] Cole, C., Wentz, E., and Christensen, P. (2005). Expert system approach for classifying land cover in New Delhi India using ASTER imagery, 3rd International Symposium on Remote Sensing and Data Fusion Over Urban Areas (URBAN 2005), Tempe, AZ, USA, 14–16 March 2005.

[12] Liao, S.-H.(2005)" Expert system methodologies and applications—a decade review from 1995 to 2004" *Expert Systems with Applications* 28 (2005) 93–103

[13] Li,X. and Yeh, A.G.(2004) "Multitemporal SAR images for monitoring cultivation systems using case-based reasoning" *Remote Sensing of Environment* 90 (2004) 524–534

[14] Attema, E. (1992) Science requirements for the calibration of the ERS-1 synthetic aperture radar. *Proceedings of GEOS SAR calibration workshop*, 21– 25 September, Ottawa, Canada.

[15] Dobson, M. C., Ulaby, F. T., and Pierce, L. E.(1995)" Land-cover classification and estimation of terrain attributes using synthetic aperture radar" *Remote Sensing of Environment*, 51, 191–214.

[16] Huang, X. Q., and Jensen, J. R. (1997). A machine-learning approach to automated knowledge-base building for remote sensing image analysis with GIS data. *Photogrammetric Engineering and Remote Sensing*, 63(10), 1185–1194.

[17] Nangendo, G., Skidmore, A.K., Oosten, H. V.(2007) " Mapping East African tropical forests and woodlands -A comparison of classifiers" *ISPRS Journal of Photogrammetry and Remote Sensing* 61 (2007) 393–404

[18] Yunyan, D., Wei,W., Feng,C., Min, J.(2010) "case-based reasoning approach for land use change prediction" *Expert Systems with Applications* 37 (2010) 5745–5750

[19] Heyman,O. , (2000) tomatic Extraction of Natural Objects from 1-m Remote Sensing Images http://www.cobblestoneconcepts.com/ucgis2summer/heyman/heyman.htm

[20] McCarthy, J. D., Graniero, P. A. and Rozic, S. M. (2008) "An Integrated GIS-Expert System Framework for Live Hazard Monitoring and Detection" *Sensors* 2008, 8, 830-846

[21] Loannidis, C., Psaltis, C., Potsiou, C. (2009)"Towards a strategy for control of suburban informal buildings through automatic change detection" *Computers, Environment and Urban Systems* 33 (2009) 64–74

[22] Quinlan, J.R.(1987)"Applications of Expert Systems"based on the proceedings of the Second Australian Conference Additions-Wesley publishersLimited-Winston P.H. The commercial debut of artificial intelligence

[23] Durkin, J.(1994)"Expert systems design and developments"Macmillan publishing company USA

[24] Kim,H. and Ku, C.Y. (2008)A machine learning approach for knowledge base construction incorporating gis data for land cover classification of Landsat ETM+ *Image Journal of the Korean Geographical Society*,Vol43,No . 5,2008

[25] Elshehaby, A. R. and Taha, L. G. (2009)"new expert system module for building detection in urban areas using spectral information and LIDAR data" *Applied Geomatic* Vol.1 No.4 December 2009

[26] Song, M. and Civco, D.L.(2002)A knowledge-based approach for reducing cloud and shadow 2002 ASPRS-ACSM Annual Conference and FIG XXII Congress

In: Expert System Software
Editors: Jason M. Segura and Albert C. Reiter

ISBN: 978-1-61209-114-3
© 2012 Nova Science Publishers, Inc.

Chapter 4

DOMAIN-WIDE EXPERT SYSTEM APPLICATIONS

*Neil Dunstan**

School of Science and Technology,
University of New England, Australia

ABSTRACT

This chapter addresses the use of multiple expert systems and varieties of multiple expert systems are categorized. A special category is described of multiple expert systems that belong to the same problem domain and have certain characteristics. A notion of equivalent entities is developed that permits a linkage between the expert systems in such a way that they may be used in combination. A distinction is made between domain-level procedures (or queries) that may be applied to any individual expert system in the domain, and domain-wide procedures that are applied using all, or more than one expert system. Domain-wide procedures make use of domain-specific equivalence functions. Examples are drawn from two quite different areas – namely transport and academia, and equivalence in these areas is discussed. XML is used to define the problem domains and Prolog is used to implement knowledge bases, equivalence functions and procedures.

Keywords: Expert systems, multiple expert systems, Prolog, XML.

INTRODUCTION

Expert Systems continue to be a popular method of providing computer-based information systems able to solve domain-specific problems in the absence of human experts. The range of application areas is large and ever-expanding. Recent examples include land use planning [Witlow, 2005]; marine technology [Helvacioglu and Insel, 2008]; and sheet metal construction [Babu et al., 2010]. The World Wide Web has added further impetus, enabling a

---

∗ E-mail: neil@cs.une.edu.au.

greater level of access and services to expert systems applications [Duan et al., 2005]. Expert systems research has investigated the task of combining expert systems in various ways. For example: Fraser et al. [1989] developed conflict resolution methods for competing expert systems; Zhang [1991] developed methods to manage cooperating heterogeneous expert systems from the same or overlapping domains; Izumi at al. [1999] proposed expert systems that could improve their performance by learning from others; and Santo et al. [2003] and Conti et al. [1991] developed complex expert systems composed of smaller expert systems each devoted to a separate sub-domain.

In this chapter, the various ways in which multiple expert systems might be used are categorized. A specialized category is described in which multiple expert systems have separate knowledge bases within the same domain. In this category, expert systems belonging to the same domain have shared entities and semantics. It has been shown that a domain can be defined by an XML Document Type Definition (DTD) and that the knowledge base of an expert system can be represented as an XML data file [Dunstan, 2008]. Furthermore, knowledge in XML format can be converted to artificial intelligence languages such as Prolog by domain-specific XML parsers [Dunstan, 2010]. Procedural rules represent the queries that may be applied to expert systems. The chapter shows that there are two distinct levels: domain-level queries that are applied to any expert system in the domain; and domain-wide queries that are applied using more than one expert system from the domain. Domain-wide queries are enabled by the notion of equivalent entities, which link expert systems from different sub-sections of the domain. Two examples are used to illustrate these concepts. The first is a passenger transport domain of passenger services between a set of towns. Each of a number of companies offering services is represented by a separate expert system. Their networks of connections may include some of the same towns. The second domain is the domain of university degrees where degrees are composed of units/subjects and have their own completion requirements and degree rules. Even though they may come from different universities, it is possible that some units have sufficient similarity to be deemed equivalent.

This chapter is organized as follows: Classifications of expert systems are discussed with an emphasis on categories of multiple expert systems. Three categories of multiple expert system structures are described. XML DTD's are given for the two example problem domains along with sample expert systems, their knowledge bases in XML format, corresponding Prolog code and domain-level procedural rules. The concept of domain-wide applications that utilize more than one expert system from the problem domain are introduced. A special category of multiple expert systems is described that relies on the notion of equivalent entities. Equivalence functions for the two example domains are discussed along with how they are able to provide linkage of expert systems in their domains. Examples of domain-wide procedural rules are shown that use the equivalence functions. These are implemented in Prolog and applied to the example expert systems. Conclusions and future work are discussed.

CLASSIFICATION OF EXPERT SYSTEMS

Expert systems may be classified in various ways, such as: by application area; implementation language; and structural methodology. Liao [2005] surveyed expert system publications from 1995 to 2004 and classified the methodologies used into eleven categories. Three of these are briefly discussed:

- Rule-based systems represent expertise as IF_THEN rules and this forms the basis for computer programs to make inferences and formulate solutions.
- Knowledge-based systems come from Artificial Intelligence research. They consist of components that include a knowledge base and an inference engine. Artificial Intelligence languages like Lisp and Prolog are traditionally the way to build knowledge-based expert systems. While knowledge facts and inference rules can be represented in these languages, the Prolog backtracking algorithm provides an effective means of investigating alternative subgoals in order to arrive at a solution and to discover alternative solutions.
- Fuzzy expert systems use fuzzy logic to arrive at solutions in contexts were there is uncertainty.

Giarratano and Riley [1998] describe expert systems as operating within a problem domain – a specific problem area such as medicine or finance. They further describe an expert system as having a specific knowledge base within that problem domain. More than one expert system may address the same problem domain and their respective knowledge bases might overlap. Though applications typically use a sole expert system for a problem domain, the use and cooperation of multiple expert systems in the same problem domain has been an interesting area of research. Expert systems from the same problem domain may be heterogeneous in that they use different methodologies or have different implementations. Utilizing a combination of expert systems from the same problem domain may require techniques to resolve their heterogeneous nature and conflicting solutions. Categories of such multiple expert systems are now described.

COMPETING EXPERT SYSTEMS

Competing expert systems occupy the same problem domain and the same knowledge domain. Their use in solving problems requires that their individual responses are resolved to form a single final solution. Competing expert systems are illustrated in Figure 1.

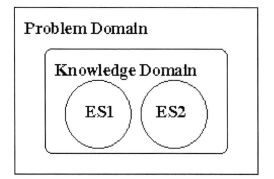

Figure . Competing Expert Systems.

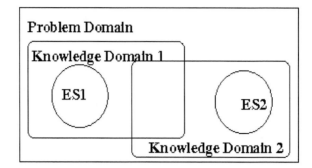

Figure 2. Cooperating Expert Systems.

COOPERATING EXPERT SYSTEMS

Cooperating expert systems occupy the same problem domain but have overlapping knowledge domains. That is, one may be able to provide solutions given knowledge unknown to others, though all share some areas of knowledge. Use of such systems requires both resolution of conflicting solutions and the ability to combine expertise to solve a wider class of problems then any one expert system can provide. Figure 2 illustrates.

COMBINED EXPERT SYSTEMS

Combined expert systems do not share knowledge domains but in combination may be able to solve problems neither can solve individually. No conflict resolution is required. Figure 3 illustrates.

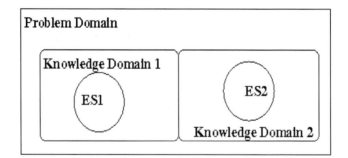

Figure 3. Combined Expert Systems.

DOMAIN-SPECIFIC EXPERT SYSTEMS

XML Document Type Definitions are an effective method of defining a problem domain. This method has been used in Dunstan [2008] and Dunstan [2010] to develop a procedure for generating web-based domain-specific expert systems utilizing domain-specific XML parsers that convert conforming XML data to Prolog and web modules. That is, the domain knowledge of an expert system can be represented as an XML file conforming to the problem domain XML DTD. Expert systems for the problem domain will share entities and semantics both in their XML data files and in the corresponding Prolog conversions. This makes it possible for domain-level procedural rules to be applied to any expert system in the domain.

Two examples are given in this chapter to illustrate the concepts.

THE PASSENGER NETWORK DOMAIN

The first is a problem domain for passenger transport services. The DTD is:

```
<!ELEMENT passenger_network (service*)>
<!ELEMENT service (name, number, connection*)>
<!ELEMENT connection (source, days, depart, destination, arrive)>
<!ELEMENT name (#PCDATA)>
<!ELEMENT number (#PCDATA)>
<!ELEMENT source (#PCDATA)>
<!ELEMENT days (#PCDATA)>
<!ELEMENT depart (#PCDATA)>
<!ELEMENT destination (#PCDATA)>
<!ELEMENT arrive (#PCDATA)>
```

That is, a passenger network is composed of services that provide connections between source and destination locations. A service may have a number of connections. They are the stops that the service makes. A connection may be available only on particular days, and has departure and arrival times. Of course there may be many other details included.

An example of a knowledge domain – representing the knowledge base for a train network expert system of this problem domain is:

```
<?xml version="1.0">
<!DOCTYPE passenger_network SYSTEM "passenger_network.dtd">
<passenger_network>
  <service>
    <name> coastal </name>
    <number> 312 </number>
    <connection>
      <source> jervisTS </source>
      <days> [monday, wednesday, friday] </days>
      <depart> 9:00 </depart>
      <destination> nandenTS </destination>
      <arrive> 10:15 </arrive>
    </connection>
    <connection>
      <source> nandenTS </source>
```

```
      <days> [monday, wednesday, friday] </days>
      <depart> 10:30 </depart>
      <destination> seymourTS </destination>
      <arrive> 11:05 </arrive>
    </connection>
   </service>
  <service>
    <name> inland </name>
    <number> 320 </number>
    <connection>
      <source> seymourTS </source>
      <days> [monday, saturday] </days>
      <depart> 19:10 </depart>
      <destination> algonTS </destination>
      <arrive> 20:05 </arrive>
    </connection>
    <connection>
      <source> algonTS </source>
      <days> [monday, saturday] </days>
      <depart> 20:20 </depart>
      <destination> jervisTS </destination>
      <arrive> 21:25 </arrive>
    </connection>
   </service>
</passenger_network>
```

This XML data can be straightforwardly converted to Prolog:

```
service( coastal, 312, [monday, wednesday, friday],
    connection( jervis, 9:00, nanden, 10:15 ),
    connection( nanden, 10:30, seymour, 11:05 ) ).
service( inland, 320, [monday, saturday],
    connection( seymour, 19:10, algon, 20:05 ) ).
    connection( algon, 20:20, jervis, 21:25 ) ).
```

The resulting Prolog expert system can be used in problem domain queries for things like finding the departure time for travel from one location to another. More complex queries are possible that use the inference engine capacity of the expert system. For instance, should there be no direct connection between two locations it may be possible to find a route based on more than one connection and possibly from more than one service. The Prolog rule is:

```
route( Src, Src, [], _ ).
route( Src, Dest,
    [ (Src, Dtime, Dest1, Atime, Serv, Numb) | RestRoute ], Max ) :-
  Max > 0,
  Max1 is Max -1,
```

```
route( Dest1, Dest, RestRoute, Max1 ),
service( Serv, Numb, _, CL ),
member( connection( Src, Dtime, Dest1, Atime ), CL ),
not( member( ( _, _, Src, _, _, _ ), RestRoute ) ).
```

A query to find a route from locations jervisTS to algonTS limited to 4 stops has this response:

```
?- route( jervisTS, algonTS, R, 4 ).
R = [ (jervisTS, 9:00, nandenTS, 10:15, coastal, 312),
     (nandenTS, 10:30, seymourTS, 11:05, coastal, 312),
     (seymourTS, 19:10, algonTS, 20:05, inland, 320)] .
```

which shows connection details (without the days information) to make the journey. That is, from jervisTS to nandenTS to seymourTS to algonTS. The network is shown in Figure 4.

THE UNIVERSITY DEGREE PROBLEM DOMAIN

The second problem domain example is for university degree programs. The DTD is:

```
<!ELEMENT degree (dname, rules, group+, unit+)>
<!ELEMENT rules (maximum*, minimum*)>
<!ELEMENT group (gname, gunits)>
<!ELEMENT unit (uname, descr, prereq, credit)>
<!ELEMENT dname (#PCDATA)>
<!ELEMENT maximum (#PCDATA)>
<!ELEMENT minimum (#PCDATA)>
<!ELEMENT gname (#PCDATA)>
<!ELEMENT gunits (#PCDATA)>
<!ELEMENT uname (#PCDATA)>
<!ELEMENT descr (#PCDATA)>
<!ELEMENT prereq (#PCDATA)>
<!ELEMENT credit (#PCDATA)>
```

That is, a degree is composed of units which have allotted credit points and prerequisites. The units are grouped and there are rules in the form of maximum and minimum numbers of credit points from each group that are required to be met in order to complete the requirements of the degree. An example of a particular degree is:

```
<?xml version="1.0"?>
<!DOCTYPE degree SYSTEM "degree.dtd">
<degree>
 <dname> Master of Management </dname>
```

```
    <rules>
     <maximum> 2:18 </maximum>
     <minimum> 1:24 </minimum>
     <minimum> all:48 </minimum>
    </rules>
    <group>
     <gname> groupmm1 </gname>
     <gunits>
      [afm112, hums102, mm105, mm110, mm200, mm202, mm213, mm300, mm322,
mm324]
     </gunits>
    </group>
    <group>
     <gname> groupmm2 </gname>
     <gunits>
      [pdas102, pdas104, pdas301, pdas302, pdas311, pdas312]
     </gunits>
    </group>
    <unit>
     <uname> afm112 </uname>
     <descr> 'Introduction to Management Accounting' </descr>
     <prereq> [] </uprereq>
     <credit> 6 </credit>
    </unit>
    <unit>
     <uname> hums102 </uname>
     <descr> 'Learning Life-Long Academic Skills' </udescr>
     <prereq> [afm112] </prereq>
     <credit> 6 </credit>
    </unit>
    ....
   </degree>
```

That is, the Master of Management degree requires a total of 48 credit points. A minimum of 24 must come from Group groupmm1 and at most 18 from Group groupmm2. Not all the unit data are shown. All units have 6 credit points. The expert system generated from this knowledge base can be queried for typical, but complex enrolment questions such as - "Given these units that are already completed, what else is required to complete the requirements for the degree?" The answer might be something like - "18 credit points from Group 1 and 42 credit points altogether". The Prolog rule (not all code shown) is:

```
    required_for_MM( N ):-
     group( G1, groupmm1 ),
     check_min( N, G1, groupmm1, 24 ),
     group( G2, groupmm2 ),
     check_max( N, G2, groupmm2, 18 ),
```

checkmin_all(N, 48).

group(M, groupmm1):-
    M = [afm112, hums102, mm105, mm110, mm200, mm202, mm213, mm300, mm322, mm324].

group(M, groupmm2):-
    M = [pdas102, pdas104, pdas301, pdas302, pdas311, pdas312].

Here is the Prolog query and response:

?- required_for_MM([afm112]).
At least 18 more credit points required from Group groupmm1:
    hums102 mm105 mm110 mm200 mm202 mm213 mm300 mm322 mm324
At least 42 more credit points required altogether.

DOMAIN-WIDE APPLICATIONS

A special category of multiple expert systems from the same problem domain is now considered. This category might match any of the categories of multiple expert systems previously described, although the *Cooperating* or *Combined* categories are the most relevant. As in the previous section, it is required that the expert system's knowledge bases will conform to the problem domain DTD. This section investigates how multiple expert systems

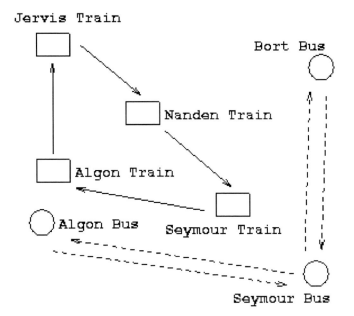

Figure 4. Train and Bus passenger Networks.

may be used to solve problems at the problem domain-wide level – that is, utilizing all, or more than one expert system from the problem domain. A possible result is that it may be possible to solve problems that no expert system can solve individually. The key point is a notion of *Equivalence* which is domain-specific. That is, this special category of multiple expert systems requires that the separate knowledge bases have some entities that are defined to be equivalent.

EQUIVALENCE IN THE PASSENGER NETWORK DOMAIN

Two independent passenger transport companies might operate services with overlapping networks in the sense that some locations (stops) are equivalent. Equivalence here means that the locations are in the same proximity – perhaps a simple measure of distance. For example, a train network has stations in various towns and a bus network has bus stops in various towns. If a train station is near a bus stop, then it is possible for passengers to transfer from one network to the other. This is illustrated in the network of Figure 4, where the solid arcs are train connections and the dotted arcs are bus connections. Note that if the function:

Equivalence(Location Train Station, Location Bus Stop)

is true, then the train and bus networks can be combined.

The combined networks enable domain-wide solutions to passenger transport problems. For example, neither network connects Jervis with Bort, but if Seymour Train Station is in the same proximity as Seymour Bus Stop, then the networks can be combined and a possible route exists. The Prolog code to find a route from source to destination in the combined network is:

```
combinedroute( Src, Src, [], _ ).

combinedroute( Src, Dest, [ (Src, 0, Dest1, 0, 0, 0) | RestRoute ], Max ) :-
  Max > 0,
  Max1 is Max -1,
  combinedroute( Dest1, Dest, RestRoute, Max1 ),
  equiv( Src, Dest1 ),
  not( member( ( _, _, Dest1, _, _, _ ), RestRoute ) ),
  not( member( ( _, _, Src, _, _, _ ), RestRoute ) ).

combinedroute( Src, Dest, [ (Src, Dtime, Dest1, Atime, Serv, Numb) | RestRoute ], Max )
:-
  Max > 0,
  Max1 is Max -1,
  combinedroute( Dest1, Dest, RestRoute, Max1 ),
  service( Serv, Numb, _, CL ),
  member( connection( Src, Dtime, Dest1, Atime ), CL ),
```

not(member((_, _, Src, _, _, _), RestRoute)).

The second combinedroute rule allows for a transfer from one network to another if there are equivalent locations. For the networks of Figure 4, the Prolog equivalence rules are:

equiv(seymourTS, seymourBS).
equiv(algonBS, algonTS).
equiv(seymourBS, seymourTS).
equiv(algonTS, algonBS).

making equivalence commutative. An example of finding a route in the combined network is:

?- combinedroute(nandenTS, bortBS, R, 4).
R = [(nandenTS, 10:30, seymourTS, 11:05, coastal, 312),
    (seymourTS, 0, seymourBS, 0, 0, 0),
    (seymourBS, 12:00, bortBS, 13:25, bortbus, 10)] ;

A refinement of this domain-wide query for the passenger network domain could also take into account days of travel for services and many other things. Further possible domain-wide queries could include finding the shortest (in time duration) route or cheapest (in combined ticket price) route.

EQUIVALENCE IN THE UNIVERSITY DEGREE DOMAIN

A common practice in universities is to grant "credit" for units completed at other universities towards degrees at their university. Such credit might be based on matching academic content and credit points. That is, *Equivalence* in this domain is whether or not a university is prepared to grant credit for a unit from another university based on its similarity to a local unit. That is, if the function

Equivalence(local unit, foreign unit)

is true, then the foreign unit can be used towards meeting the requirements of the local degree. The Prolog rule to check Master of Management degree completion requirements with a list of completed units that may contain units from another university is:

combined_required_for_MM(N) :-
 group(G1, mmgroup1),
 group(G2, mmgroup2),
 append(G1, G2, G),
 convert_units(N, G, [], N1),
 check_min(N1, G1, mmgroup1, 24),
 check_max(N1, G2, mmgroup2, 18),

```
checkmin_all( N1, 48 ).

convert_units( [], _, M, M ).

convert_units( [UH | UT], G, A, M ) :-
 member( UH, G ),
 append( A, [UH], M1 ),
 convert_units( UT, G, M1, M ).

convert_units( [UH | UT], G, A, M ) :-
 not( member( UH, G ) ),
 equiv( UH, EU ), member( EU, G ),
 append( A, [EU], M1 ),
 convert_units( UT, G, M1, M ).

convert_units( [UH | UT], G, A, M ) :-
 not( member( UH, G ) ),
 convert_units( UT, G, A, M ).
```

In this rule, the completed units are checked against the total list of units from all groups. When a unit is not from the groups, its equivalent (if it exists) is checked instead. The final converted list of units is used to check against the degree requirements. The equivalence rules for the example below are:

```
equiv( enco100, hums102 ).
equiv( hums102, enco100 ).
equiv( prof102, mm110 ).
equiv( mm110, prof102 ).
equiv( prof302, mm324 ).
equiv( mm324, prof302 ).
```
where the foreign units are enco100, prof102 and prof103, which are deemed to be equivalent to the local units hums102, mm110 and mm324 respectively.

The Prolog query and response is:
?- combined_required_for_MM([afm112, prof102, enco100, mm213]).
At least 24 more credit points required altogether.

That is, the minimum requirements for mmgroup1 are met with afm112, prof102 == mm110, enco100 == hums102 and mm213 constituting 24 credit points, leaving 24 credit points required.

Other domain-wide applications within the university domain could include searches for units with particular characteristics across the multiple universities, or finding the degree which provides for the maximum credit for a group of completed units.

CONCLUSIONS

Multiple expert systems within the same problem domain can exist for many reasons. They may represent separate sub-sections of the domain, different methodologies or the information systems of rival companies. Multiple expert systems within the same domain can be classified into categories such as Competing, Cooperating and Combined expert systems according to how their separate knowledge domains overlap. Expert systems belonging to a problem domain can represent their knowledge bases using XML data files that conform to the problem domain DTD. Thus they have shared entities and semantics. XML data can be straightforwardly converted to Prolog using domain-specific XML parsers. Domain-level procedural rules can be applied to any expert systems belonging to the same problem domain because of the shared entities and semantics. Two examples of problem domains and domain-level procedural rules were given – namely passenger transport networks and university degrees.

This chapter has described a class of multiple expert systems where there exists an equivalence of at least some entities across the knowledge bases. Examples provided were of close train and bus stations, allowing passengers to switch from the train to the bus network or vice versa, and units from different universities that are deemed to be so similar that credit can be granted for foreign units towards meeting the requirements of local degrees. This equivalence enables domain-wide procedural rules that can utilize all or at least more than one expert system in the problem domain. Domain-wide procedural rules may be able to solve a wider range of problems within the domain than by using any individual expert system. Real examples, using Prolog implementations, were given to illustrate this capacity of domain-wide procedural rules.

The Prolog implementations of equivalence used in this chapter are simple assertions though the concepts are domain-specific. Complex rules, implemented in Prolog, could be developed for each problem domain. For instance, equivalent university units could be based on the number of matching keywords in the unit description and the proportion of credit points allotted to the unit within the total number required for the degree, and other factors. It would be expected that implementations of equivalence functions in real-world domain-wide applications would themselves be complex rules.

This chapter has introduced the concept of domain-wide applications in the context of suitable types of multiple expert systems. It has used XML technology as a means of defining problem domains but also because of the important role XML now plays in providing a means of transmitting data between applications – particularly on the World Web Web. Future work will include the development of real-world domain-wide applications and particularly those that are web-based.

REFERENCES

[1] Babu, K. V., Narayanan, R. G. and Kumar, G. S., An expert system for predicting the behavior of tailored welded blanks, *Expert Systems with Applications*, December 2010, Volume 37, Issue 12, 7802-712.

[2] Conti, P., Hamoir, T., De Smet, M., Piryns, H., Vanden Driessche, N., Maris, F., Hindriks, H., Schoenmakers, P. J. and Massart, D. L., Integrating expert systems for high-performance liquid chromatographic method development, *Chemometrics and Intelligent Laboratory Systems*, May 1991, Volume 11, Issue 1, 27-35.

[3] De Santo, M., Molinara, M., Tortorella, F. and Vento, M., Automatic classification of clustered microcalcifications by a multiple expert system, *Pattern Recognition*, July 2003, Volume 36, Issue 7, 1467-1477.

[4] Duan, Y., Edwards, J. S. and Xu, M. X., Web-based expert systems: benefits and challenges, *Information and Management*, September 2005, Volume 42, Issue 6, 799-811.

[5] Dunstan, N., Generating domain-specific web-based expert systems, Expert Systems with Applications, October 2008, Volume 35, Issue 3, 686-690.

[6] Dunstan, N., ET: An Enrolment Tool for generating expert systems for university courses. In: Vizureanu, P. (editor). *Expert Systems, Croatia, Intech*, 2010, 35-46.

[7] Fraser, N. M., Hipel, K. W., Kilgour, D. M., McNeese, M. D. and Synder, D. E., An architecture for integrating expert systems, Decision Support Systems, 1989, Volume 5, 263-276.

[8] Giarratano, J. and Riley, G. (1998), Expert Systems : Principles and Programming, 3rd edition, Boston, PWS Publishing Company.

[9] Helvacioglu, S. and Insel, M., Expert system applications in marine technologies, Ocean Engineering, August 2008, Volume 35, Issues 11-12, 1067-1074.

[10] Izumi, N., Maruyama, A., Suzuki, A. and Yamaguchi, T., An interoperative environment for developing expert systems, Knowledge Acquisition Modeling and Management, Lecture Notes in Computer Science, 1999, Volume 161/1999, 335-340.

[11] Loao, S., Expert system methodologies and applications – a decade review from 1995 to 2004, *Expert Systems with Applications*, January 2005, Volume 28, Issue 1, 93-103.

[12] Witlox, F., Expert systems in land-use planning: an overview, *Expert Systems with Applications,* August 2005, Volume 29, Issue 2, 437-445.

[13] Zhang, C. and Bell, D. A., HECODES: a framework for heterogeneous cooperating expert systems, *Data and Knowledge Engineering*, May 1991, Volume 6, Issue 3, 251-273.

In: Expert System Software
Editors: Jason M. Segura and Albert C. Reiter

ISBN: 978-1-61209-114-3
© 2012 Nova Science Publishers, Inc.

Chapter 5

MODELING A PARSER AS AN EXPERT SYSTEM

*Pinaki Chakraborty**

School of Computer and Systems Sciences
Jawaharlal Nehru University
New Delhi, India

INTRODUCTION

A parser is an essential component in all compilers (Aho and Ullman, 1972). In many compilers, the parser acts as the main routine with all other components functioning in its hegemony (Chakraborty, 2007; Chakraborty and Gupta, 2008; Chakraborty *et al.*, 201x). Parsers are used not only in compilers but also in other software tools like interpreters, query processors and natural language processors. The process of parsing is a complicated one. Therefore, a large number of studies both theoretical and experimental have been undertaken over the years to standardize the process. Nevertheless, the researchers still continue working on the advancement of the science and technology of parsing.

One important direction of research on parsing is based upon employing probability and heuristic based techniques, and modeling the parsers as knowledge based systems. Several scientists have studied how the concept of probability can be applied to improve the efficiency of a formal grammar. Some of them are worth mentioning. Salomma (1969) discussed a technique for assigning probabilities to sequences of production rules of a grammar. Booth and Thompson (1973) have presented a technique for estimating the probability of occurrence of each word of in a language. Thompson has further analyzed probabilistic grammars (1974) and used them to construct a theoretical foundation for an error correcting compiler (1976). Humenik and Pinkham (1990) have proposed a method to use relative production probabilities of nonterminals in a probabilistic grammar to obtain an efficient parse. Experimental results verified that the method works well in most cases. Asveld (2005a,b) presented a theoretical framework which can be used to develop a fuzzy grammar based parser that can detect and correct erroneous programs. Quite a few studies have been carried out to model parsers and other compiler components as knowledge based

---

* E-mail: pinaki_chakraborty_163@yahoo.com.

systems. Two of them require mentioning. Simon (1963) in an exploratory study performed some experiments on the construction of a compiler that makes use of heuristic problem solving techniques such as those used in a general problem solver program. The compiler compiles program written in Information Processing Language V (IPL-V). The compiler is organized as a collection of several compiling routines like general compiler, state description compiler and functional description compiler. The study concluded that a compiling task can be modeled as a problem solving task and solved by a compiler organized as a problem solver. In another important study, Fraser (1977) developed a heuristic based code generator generator called XGEN for ALGOL-like languages. XGEN accepts the description of a machine in ISP machine description language and produces a code generator for that machine. The code generator accepts a program in a language called XL and generates code corresponding to it. XGEN is organized as a production system of rules codifying previously acquired knowledge about computer architectures and programming languages. It especially emphasizes on assembly language programming skills that humans apply tacitly. The various performance parameters were found to be encouraging for XGEN. XGEN is easy to use, it is not difficult to obtain a working code generator and most importantly the quality of the code generated is satisfactorily good. In the current study, the concepts of probability, heuristics and knowledge based systems have been amalgamated to develop a parser.

This chapter presents a parser modeled as an expert system. Modeling the parser as an expert system allows the use of different types of heuristics to facilitate the parsing process and makes it faster. The next section provides the details of the parser while the section after that discusses a compiler that uses the parser.

THE PARSER

Basic Concepts

A compiler is a program that takes as input a program written in a high level source language and generates a functionally equivalent program in a low level object language. The compiler first analyzes the source program. If the compiler detects any error in the source program, then it displays an error message. Alternatively, if the source program is correct, then the compiler synthesizes the object program. The tasks involved in analyzing the source program and synthesizing the object program are diverse and often complicated. Therefore, the tasks are properly scheduled and similar tasks are grouped into distinct phases. The working of the phases is strictly sequential, i.e., for each fragment of the source program the phases are invoked in the same order. Researchers and developers have used the concept of phases to standardize the structure of compilers over the years. The number and types of the phases vary slightly in different compilers depending upon the source language, object language and design principles of the compiler. However, in most compilers the first two phases are lexical analysis and syntax analysis.

A lexical analysis of the source program is performed by a lexical analyzer. The lexical analyzer decomposes the source program into a stream of tokens. The lexical analyzer typically uses two fields, type and value, to represent a token. The lexical analyzer passes on the tokens to the next phase, which is typically the syntax analyzer, for further processing.

The second phase of a compiler is normally a syntax analyzer. A syntax analyzer, more commonly known as a parser, groups successive tokens into syntactic structures. Simple syntactic structures are combined together to form complex ones and finally the whole program is obtained as a single syntactic structure. The parser generates a hierarchical representation of the source program, called the parse tree, which is used by the subsequent phases of the compiler. The parser also often monitors the flow of control and data to the subsequent phases. This makes the parser the central routine in many compilers. Over the years, many parsing techniques have been developed. These parsing techniques are classified either as top-down parsing techniques or bottom-up parsing techniques. Each such parsing technique has its own merits and may be preferred for a particular type of source languages or even a particular part of a source program. Consequently, a parser may use one or more of these parsing techniques.

The functioning of a parser is governed by a preselected formal grammar. The grammar is generally a context free grammar. The grammar is defined in terms of nonterminals, terminals, a start symbol and production rules as usual. The parser generates a parse tree for a program if and only if it follows the grammar.

The Parser of the iXC85 Cross Compiler

The iXC85 cross compiler is an experimental compiler developed to study several practical aspects of compiler construction including the scope of modeling a parser as an expert system (Chakraborty, 2009). The source language of the compiler is a subset of C++ called C85++. C85++ emphasizes on operator mathematics. As a result, most of the operators of C++ have been included in C85++. However, C85++ supports fewer constructs for data abstraction and control flow. This makes C85++ a much simpler language than C++.

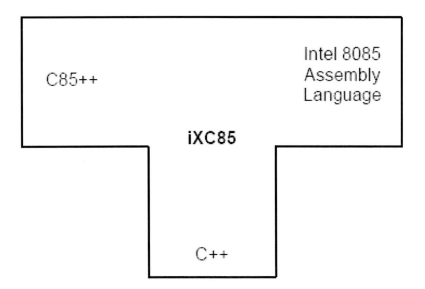

Figure 1. T-diagram of the iXC85 cross compiler.

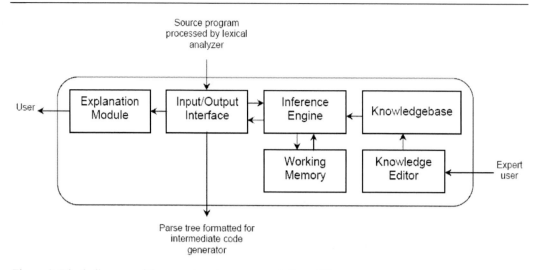

Figure 2. Block diagram of the expert system representation of the parser.

The object language of the compiler is Intel 8085 assembly language. It can be seen quite evidently that the name of the target machine has influenced the names of the compiler and the source language. The iXC85 cross compiler has been implemented in C++ and Figure 1 shows its T-diagram.

The parser used in the iXC85 cross compiler is a shift-reduce parser, a type of bottom-up parser. The parser strictly follows the grammar of the C85++ language which is a context free grammar. The grammar is defined in terms of 17 nonterminals, 50 terminals and 66 production rules. A nonterminal, named **program**, is the start symbol of this grammar. According to their usage, the production rules of the grammar have been logically classified in three categories as follows.

1. *Program related production rules.* These are the highest level production rules that are used to construct a program from statements, e.g., **program → statement-sequence**.
2. *Expression related production rules.* These are the lowest level production rules that are used to construct basic expressions, e.g., **multiplicative-expression → multiplicative-expression * unary-expression**.
3. *Statement related production rules.* These are middle level production rules that are used to construct statements using the expressions, e.g., **statement → while (expression) {statement-sequence}**.

The Architecture of the Parser

The parser of the iXC85 cross compiler has been developed as an expert system with a rule based system architecture (Figure 2). The knowledge is stored in the form of production rules and associated metadata. This architecture allows using a nondeterministic parsing technique to parse the source programs. The term nondeterministic denotes that the order in which the production rules are applied is dynamic instead of being predetermined as in most compilers. The nondeterminism is implemented using probability and heuristic based techniques. The nondeterministic parsing technique facilitates automatic learning and produces an efficient parse for most source programs. The expert system representation of the parser, as explained in detail by Chakraborty (2008), has six important components as follows.

1. *Input/output interface.* The input/output interface of the expert system receives the source program after being processed by the lexical analyzer. The input/output interface also formats the output of the parser such that it can be used by the next phase, the intermediate code generator.

2. *Inference engine.* The inference engine begins with loading the source program on to the working memory and attempts to parse it. The production rules, which are presorted according to their priorities, are used in an iterative process of matching, selecting and executing. The current problem state is matched with the production rules. The matching production rule is selected. The current problem state is reduced according to the selected production rule. Then, the priorities of the production rules are updated as explained in the next subsection. At last, the production rules are sorted by their priorities for the use in the next iteration. This process is carried out till the goal state is reached, i.e., the entire source program is parsed.

3. *Knowledgebase.* The knowledgebase contains the production rules of the C85++ grammar and associated metadata in a suitably encoded format. The encoded format facilitates fast knowledge retrieval.

4. *Knowledge editor.* The knowledge editor can be used by an expert user to modify the knowledge stored in the knowledgebase. Editing this knowledge changes the order in which the production rules are used in the parsing process. The knowledge editor is primarily meant for editing the heuristic knowledge associated with the production rules so that the parser can be fine-tuned to obtain an efficient parse. However, the production rules themselves can be also edited.

5. *Working memory.* The working memory contains the source program being parsed. In this expert system, the working memory is implemented primarily in the runtime stack of the compiler.

6. *Explanation module.* The explanation module of the expert system provides the user an explanation of the parsing process which is actually a simplified and human readable representation of the parse tree.

The Heuristics

Heuristics can be used to improve the efficiency of a parser. There are various types of heuristics that can be used in a parser (Chakraborty, 2008). However, most of the available heuristics perform well only for particular types of source programs. Nevertheless, there exist some heuristics that work satisfactorily well for parsing a large number of source programs of different types. Such heuristics can be called General Purpose Parsing Heuristics (GPPH). Three such GPPH, as listed below, have been implemented in the parser of the iXC85 cross compiler.

- *GPPH 1.* In every grammar, some production rules have more probability of being used than the others. So, each production rule is assigned an initial priority according to its relative likelihood of being used. In the matching process, a production rule with a higher priority is given precedence over another with a lower priority. For example, the production rule postfix-expression → identifier++ is used more often than the production rule postfix-expression → ++identifier. Therefore the first production rule has been assigned an initial priority of 760 against the initial priority of 750 of the latter.

- *GPPH 2.* If a particular production rule is used in parsing a source program, then it is normally used more than once. So, every time a production rule is used, its priority is increased by one. Thus, the priorities of the most frequently used production rules increase steadily. For example, to parse the expression a+b+c+d+e the production rule additive-expression → additive-expression + multiplicative-expression is used four times in quick succession. So, after every use of the production rule its priority is increased by one.

- *GPPH 3.* It has been observed that some production rules are typically used in cascade. The use of a production rule in such a cascade can predict the use of the next production rule in the cascade. In such a case, the priority of the predicted production rule is increased by two. For example, use of the production rule multiplicative-expression → multiplicative-expression * unary-expression is followed in many occasions by the use of the production rule additive-expression → multiplicative-expression. Therefore, after every use of the production rule multiplicative-expression → multiplicative-expression * unary-expression, the priority of the production rule additive-expression → multiplicative-expression is increased by two.

Implementation Issues

The parser of the iXC85 cross compiler is a nondeterministic shift-reduce parser. As already stated, the term nondeterministic denotes that the order in which the production rules are used in the parsing process is dynamic instead of being predetermined. The nondeterminism is realized by associating priorities with each production rule and then applying the production rules in a non-increasing order of their priorities. The priorities of the production rules are updated automatically during the parsing process adding to the nondeterministic behavior. The priorities of the production rules are represented using whole numbers between 0 and 899 in the knowledgebase.

The production rules have been divided into 18 distinct classes. A production rule in a class can have 50 values for its priority. The priority of a production rule increases when it is used or its use in near future is predicted by another production rule. There is, however, no way to decrease the priority of a production rule. Since, the priority of a production rule can only increase and there is no mechanism to decrease its value, it may easily reach the maximum limit for that class. Once the priority of the production rule reaches the maximum limit of that class, it cannot be increased anymore. As a result, this prioritization approach works well for programs of up to 3000 lines of code but becomes less effective for larger programs.

The production rules need to be encoded in some form so that the parser can easily read them and modify their priorities. So, each production rule is represented as a sequence of its rule number, priority, predicted next production rule, nonterminal on left hand side and terminals and nonterminals on right hand side. Each of these values is denoted as 3-digit codes (Figure 3). Unique 3-digit codes have been assigned to each terminal and nonterminal. A special code (000) is used to denote the end of a production rule. The production rules thus encoded are stored in the knowledgebase. The knowledgebase is provided separately from the executable program so that the user may modify the heuristic knowledge to parse their programs more effectively.

The parser may encounter two types of errors. The first occurs when the knowledgebase is missing. The second type of errors is parsing errors, i.e., a source program not following the grammar. On encountering either type of errors, the parser generates suitable error messages. On successful parsing of a source program, the parser generates the parse tree as its output. The output is generated in two formats. The first is a binary format meant to be used by the next phase of the compiler. The second format is a simplified human intelligible format.

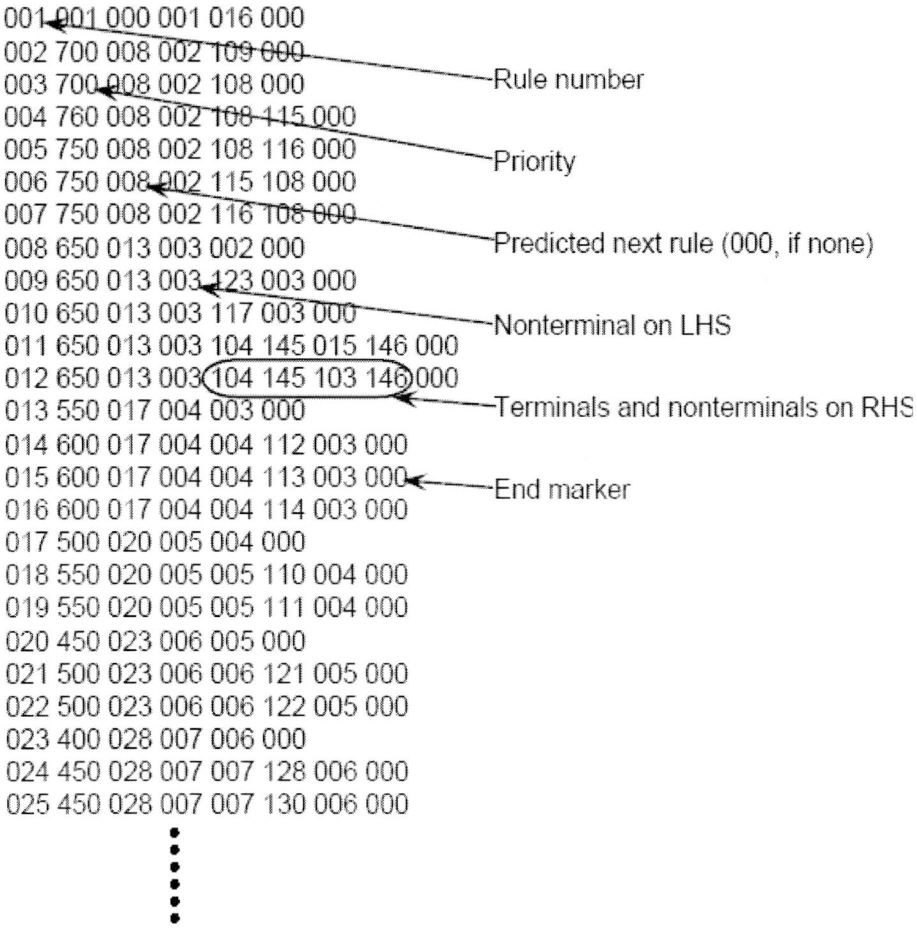

```
001 001 000 001 016 000
002 700 008 002 109 000
003 700 008 002 108 000                    Rule number
004 760 008 002 108 115 000
005 750 008 002 108 116 000                Priority
006 750 008 002 115 108 000
007 750 008 002 116 108 000
008 650 013 003 002 000                    Predicted next rule (000, if none)
009 650 013 003 123 003 000
010 650 013 003 117 003 000                Nonterminal on LHS
011 650 013 003 104 145 015 146 000
012 650 013 003 104 145 103 146 000
013 550 017 004 003 000                    Terminals and nonterminals on RHS
014 600 017 004 004 112 003 000
015 600 017 004 004 113 003 000            End marker
016 600 017 004 004 114 003 000
017 500 020 005 004 000
018 550 020 005 005 110 004 000
019 550 020 005 005 111 004 000
020 450 023 006 005 000
021 500 023 006 006 121 005 000
022 500 023 006 006 122 005 000
023 400 028 007 006 000
024 450 028 007 007 128 006 000
025 450 028 007 007 130 006 000
                    ⋮
```

Figure 3. Encoding the production rules.

THE COMPILER

Design of the Compiler

The iXC85 cross compiler consists of five phases and two modules as listed below. Each phase generates its output in two forms. The first is in a compressed binary format and is used by the next phase. Alternatively, the second contains the same information in a textual format intelligible to the user.

1. *Lexical analyzer.* The lexical analyzer reads the source program sequentially and groups the characters into tokens. To ease the task of the lexical analyzer, a preprocessor has been also implemented. The preprocessor replaces all macros in the source program with appropriate source language statements. The preprocessor also deletes the comments and redundant whitespaces. The lexical analyzer classifies the recognized tokens as keywords, identifiers, constants, operators and punctuators. On recognizing an identifier, the lexical analyzer invokes the bookkeeper module to install the identifier in the symbol table if it is not there already. The lexical analyzer generates as output a stream of tokens where each token is represented by a pair of type and value fields.

2. *Syntax analyzer.* The stream of tokens generated by the lexical analyzer is fed to the syntax analyzer or the parser. As discussed in the previous section, the parser generates a parse tree for the source program as its output. The parse tree is represented by a list of nodes in which each node is denoted by a type, production rule used to derive it, number of children nodes and a list of child nodes.

3. *Intermediate code generator.* The intermediate code generator transforms the information stored in the parse tree into a list of three address instructions implemented as quadruples of operator, operand1, operand2 and result fields. The intermediate code generator also creates temporary objects in the symbol table to store intermediate results.

4. *Code optimizer.* The code optimizer uses some simple machine independent code optimizing techniques to improve the three address instructions generated by the intermediate code generator.

5. *Code generator.* The code generator translates the three address instructions to their Intel 8085 assembly language equivalents. A single three address instruction may be translated to one or more Intel 8085 assembly language instructions. The instructions generated by the code generator are machine specific and are defined in terms of actual registers.

6. *Bookkeeper module.* The bookkeeper module uses a symbol table to store information about all the identifiers that appear in the source program.

7. *Error handler module.* On detection of an error, of whatsoever type, a phase or a module invokes the error handler module with necessary arguments. The error handler module generates error messages that are simple and easy to understand.

Working of the Compiler

The working of the iXC85 cross compiler can be best explained using an example. Consider the source program statement given below.

```
a=b+c*1;
```

The lexical analyzer decomposes this statement into a stream of tokens represented as follows.

```
Type   Value
  8     10
 15      1
  8     11
 10      1
  8     12
 10      3
  9      1
```

The parser generates the parse tree for this statement which is represented by a list of nodes as follows.

```
Node No.   Type   Rule   No. of Children   Children
  10       108     0      0
  11       132     0      0
  12       108     0      0
  13       110     0      0
  14       108     0      0
  15       112     0      0
  16       109     0      0
  17       150     0      0
  18       003     3      1                   10
  19       003     3      1                   12
  20       003     3      1                   14
  21       002     2      1                   16
  22       015    14      3                   20    15   21
  23       015    18      3                   19    13   22
  24       015    42      3                   18    11   23
  25       017    58      2                   24    17
  26       016    57      1                   25
  27       001     1      1                   26
```

Form the parse tree, the intermediate code generator produces the following three address instructions. Values enclosed between pairs of '[' and ']' denote addresses in the symbol table.

```
Operator   Operand1   Operand2   Result
   7        [ 12]         1       [ 20]
   3        [ 11]       [ 20]     [ 21]
   2        [ 21]         0       [ 10]
```

The code optimizer improves this sequence of three address instructions as follows.

```
Operator   Operand1   Operand2   Result
   3        [ 11]       [ 12]     [ 21]
   2        [ 21]         0       [ 10]
```

Finally, the code generator translates these three address instructions to the following Intel 8085 assembly language instructions.

```
LDA 8001
MOV B,A
LDA 8002
ADD B
STA 8000
```

CONCLUSION

The current study demonstrated that it is feasible to design and implement a parser modeled as an expert system. The parser developed in this study is able to parse most source programs quite efficiently. The current study was just an exploratory study. The real benefits of modeling a parser as an expert system will be realized in the case of a compiler for a more complex source language and an advanced target machine.

ACKNOWLEDGMENTS

The author is grateful to S. Taneja, late Prof. R. G. Gupta, Prof. P. C. Saxena and Prof. C. P. Katti for their guidance during the course of this study. The author would also like to thank Frank Columbus of Nova Science Publishers, Inc. for inviting him to write this chapter.

REFERENCES

Aho, A. V. and Ullman, J. D. 1972. The Theory of Parsing, Translation, and Compiling, Vol. I: Parsing, Prentice-Hall.

Asveld, P. R. J. 2005a. Fuzzy context free languages – Part 1: Generalized context free grammars, *Theoretical Computer Science*, 347(1-2): 167-190.

Asveld, P. R. J. 2005b. Fuzzy context free languages – Part 2: Recognition and parsing algorithms, *Theoretical Computer Science*, 347(1-2): 191-213.

Booth, T. L. and Thompson, R. A. 1973. Applying probability measures to abstract languages, *IEEE Transactions on Computers*, C-22(5): 442-450.

Chakraborty, P. 2007. A language for easy and efficient modeling of Turing machines, *Progress in Natural Science*, 17(7): 867-871.

Chakraborty, P. 2008. Use of heuristics in shift-reduce parsers, Proceedings of the International Conference on Data Management, pp. 103-109.

Chakraborty, P. 2009. Design and implementation of a cross compiler, *Journal of Multidisciplinary Engineering Technologies*, 3(2): 6-15.

Chakraborty, P. and Gupta, R. G. 2008. A simple object oriented compiler, Proceedings of the National Conference on Information Technology and Competitive Dynamics, pp. 203-215.

Chakraborty, P., Saxena, P. C. and Katti, C. P. 201x. A compiler based toolkit to teach and learn finite automata, *Computer Applications in Engineering Education*, In Press.

Fraser, C. W. 1977. A knowledge based code generator generator, *ACM SIGPLAN Notices*, 12(8): 126-129.

Humenik, K. and Pinkham, R. S. 1990. Production probability estimators for context free grammars, *Journal of Systems and Software*, 12(1): 43-53.

Salomaa, A. 1969. Probabilistic and weighted grammars, *Information and Control*, 15(6): 529-544.

Simon, H. A. 1963. Experiments with a heuristic compiler, *Journal of the ACM*, 10(4): 493-506.

Thompson, R. A. 1974. Determination of probabilistic grammars for functionally specified probability measure languages, *IEEE Transactions on Computers*, C-23(6): 603-614.

Thompson, R. A. 1976. Language correction using probabilistic grammars, *IEEE Transactions on Computers*, C-25(3): 275-286.

In: Expert System Software

Editors: : Jason M. Segura and Albert C. Reiter

ISBN: 978-1-61209-114-3

© 2012 Nova Science Publishers, Inc.

Chapter 6

EMBEDDED EXPERT SYSTEM FOR COGNITIVE CONGESTION AND FLOW CONTROL IN WLANS

Tapio Frantti and *Mikko Majanen*[†]

VTT Technical Research Centre of Finland

Abstract

This chapter introduces an embedded expert system for flow control of delay sensitive real-time traffic in Wireless Local Area Networks (WLANs). The expert system is based on the fuzzy set theory. It adjusts tranceivers' traffic flow(s) for prevailing network conditions to achieve maximum throughput in required application dependent delay limits. In wireless networks delay and throughput are very much dependent on the packet size, packet transmission interval, and the node connection density. Therefore, the expert system on the destination node monitors congestion by measuring an average one-way delay and a change of one-way delay of the incoming traffic. Thereafter it adjusts packet size and transmission interval of the source node by transmitting a control command to the source.

A linguistic decision making model of the expert system is described by linguistic relations. The linguistic relations form a rule base that is converted into numerical equations for tranceiver's computational efficiency. The developed congestion and flow control method does packet size definition by at most 56 computations. In the system level, the feedback control increases only lightly communicational load by transmitting application level acknowledgements after every 200 received packets.

The model was valitated by simulating User Datagram Protocol (UDP) traffic in OMNeT++ network simulator. The achieved results demonstrate that the developed expert system is able to regulate packet sizes and transmission intervals to the prevailing optimum level very fast, accurately and with minimal overshoot and to increase overall throughput of the network. Even if this work is mainly motivated by the congestion and flow control of WLAN systems and the simulations and results were performed for the IEEE 802.11b system, the approach and the techniques are not limited to these systems, but are easily applicable for other Packet Switched Access Networks (PSANs), too.

---

[*]E-mail address: tapio.frantti@vtt.fi

[†]E-mail address: mikko.majanen@vtt.fi

Keywords: expert systems, flow control, congestion control, packet size control, real-time traffic, PID, fuzzy control.

1. Introduction

The Internet has two independent flow problems. Internet protocols need end-to-end *flow control* and a mechanism for intermediate nodes, like routers and access points, to control the amount of traffic known as the *congestion prevention and control* mechanism. *Flow control* is closely related to the point-to-point traffic between a sender and a receiver. It guarantees that a fast sender cannot continually send datagrams faster than a receiver can absorb them. *Congestion* is a condition of severe delay caused by an overload of datagrams at intermediate nodes. Usually congestion arises for two different reasons: a high-speed computer may be able to generate traffic faster than a network can transfer it or many computers send datagrams simultaneously through a single router, even though no single computer causes the problem. Hence, the congestion control can be considered more as a global issue whereas flow control is more a local, point to point, issue with some direct feedback from the receiver to the sender.

Wireless Local Area Networks (WLANs) typically consist of an access point (AP) and wireless nodes around it. Nodes transmit data to the nearest access point, which delivers it either to another node in the coverage area or to some other node(s) on the Internet. In WLANs nodes can transmit only when a communication channel is unoccupied. The channel access is regulated by media access control (MAC) protocols, which are typically contention-based protocols. In contention-based MACs, the transmission bursts intervals for nodes are irregular (transmission jitter) and vary according to the type of transmitted traffic and the number of nodes competing or reserving the channel. The packet interval is also dependent on the packet length and the optimum packet size for the maximum throughput and minimum delay is dependent on the channel conditions.

In our earlier publications (Frantti et al., 2010; Frantti and Majanen, 2010) were presented and compared PID (Proportional, Integral, Derivative) and fuzzy control systems, which adjust packet size of UDP (User Datagram Protocol) based uni- or bidirectional traffic flow on WLANs according to prevailing channel conditions. The aim of this chapter is to enhance and deepen the analysis of the previously presented fuzzy expert system to adapt to various application level requirements, like the maximum acceptable delay time, with minimum computational complexity. The target of the developed embedded expert system for cognitive congestion and flow control is to optimize packet sizes of real-time traffic flows for the prevailing connection for higher end-to-end throughput by fulfilling the overall application dependent delay requirement. Even if the expert system was developed here to WLAN systems and the simulations and results were performed for the IEEE 802.11b system, the approach and the techniques are not limited to these systems, but are easily applicable for other packet switched access networks, too.

The organization of the rest of the chapter is as follows. Section 2. presents a literature review of the expert systems and packet size optimization for congestion and flow control in wireless networks. Section 4. introduces the principles of congestion control and prevention. In Section 3. is briefly summarized the structure and channel access of the WLANs. In

Sections 7. and 8. are briefly summarized the basic principles of the developed control systems. Section 9. depicts the developed simulation model. Section 10. comprises achieved results with the controllers. Finally, conclusions are presented in Section 11..

2. Literature Review

The term *cognition* (Latin: cognoscere, "to know", "to conceptualize" or "to recognize") refers to a faculty for the processing of information, applying knowledge, and changing preferences. In the communication networks, cognition can be used to improve the performance of resource management, quality of service, security, control algorithms, or many other network goals. *Cognitive network* is defined, *e.g.*, in Thomas et al. (2006) as cognitive process that can perceive current network conditions, and then plan, decide, and act on those conditions. The network can learn from these adaptations and use them for future decisions, all while taking into account end-to-end goals. End-to-end denotes all the network elements involved in the transmission of a data flow. In other words, unlike current data networks, cognitive networks can observe, act, and learn (use observations of the network performance) in order to optimize their performance.

2.1. Expert Systems and Communication Networks

Cognitive techniques for reasoning and decision making in communication networks have been limited previously to bounded problems. Steinder and Sethi (2004), for example, present a survey of the expert system techniques for fault localization to deduce the exact source of a failure from a set of observed failure indications. Patel et al. (1989) state that expert systems were the most widely used techniques in the field of fault localization and diagnosis in complex communication systems already at the end of 1980's. Habetha and Walke (2002) present a mobility and load management scheme, which is based on a rule-based fuzzy inference engine, for self-organizing cluster-based wireless networks. Shen et al. (2000) propose an adaptive fuzzy logic inference system to estimate and predict the mobility information of users on the future moments in cellular network. Kwon et al. (2005) identify key considerations for future decision support systems (DSSs) to enable ubiquitous computing technologies as tools for resolving conventional DSSs' limits. Giupponi et al. (2008) presents a fuzzy neural network based decision support algorithm to perform joint radio resource management in the context of heterogeneous radio access networks. Authors in () present a fuzzy decision support system for wireless ad hoc network. They use fuzzy logic theory for best-effort traffic regulation, and proposes schemes for real-time traffic regulation, and admission control. Chan et al. (2001) apply fuzzy set theory to employ decision criteria such as user preferences, link quality, cost, or QoS for handover decision scheme. We have considered in our previous publications embedded fuzzy expert systems, for example, for transmission power control (Frantti and Mahonen, 2001b; Frantti, 2006) in cellular networks, gesture recognition (Frantti and Kallio, 2004) in mobile terminals, active queue management (Frantti, 2005) in TCP/IP network, and for adaptive weighted fair queueing and service classification (Frantti and Jutila, 2009).

2.2. Congestion and Flow Control

Authors in (Wu and Djemame, 2003) claim that the Internet congestion control problem is one of those practical problems where conventional control does not offer a satisfactory solution. Therefore, they propose a structure for Expert Congestion Controller (ECC) and apply this structure for an AQM algorithm in data networks. Kang et al. (2009) propose a TCP Vegas-like expert-controlled multicast congestion control mechanism in which the network congestion state is detected according to network relative queuing delay and packet loss. The packet loss reason is distinguished between wireless link errors and network congestion, and the current state of the network is judged for different multicast source control strategies to adjust the sending rate. Jammeh et al. (2007) propose a fuzzy-logic congestion controller which changes the sending rate of a video transcoder without feedback of packet loss, using packet dispersion instead. It is a sender-based system for unicast flows. The receiver returns a feedback message that indicates time-smoothed and normalized changes to packet inter-arrival time. These allow the sender to compute the network congestion level through pre-designed fuzzy models. The sender then applies a control signal to the transcoder's quantization level, as a reflection of the anticipated congestion.

2.3. Packet Size Optimization for Congestion Control

Korhonen and Wang (2005) have studied the effect of packet size on loss rate and delay in IEEE 802.11 based WLAN. The analysis shows that there is a straightforward connection between bit error characteristics and observed delay characteristics. This information can be useful in adjusting application level framing under different network conditions. For example, an intelligent streaming application could optimize end-to-end delay and wireless resource utilization by analyzing the delay pattern for packets with different lengths. In general, it is shown throughout the literature that the performance of wireless networking is sensitive to the packet size, and that significant performance improvements are obtained if a "good" packet size is used. For example, authors in (Bakshi et al., 1997) show this for TCP traffic over wireless network. Chee and David (1989), Lettieri and Srivastava (1998), and Chien et al. (1999) do study of the relationship between frame length and throughput, but they do not propose any exact method to dynamically control the frame length. Packet size optimization has been studied also in several other perspectives, like energy efficiency in (Sankarasubramaniam et al., 2003) and security in (Younis et al., 2009), but these solutions are statistical in nature, meaning that the packet size is optimized beforehand. Work done in (Smadi and Szabados, 2006) is somehow related to our work, but even in this article the focus is different, error recovery in communication rather than optimal packet size in the first place. PLFC (Sheu et al., 2000) is the most similar to our approach presented in this chapter. PLFC is a fuzzy packet length controller for improving the performance of WLAN under the interference of microwave oven. The input parameters for the fuzzy controller are the packet length and the packet error rate. It is shown that PLFC improves the throughput of UDP traffic compared to using fixed length packets.

In the most recent of our publications (Frantti et al., 2010; Frantti and Majanen, 2010) were presented and compared PID and fuzzy control systems, which adjust packet size of UDP based uni- or bidirectional traffic on WLANs according to prevailing channel conditions. In other words, in Frantti et al. (2010); Frantti and Majanen (2010) was considered flow control for a fixed delay requirements. The delay can be defined as the time taken by a packet to traverse the network. Here we enhance the previously presented fuzzy expert system (FES) to adapt to various application level requirements, like an application dependent delay limit, with minimum computational complexity. The target of the developed embedded expert system for cognitive flow and congestion control is to optimize packet size of real-time traffic for the prevailing connection for higher throughput of the flow and by fulfilling the overall delay requirement of the flow. The FES controls end-to-end flow(s) by commanding a sender to transmit at on correct frequency and prevents a condition of severe delay (congestion) caused by an overload of datagrams at a network by controlling the amount of data in the flow(s) for acceptable delay.

3. Wireless Local Area Network

The market for wireless communications has grown rapidly since the introduction of the 802.11b, g, and a WLANs standards offering performance almost comparable to the Ethernet. The 802.11b, g, and a standards specify the lowest (physical) layer of the OSI reference model and a lower part (MAC) of the next higher layer (data link layer). The standards specify also the use of the 802.2 link layer control protocol, which is the upper portion of the data link layer.

The IEEE 802.11b wireless local area networks use the 2.4 GHz ISM (Industrial, Science and Medical) license-free frequency band, which is divided into 11 usable channels. Any particular network can use only less than half of these in operation, but all network hardware is built to be able to listen to and transmit on any of the channels. The sender and receiver must be on the same channel to communicate with each other.

The IEEE 802.11b network can be set to work in an Independent Basic Service Set (IBSS), in a Basic Service Set (BSS) or in an extended service set (ESS) mode. The IBSS is an ad hoc group of independent wireless nodes which communicate on a peer-to-peer basis. A standard refers to a topology with a single access point as a BSS. The arrangement with multiple access points is called an ESS (B. Bing, 2002). In ESS nodes transmit data to the nearest access point, which delivers it either to another node in the coverage area or to some other node(s) on the Internet. In WLANs nodes can transmit only when a communication channel is unoccupied. The channel access is regulated by media access control (MAC) protocols, which are typically contention-based protocols. The IEEE 802.11 b MAC supports two modes of operation: the Point Coordination Function (PCF) and the Distributed Coordination Function (DCF). The PCF provides contention free access, while the DCF uses the carrier sense multiple access with collision avoidance (CSMA/CA) mechanism for contention based access. Here we consider only DCF mode, because PCF mode is not commonly used and it is not a part of, $e.g.$, the Wi-Fi Alliance's interoperability standard (Leung et al., 2002; Li and Ni, 2005). In contention-based MACs, the transmission bursts intervals for nodes are irregular (transmission jitter) and vary according to the type of transmitted traffic and the number of nodes competing or reserving the channel. The packet interval is also dependent on the packet length. Therefore, the packet transmission interval and the channel access time are decreased, when the packet size is reduced. This increases channel reservation competition and may lead to the network congestion and decreased throughput of the network. On the other hand, when the packet payload is increased, the number of packets sent from the source node is reduced and the packet interval becomes longer. Then the channel is free for a longer period of time between packets, which reduces the channel reservation competition and increases the probability of getting a free channel. However, when the packet size increases the bit errors caused by the channel increase the probability of a packet error, which increases packet loss and decreases throughput. The channel access time depends also the type of traffic exchange. For example, in connection-oriented communication also acknowledgement (ACK) frames have to compete the channel access time in reverse direction, which decreases network node's channel access time in forward direction, too.

4. Congestion Prevention and Control

For the Internet congestion and resource control has been a research challenge for a long time. Congestion occurs when the aggregate demand for a resource exceeds the available capacity of the resource, *i.e.*, congestion conditions occur when a network cannot handle all the traffic that is offered. An increase of the offered load does not necessarily imply an increase of throughput but it may even happen in congestion condition that the throughput is reduced as the offered load increases due to, *e.g.*, the aggressive retransmission techniques used by some network protocols to compensate packet loss. Resulting effects include long delays, wasted resources due to lost or dropped packets, or even possible congestion collapse, in which all communications in the entire network ceases. Therefore, it is evident that certain mechanisms is required to maintain good network performance and to prevent the network from being congested.

For the congestion handling there are two main approaches, namely *congestion control* and *congestion prevention*. Congestion control is a reactive method and comes into play after the network is overloaded. Congestion control involves the design mechanisms to limit the demand-capacity mismatch and dynamically control traffic sources when such a mismatch occurs. Especially for real-time traffic, it is important to understand how congestion arises and find efficient ways to keep the network operating within its capacity. The basic design issues of the congestion control are what to feedback to sources and how to react to the feedback. However, endpoints, *i.e.*, the source and destination do not usually have the details of congestion point(s) and reason(s). Intermediate nodes, on the other hand, can use network layer techniques like ICMP (Internet Control Message Protocol, one part of the Internet protocol family) to inform hosts that congestion has occured.

Congestion prevention is a proactive approach and it acts before the network is overloaded. Congestion prevention aims to reduce congestion by designing good protocols and it takes proactive actions without relying on the network status. It plays a major role before the network faces congestion. Congestion prevention covers different policies at the transport, network, and data link layer such as retransmission, acknowledgement, flow control, admission control, and routing algorithm. The end systems typically negotiate with the network and after that systems act independently. The end-systems get no information from the network about the current traffic and network status but intermediate nodes, such as routers, can monitor their output lines' load. Hence, whenever the utilisation of a line approaches a specified threshold level, the router transmits *choke* datagrams to the sources in order to give warning signals to them. The source nodes or hosts are required to reduce transmission rate to the specified destination by n percentage. Another paradigm that has been suggested for use in congestion prevention is *weighted fair queuing*, where a router selects datagrams from multiple queues in a round robin way to the idle output line. The router weights more bandwidth to some services than others. In packet switched networks it is also possible to allow new virtual circuits by routing traffic via a different, uncongested, route. Another alternative solution is to negotiate an agreement between the hosts and network during the connection set up by specifying the volume and the shape of the traffic as well as quality of service requirements.

In wireless networks, admission control and resource reservation mechanisms are commonly proposed for congestion prevention. In admission control, after congestion has been signalled, no more connections are allowed to be set up until the congestion has gone away. Admission control is crude but simple and robust to implement, and has been used in telephone systems for decades. In congestion prevention it is also suggested to use media access layer solutions, like decreasing excessive overhead, retransmissions and auto-rate fallback.

If congestion does not disapper with the preventive actions, routers can throw away datagrams they cannot handle (*load shedding*). They can do it either randomly or in a rational way, for example, when dropping a file transfer, a newer one is more rational than an older one due to acknowledgement and retransmission procedures. On the contrary, in real-time data transfer newer ones are more valuable than older ones.

The most widely used congestion control mechanisms are *drop-tail*, *active queue management*

5. Flow Control

Problems of congestion control, like congestion collapse, are largely related to the flow control of TCP (Transmission Control Protocol). TCP adjusts a source node's transmission rate according to the rejected number of datagrams (TCP considers it as a congestion measure) in the network. During the flow control of TCP session, a sender transmits W (W=size of the transmission window) datagrams per time unit and starts to wait for acknowledgements from the receiver. The receiver sends an acknowledgement signal for each datagram, which it has received. If all the datagrams are received, the source increases the size of the window (additive increment), while if a datagram is dropped the size of W is halved (multiplicative decrement). This is also called a *drop-tail* mechanism. The drawback of drop-tail is that the transmission rate is decreased only after the detection of datagrams losses, which causes a time delay (due to round trip time, RTT) and results in buffer overflows in routers and further losses of datagrams. Hence, it is obvious that the flow control of TCP with the sliding window scheme is not sufficient for flow and congestion control in terms of the network performance and overall quality of service (QoS).

On the other side, real-time flows with stringent delay requirements make use of UDP (User Datagram Protocol), which lacks the mechanism to regulate the amount of data being transmitted. UDP does not return acknowledgements and cannot signal congestion to the sender. Therefore, for the UDP sessions, applications have to provide some form of flow control on their own. The inability of UDP flows to regulate transmission rate at the transport layer makes them especially vulnerable to congestion.

6.   Congestion and Flow Control in WLANs

In access networks, like WLANs, congestion occurs when the load on the network is temporarily greater than the resources. Congestion typically causes packet loss due to collisions, which arises when several nodes try to send at the same time, *i.e.*, try to do channel reservation at the same time with CSMA/CA MAC, decreasing significantly transmission rate and increasing dramatically delay. However, the nodes do not know whether the cause of the packet loss is due to congestion or low signal to noise ratio.

In WLANs delay and throughput are very much dependent on the packet size, packet transmission interval, and the node connection density. Therefore, in a congested state one can either decrease load by denying and/or degrading services or reduce channel access competition by access control and/or packet size and transmission interval control. Congestion can be identified via monitoring, *e.g.*, the *percentage share of discarded datagrams*, *average queue lengths*, and the *percentage share of datagrams that are timed out and retransmitted* on access points, and monitoring the *average value* and *variance of a datagram's delay* on destination nodes. A natural step after monitoring and identification is to transfer information from the congested places (destination nodes, access points) to places where control actions can be performed (source nodes, access points).

Here we use an embedded fuzzy expert system on the destination nodes to shape real-time traffic on WLANs. In our system the destination node monitors congestion by measuring *average one-way delay error* and the *change of one-way delay error* as congestion information, defines packet size increment according to them, and delivers packet size information to the source node.

7.   Proportional-Integral-Derivative Packet Size Controller

A proportional-integral-derivative (PID) control is a widely used feedback control mechanism. A PID controller calculates an error value as the difference between a measured process variable and a desired setpoint and attempts to minimize the error by adjusting the process control inputs. The *proportional* value determines the controller's reaction to the current error, the *integral* value determines the reaction based on the sum of recent errors, and the *derivative* value defines the reaction to the rate at which the error has been changing. The weighted sum of these three actions is used to adjust the process, such as the packet payload size of the transmitter, via a control element.

In the developed PID controller, one-way delay error (E_d = proportional value = delay - set value (100 ms)), sum of the recent errors (I_d = integral value), and the change of error (ΔE_d = derivative value) are used as the input values. The output value of the controller is the change of the packet payload size. The new packet payload size is the change of the packet payload size + earlier packet size. The developed controller can be presented in the equation form as follows:

$$P_i(t) = K_p \times E_d(t) + K_i \times \int_{-3}^{0} E_d(t)\,dt + K_d \times \frac{\Delta E_d(t)}{dt}, \tag{1}$$

where P_i is the change of the packet payload size, K_p (=0.75) is a proportional amplifier, K_i (=0.20) is an integration amplifier, K_d (=0.1) is a derivation amplifier, and t is time.

The controller is located at the user terminal. The controller was designed to update the transmission packet size in order to reach an application dependent target end-to-end delay with the maximum throughput in the prevailing channel conditions. For example in VoIP calls (Andrews et al., 2007) and in action games (Balakrishnan and Sadasivan, 2007), it is preferred that the absolute one-way delay should remain below 100 ms. Maximum through-put instead of the fixed minimum required throughput is needed for example for the video conversations with scalable video coding. Video conversations have a strict end-to-end de-lay requirement but flexible throughput requirement. Therefore, with higher throughput it is possible to use better video coding for higher quality of videos.

8.   Fuzzy Packet Size Controller

Fuzzy set theory was originally presented by L. Zadeh in his seminal paper "Fuzzy Sets" in *Information and Control 1965* (Zadeh, 1965). Fuzzy logic was developed later from fuzzy set theory primary to reason with uncertain and vague information and secondary to represent knowledge in operationally powerful form. In the fuzzy set theory the name *fuzzy sets* are used to distinguish them from the *crisp sets* of the conventional set theory. The characteristic function of a crisp set C, $\mu_C(u)$, assigns a discrete value (usually either 0 or 1) to each element u in the universal set U, *i.e.*, it discriminates members and non-members of the crisp set (then for each element u of U, either $u \in C$ or $u \notin C$). The characteristic function can be generalized in fuzzy set theory so that the values assigned to the elements u of the universal set U fall within a prespesified range (usually to the unit interval [0, 1]) indicating the membership grade of these elements in the fuzzy set F. Then it is not necessary that either $u \in F$ or $u \notin F$. The generalized function is called *membership function* and the set defined with the aid of it is a *fuzzy set*, respectively. The membership function assigns to each $u \in U$ a value from the unit interval [0, 1] instead of dual value set $\{0,1\}$.

A fuzzy control was originally developed to include a human operator's or system engi-neer's expertise, which does not lend itself to being easily expressed in PID -parameters or differential equations but rather in situation/action rules. In this study a fuzzy expert system based controller was developed to handle the problems of large overshoot, large steady state error and long-rise time that are evident in the classical systems (Chang and May, 1996). Li and Lau (1989) have shown that the fuzzy proportional-integral controller is less sensitive to large parametric changes in the process and is comparable in performance to the conven-tional PI controller for small parametric changes. In the fuzzy control system the input and output variables are represented in linguistic form after fuzzyfication of physical values into linguistic form. In this application the input variables are the *average one-way delay error* and the *change of one-way delay error*, the output value is the *packet size increment*. This is so called *two-input, single output control strategy* .

The major components of an expert system are the knowledge base and inference en-gine. The knowledge base contains the expert-level information necessary to solve domain specific problems, *i.e.*, the knowledge bases are domain specific and nontrasferable. The information is generally presented in the rule form, although, *e.g.*, semantic nets and belief networks are also used. In fuzzy expert system based control applications, a rule base in-cludes a control policy, which is usually presented with linguistic conditional statements, *i.e.*, if-then rules. Here we present the rule base in the matrix form and the reasoning is done by linguistic equations, see Juuso (1992) and Frantti and Mahonen (2001a). The main advantages of the linguistic equations are the compact size of rule base and computational efficiency. In the inference engine, the control strategy produces the linguistic control output, which is transformed back into the physical domain in order to find the crisp control output value for the packet size increment. Interested reader finds more information about fuzzy controllers, for example, from (Driankov et al., 1994).

8.1. Fuzzy Expert System

The leading idea of fuzzy logic based modelling is the use of domain experts' knowledge for the rule base creation. In the developed fuzzy expert system based controller, the fuzzy proportional, integral, and derivative parts (FPID) are included to improve the controller's performance. The structure of the developed fuzzy controller for the packet size definition is presented in Figure 1. The fuzzy controller monitors incoming traffic, defines the change of packet size for the source node, and transmits a packet size control command to the source node by acknowledgements. The actual fuzzy system, which is located at the user terminal, has three modules: a fuzzyfication module, a reasoning module and a defuzzyfication module.

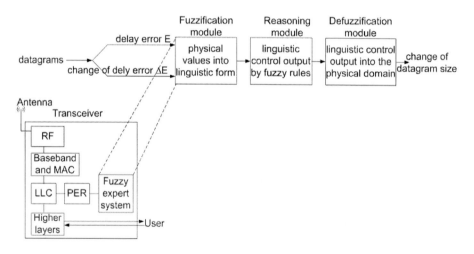

Figure 1. Fuzzy model for packet size control.

The one-way delay error (E_d) and the change of it (change of the delay error, ΔE_d) are used as the input values for the fuzzy reasoning model. Input variables are represented in linguistic form after fuzzyfication in the fuzzyfication module. Fuzzyfication procedure is illustrated in Figures 2 and 3. In Figure 2, the delay error E_d is -24.92 ms, which is *negative big* at the grade of 0.48 and *negative small* at the grade of 0.52. The change of delay ΔE_d is 6.46 ms, which from one's part is *zero* at the grade of 0.77 and from other part is *positive small* at the grade of 0.23, see Figure 3.

In fuzzy set theory reasoning can be done either using *composition based* or *individual based inference*. In the former all rules are combined into an explicit relation and then fired with fuzzy input whereas in the latter rules are individually fired with crisp input and then combined into one overall fuzzy set. Here we used individual based inference with Mamdani's implication (Driankov et al., 1994). The main reason for the choice was its easier implementation (the results are equivalent for both methods when Mamdani's implication is used).

In this application, a linguistic model of a system was described by linguistic relations. The linguistic relations form a rule base (25 rules, see Figure 5) that can be converted into numerical equations. Suppose, as an example, that X_{ij}, $i=1,2$; $j = 1,..., m$ (j is uneven number), is a linguistic level (*e.g.,negative big, negative small, zero, positive small, and positive big*) for a variable X_i. The linguistic levels are replaced by integers $\frac{-(j-1)}{2}, ..., -2, -1, 0, 1, 2, ..., \frac{(j-1)}{2}$. The direction of the interaction between fuzzy sets is presented by coefficients $A_{ij}=\{-1, 0, 1\}$, $i=1,2$; $j = 1,..., m$. This means that the directions of the changes in the output variable decrease or increase depending on the directions of the changes in the input variables (Juuso, 1993). Thus a compact equation for the output Z_{ij} is:

$$\sum_{j=1}^{m} \sum_{i=1}^{2} A_{ij} X_{ij} = Z_{i,j}. \tag{2}$$

The mapping of linguistic relations to linguistic equations for this application is described in Figure 5. For example, we can read from Figure 5 that *IF E_d IS negative small AND ΔE_d IS zero THEN the change of packet size IS positive small*. In linguistic equations this can be presented as $\lceil \frac{(-1*-1+-1*0)}{2} \rceil = 1$. A more detail reasoning example is given in Section 8.2..

In the defuzzyfication module the control strategy produces the linguistic control output, which is transformed back into the physical domain to find the crisp output value for the change of packet size. In the defuzzyfication phase the center of area method (CoA) was used. The defuzzyfication procedure is illustrated in Figure 4. From Figure 4 it can be seen that the change of packet size is *positive small* at the grade of 0.52 and *positive big* at the grade of 0.48. The crisp output value is the center of the area, *i.e.*, the new packet size is 43 bits bigger than the earlier value.

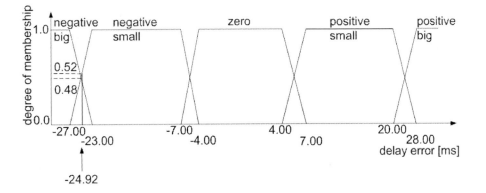

Figure 2. Fuzzy membership functions for the E_d.

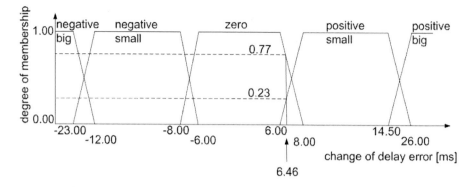

Figure 3. Fuzzy membership functions for the ΔE_d.

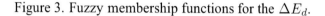

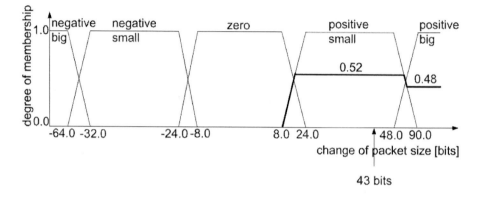

Figure 4. Fuzzy membership functions for the change of packet size.

8.2. Reasoning Example

The developed fuzzy expert system was designed to update the transmission packet size in order to reach a target end-to-end delay with the maximum throughput in the prevailing channel conditions. Consider as an example, that the E_d is -24.92 ms, which is after fuzzyfication in linguistic form *negative big* at the grade of membership 0.48 and *negative small* at the grade of membership 0.52 (see Figure 2). Suppose that the ΔE_d is 6.46 ms, which is after fuzzyfication in linguistic form *zero* at the grade of membership 0.77 and *positive small* at the grade of membership 0.23 (see Figure 3). Now we can read from Figures 2, 3 and 5 that

IF E_d IS NB at the grade 0.48 AND ΔE_d IS ZE at the grade 0.77 THEN the change of packet size IS PB at the grade 0.48

IF E_d IS NB at the grade 0.48 AND ΔE_d IS PS at the grade 0.23 THEN the change of packet size IS PB at the grade 0.23

IF E_d IS NS at the grade 0.52 AND ΔE_d IS ZE at the grade 0.77 THEN the change of packet size IS PS at the grade 0.52

mapping of the linguistic relations to the linguistic equations

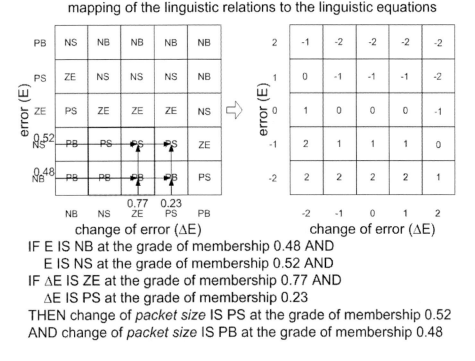

IF E IS NB at the grade of membership 0.48 AND
E IS NS at the grade of membership 0.52 AND
IF ΔE IS ZE at the grade of membership 0.77 AND
ΔE IS PS at the grade of membership 0.23
THEN change of *packet size* IS PS at the grade of membership 0.52
AND change of *packet size* IS PB at the grade of membership 0.48

Figure 5. Fuzzy rule base and mapping of the linguistic relations to the linguistic equations.

IF E_d IS NS at the grade 0.52 AND ΔE_d IS PS at the grade 0.23 THEN the change of packet size IS PS at the grade 0.23

In linguistic equations this can be presented as follows:

$$\lceil \tfrac{(-2*-2+-1*0)}{2} \rceil = 2 \text{ at the grade } \min(0.48,0.77)$$

$$\lceil \tfrac{(-2*-2+-1*1)}{2} \rceil = 2 \text{ at the grade } \min(0.48,0.23)$$

$$\lceil \tfrac{(-2*-1+-1*0)}{2} \rceil = 1 \text{ at the grade } \min(0.52,0.77)$$

$$\lceil \tfrac{(-2*-1+-1*1)}{2} \rceil = 1 \text{ at the grade } \min(0.52,0.23)$$

where $\lceil \; \rceil$ returns the next highest integer value by rounding up the value if necessary. Using individual based inference with Mamdani's implication the weight value is *positive big* at the grade of membership 0.48 (max(0.48,0.23)) and *positive small* at the grade of membership 0.52 (max(0.52,0.23)). Therefore, the crisp output value is 43 bits (see Figure 4), which is used in the user equipment to update a new packet size to be 43 bits bigger than earlier. The rule base keeps the packet size between [256, 11520] bits.

8.3. Computational Complexity

The definition of the packet size on the mobile nodes increases node's computational complexity. The implementation decision of the fuzzy control method is a trade-off between complexity, required computational time, required RAM (Random Access Memory) and program memory and achieved advantages of the algorithm. The fuzzy feedback control also lightly increases communicational load by transmitting application level acknowledgements after every 200 received packets. Fuzzyfication phase requires at the most two × nine comparisons, two × two addition and two × one multiplications. In the comparisons crisp input values are compared to the parts of the membership functions, which cover the dynamic ranges of the input variables, see Figure 2. After the comparisons, when the fired fuzzy label(s) are identified, the degree of membership is defined by multiplying the interval of corner point and crisp value by the angle of the line. Multiplication is not needed if the crisp point sets to the top area, *i.e.*, the degree of membership is 1.0. Reasoning process for linguistic equations requires in the worst case eight multiplications, four additions, four divisions, and six min/max comparisons. In the defuzzyfication phase, it is required at most two × two additions and two × five multiplications for the definition of horizontal component of the center of area. All in all, the developed control method increases at most 56 computations for fuzzy packet size definition. According to Koomey (2010) it can be estimated that one operation requires 1.2-1.8 nJ and thus 56 operations requires about 84 nJ, if the value 1.5 nJ/operation is used. The estimated energy consumption per transmitted packet is then $\frac{84}{200}$ nJ = 0.42 nJ, which is less than or equal to $\frac{1}{3}$ of the energy consumption one elementary operation requires.

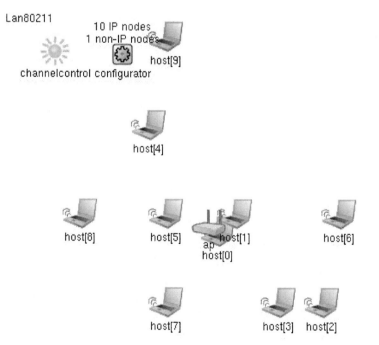

Figure 6. The simulation scenario.

Table 1. Parameters for the simulations. BG = Background

Parameter	Value
Simulation time	200 s
Wireless hosts	10
Protocols	IP/UDP
MAC	CSMA/CA
MAC data rate	11 Mbit/s
carrier frequency	2.4 GHz
transmitter power	2.0 mW
thermal noise	-110 dBm
sensitivity	-85 dBm
snirThreshold	4 dB
Simulation area	600 x 400 m
BG traffic packet interval	uniform(0.01,0.09/0.085/0.08/0.075/0.07) s

9. Network Simulations

The simulation studies were done with OMNeT++ 4.0 simulator (http://www.omnetpp.org) with the INETMANET framework. The conducted simulations measured delay and throughput with different background traffic levels. The simulation scenario consisted of 10 wireless hosts in an infrastructure (BSS) mode and one IEEE 802.11b WLAN access point. The nodes were distributed randomly around the AP, as depicted in Figure 6. The nodes were not moving. Host1 had an application that sent a UDP packet to Host0 every 1 ms starting with the packet size of 256 bits. Host0 measured the delay for the packets, used the developed packet size optimization algorithms to calculate the optimum packet size, and reported it to the Host1 after every 200 packets by sending an UDP acknowledgement message. It was assumed that the nodes were synchronized using, *e.g.*, access point's beacon message. The other hosts, host2-host9, generated the background traffic that interfered with the communication between host1 and host0. The background traffic consisted of bi-directional constant bit rate (CBR) UDP traffic between pairs of hosts 2-9, *i.e.*, host2 sent CBR traffic to host3, and *vice versa*, host4 sent traffic to host5, *etc.*. The packet intervals were randomly selected from uniform distributions. The background traffic packet size was a constant 2496 bits. The measurements were done with 5 different background traffic levels. The background traffic was increased by decreasing the packet interval. The most important simulation parameters are shown in Table 1.

10. Results

10.1. Throughput

The developed controllers were designed to update the transmission packet size in order to reach an application dependent target end-to-end delay with the maximum throughput in

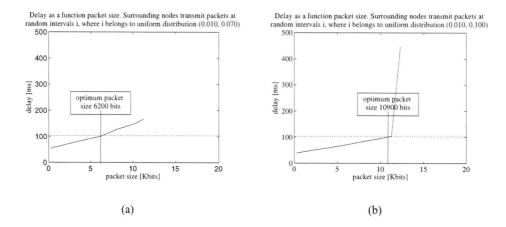

(a)   (b)

Figure 7. Delay as a function of packet size when a.) surrounding nodes transmit packets at random intervals $i \in [0.010\ s, 0.070\ s]$ and b.) surrounding nodes transmit packets at random intervals $i \in [0.010\ s, 0.100\ s]$.

Table 2. Throughputs and corresponding averaged packet sizes with different amount of background traffic. Delay limit was 100 ms. Initial packet size was 256 bits. OF = Optimized fixed

Background traffic	Average packet size			Throughput		
	OF [bits]	FPID [bits]	PID [bits]	OF [Kbit/s]	FPID [Kbit/s]	PID [Kbit/s]
(0.010,0.100)	10900	10552	10538	1518	2149	2130
(0.010,0.090)	9750	9366	9324	1285	1907	1874
(0.010,0.085)	8800	8897	8455	1180	1804	1763
(0.010,0.080)	8200	8276	7876	1051	1686	1593
(0.010,0.075)	7100	7103	7034	900	1457	1429
(0.010,0.070)	6200	6207	5793	715	1255	1175

the prevailing channel conditions. Therefore, in the conducted simulations were measured delay and throughput with the different background traffic level when the packet payload size was fixed, adjusted by the developed PID controller, and adjusted by the developed fuzzy controller. The optimum packet size value depends on the amount of traffic on the network. For example, Figure 7 a presents delay as a function of packet size, when surrounding nodes transmit packets at random intervals i, where $i \in [0.010\ s, 0.070\ s]$ and Figure 7 b presents delay as a function of packet size, when $i \in [0.010\ s, 0.100\ s]$. In Figure 7 the optimum values are 6200 bits and 10900 bits for 100 ms delay, respectively. For 50 ms target delay, the respective optimum values are 150 bits and 2220 bit, see Table 3. Tables 2 and 3 present averaged packet sizes and respective throughputs for one-directional traffic from a single transmitter to a single receiver when the packet transmission interval of surrounding nodes is varied from $i \in [0.010\ s, 0.070\ s]$ to $i \in [0.010\ s, 0.100\ s]$ and the target delays are 100 ms and 50 ms, respectively. Table 4 presents averaged packet sizes

Table 3. Throughputs and corresponding averaged packet sizes with different amount of background traffic. Delay limit was 50 ms. Initial packet size was 256 bits. OF = Optimized fixed

Background traffic	Average packet size			Throughput		
	OF [bits]	FPID [bits]	PID [bits]	OF [Kbit/s]	FPID [Kbit/s]	PID [Kbit/s]
(0.010,0.100)	2220	2443	2313	1415	1526	1323
(0.010,0.090)	1720	1957	1638	1053	1192	1049
(0.010,0.085)	1170	1614	1264	721	987	842
(0.010,0.080)	910	1348	993	541	656	525
(0.010,0.075)	460	913	515	269	455	318
(0.010,0.070)	150	536	379	79	259	192

Table 4. Throughputs and corresponding averaged packet sizes of tranceiver pair with different amount of background traffic. Delay limit was 100 ms. Initial packet size was 256 bits. OF = Optimized fixed

Background traffic	Average packet size			Throughput		
	OF [bits]	FPID [bits]	PID [bits]	OF [Kbit/s]	FPID [Kbit/s]	PID [Kbit/s]
(0.010,0.100)	3570	2960	2449		1123	931
(0.010,0.090)	2712	1983	1888		685	684
(0.010,0.085)	2048	1833	1378		607	464
(0.010,0.080)	1045	1293	1035		398	333
(0.010,0.075)	288	807	546		214	151
(0.010,0.070)	nan	687	472		140	107

Table 5. Average delay of received packets with different amount of background traffic when optimized fixed (OF) packet size, FPID controlled and PID controlled packet sizes were used. Delay limit was 100 ms. Initial packet size was 256 bits

Background traffic	Average delay		
	OF [ms]	FPID [ms]	PID [ms]
(0.01,0.100)	101.50	94.75	94.43
(0.01,0.090)	101.90	93.95	94.30
(0.01,0.085)	99.51	94.71	94.26
(0.01,0.080)	100.34	95.62	93.33
(0.01,0.075)	100.60	97.79	95.22
(0.01,0.070)	103.70	97.79	95.29

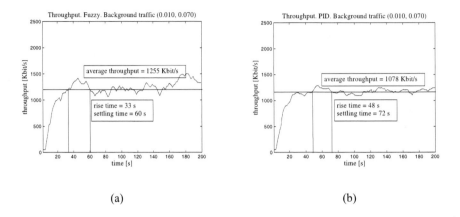

(a)   (b)

Figure 8. Throughput as a function of time when the packet size was adjusted by a.) the FPID and b.) the PID controller and the surrounding nodes transmit packets at random intervals i, where $i \in [0.010\,s, 0.070\,s]$.

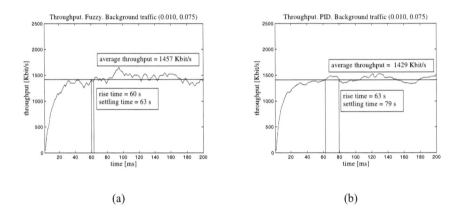

(a)   (b)

Figure 9. Throughput as a function of time when the packet size was adjusted by a.) the FPID and b.) the PID controller and the surrounding nodes transmit packets at random intervals i, where $i \in [0.010\,s, 0.075\,s]$.

and respective throughputs for a tranceiver pair when the packet transmission interval of surrounding nodes is varied from $i \in [0.010\,s, 0.070\,s]$ to $i \in [0.010\,s, 0.100\,s]$ and the target delays is 100 ms. The packet size adjustment was performed after every 200 received packets. As can be seen from the Tables 2-4 throughputs with PID and FPID controlled packet sizes are significantly higher than with the optimally chosen fixed (OF) packet sizes. This is probably due to controllers ability to adapt fast to prevailing channel conditions and exploit available transmission capacity. In practise, the amount of background traffic changes as a function of time and it is not possible to manually choose optimal fixed packet sizes for the current background traffic level. This further enhances the superiority of the control to uncontrolled situation.

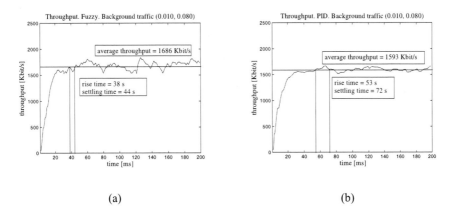

Figure 10. Throughput as a function of time when the packet size was adjusted by a.) the FPID and b.) the PID controller and the surrounding nodes transmit packets at random intervals i, where $i \in [0.010 \, s, 0.080 \, s]$.

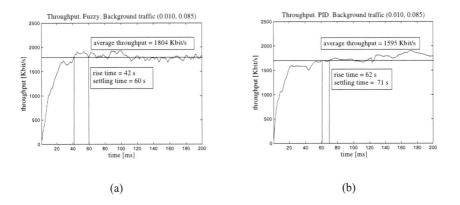

Figure 11. Throughput as a function of time when the packet size was adjusted by a.) the FPID and b.) the PID controller and the surrounding nodes transmit packets at random intervals i, where $i \in [0.010 \, s, 0.085 \, s]$.

10.2. Delay

The mean packet delay for 100 ms target delay when there was one-directional traffic from a single transmitter to a single receiver (see Table 5) was varied between 99.51 ms - 103.70 ms, 93.95 ms - 97.79 ms, and 93.33 ms - 95.29 ms for the optimum fixed packet sizes, for the FPID controller, and for the PID controller, respectively. For 50 ms target delay (see Table 6) the respective values were 49.9 ms - 52.27 ms, 46.28 ms - 50.19 ms, and 46.35 ms - 49.04 ms. For a tranceiver pair (Table 7) the values were xx ms - yy ms, 89.91 ms - 109.49 ms, and 87.25 ms - 115.51 ms. Both of the controllers managed to keep the average delay value below the target value except for the transitter pair with highest amount background traffic. The reason for exceeded target value was networks uncapability to reach target value in any packet size.

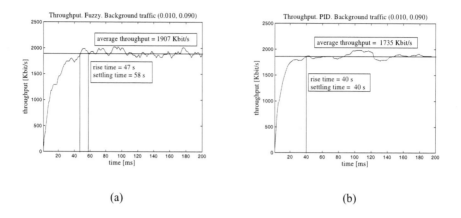

Figure 12. Throughput as a function of time when the packet size was adjusted by a.) the FPID and b.) the PID controller and the surrounding nodes transmit packets at random intervals i, where $i \in [0.010\ s, 0.090\ s]$.

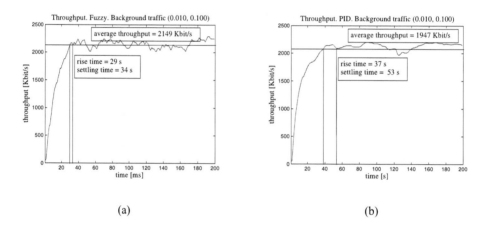

Figure 13. Throughput as a function of time when the packet size was adjusted by a.) the FPID and b.) the PID controller and the surrounding nodes transmit packets at random intervals i, where $i \in [0.010\ s, 0.100\ s]$.

As was shown above in Tables 2-4, they also keep throughputs significantly higher than with the optimally chosen fixed packet sizes. The delay variance for 100 ms target delay when there was one-directional traffic from a single transmitter to a single receiver (Table 8) was varied between 0.72 ms - 3.08 ms, 1.08 ms - 2.44 ms, and 1.10 ms - 2.88 ms for the optimum fixed packet sizes, for the FPID controller, and for the PID controller, respectively. The respective values for the 50 ms target delay were 0.38 ms - 1.10 ms, 0.29 ms - 1.41 ms, and 0.24 ms - 0.98 ms. For a tranceiver pair (Table 10) the values were xx ms - yy ms, 1.12 ms - 6.33 ms, and 1.10 ms - 5.46 ms. The delay variance is mainly due to corrupted acknowledgements in a noisy feedback channel preventing control actions on source nodes. The minor delay variances also prove that the controllers are suitable to

Table 6. Average delay of received packets with different amount of background traffic when optimized fixed (OF) packet size, FPID controlled and PID controlled packet sizes were used. Delay limit was 50 ms. Initial packet size was 256 bits

Background traffic	Average delay		
	OF [ms]	FPID [ms]	PID [ms]
(0.01,0.100)	49.49	49.04	50.13
(0.01,0.090)	50.10	48.59	50.02
(0.01,0.085)	48.90	48.05	50.19
(0.01,0.080)	49.68	47.18	49.98
(0.01,0.075)	49.62	46.39	49.08
(0.01,0.070)	52.27	46.35	46.28

Table 7. Average delay of received packets of tranceiver pair with different amount of background traffic when optimized fixed (OF) packet size, FPID controlled and PID controlled packet sizes were used. Delay limit was 100 ms. Initial packet size was 256 bits

Background traffic	Average delay		
	OF [ms]	FPID [ms]	PID [ms]
(0.01,0.100)		92.29	87.77
(0.01,0.090)		89.91	87.25
(0.01,0.085)		97.05	92.21
(0.01,0.080)		98.67	96.84
(0.01,0.075)		99.49	95.61
(0.01,0.070)		109.49	115.51

maximize throughput for delay constrained real-time traffic.

10.3. Response Times

The conducted simulations measured also rise and settling times of the controllers with the different level of the background traffic. For example, Figures 8 - 13 a and b present throughput as a function of time, when the packet size was adjusted by the FPID and PID controllers and the target delay was 100 ms. The packet transmission interval of surrounding nodes is varied in Figures 8 - 13 from $i \in [0.010\,s, 0.070\,s]$ to $i \in [0.010\,s, 0.100\,s]$.

Table 11 presents rise and settling times of the controllers with 100 ms target delay when the packet transmission interval of surrounding nodes is varied from $i \in [0.010\,s, 0.070\,s]$ to $i \in [0.010\,s, 0.100\,s]$. The average (averaged over the different amount of disturbing background traffic of surrounding nodes) rise and settling times were 41.5 s and 53.2 s for

Table 8. Delay variance of optimized fixed (OF) packet size, FPID and PID controlled packet sizes. Delay limit was 100 ms. Initial packet size was 256 bits

Background traffic	Delay variance		
	OF [ms]	FPID [ms]	PID [ms]
(0.01,0.100)	0.72	1.08	1.10
(0.01,0.090)	1.31	1.43	1.40
(0.01,0.085)	1.45	1.60	1.50
(0.01,0.080)	1.73	1.54	1.36
(0.01,0.075)	1.77	2.44	2.09
(0.01,0.070)	3.08	2.44	2.88

Table 9. Delay variance of optimized fixed (OF) packet size, FPID and PID controlled packet sizes. Delay limit was 50 ms. Initial packet size was 256 bits

Background traffic	Delay variance		
	OF [ms]	FPID [ms]	PID [ms]
(0.01,0.100)	0.38	0.39	0.24
(0.01,0.090)	0.48	0.29	0.48
(0.01,0.085)	0.53	0.39	0.36
(0.01,0.080)	0.64	0.69	0.46
(0.01,0.075)	0.56	0.92	0.85
(0.01,0.070)	1.10	1.41	0.98

Table 10. Delay variance of optimized fixed (OF) packet size, FPID and PID controlled packet sizes. Delay limit was 100 ms. Initial packet size was 256 bits

Background traffic	Delay variance		
	OF [ms]	FPID [ms]	PID [ms]
(0.01,0.100)		1.12	1.10
(0.01,0.090)		1.22	1.88
(0.01,0.085)		1.80	2.19
(0.01,0.080)		2.24	2.01
(0.01,0.075)		3.83	3.64
(0.01,0.070)		6.33	5.46

the FPID controller, and 58.5 s and 78.3 s for the PID controller. The developed controllers

Table 11. Rise and settling times of controllers with different amount of background traffic. Initial packet size was 256 bits. Delay limit was 100 ms

Background traffic	Rise time		Settling time	
	FPID [s]	PID [s]	FPID [s]	PID [s]
(0.01,0.100)	29	37	34	53
(0.01,0.090)	47	88	58	123
(0.01,0.085)	42	62	60	71
(0.01,0.080)	38	53	44	72
(0.01,0.075)	60	63	63	79
(0.01,0.070)	33	48	60	72

manage to set packet payload size values to the prevailing optimum level very fast and accurately. However, the rise and settling times of the FPID controller are about 29 % and 32 % lower than for the PID, *i.e.*, it can be stated that the FPID controller adapts faster and adjust better to traffic load changes, which is an important feature especially in congestion situation.

11. Conclusion

This chapter considered embedded fuzzy expert system for cognitive flow and congestion control. The expert system regulates source nodes packet sizes for prevailing network conditions in order to achieve maximum throughput and minimum application dependent target delay for real-time UDP based traffic in WLANs. The expert system was compared to conventional PID control systems. The controllers were located at user terminals. The models were validated by simulating real-time traffic over UDP in WLAN environment with OMNeT++ network simulator. The fuzzy expert system controls end-to-end flow(s) by commanding a sender to transmit at on correct frequency and prevents a condition of severe delay (congestion) caused by an overload of datagrams at a network by controlling the amount of data in the flow(s) for acceptable delay. The results proved that throughputs with controlled packet sizes are significantly higher than with the optimally chosen fixed packet sizes. The results also showed that the developed controllers manage to set packet payload size values to the prevailing optimum level very fast and accurately and they also managed to keep average delay below the target value. The developed models enable WLANs to increase the number of concurrent users and improve quality of the connections with the minimum delay. The fuzzy expert system also adapt to various application level requirements, like an application dependent delay limit, with minimum computational complexity.

Acknowledgement

This work was partially funded by the Commission of the European Union within the ICT FP7 project 4WARD (Ref. No. 216041) and by TEKES (Finnish Funding Agency for

Technology and Innovation) as part of the Future Internet programme of TIVIT (Finnish Strategic Centre for Science, Technology and Innovation in the field of ICT). Authors are grateful to Prof. Kauko Leiviskä and Prof. Yoshito Tobe for their review comments and corrections.

References

Andrews, J., Ghosh, A., Muhamed, R., 2007. *Fundamentals of WiMAX - Understanding Broadband Wireless Networking*, 1st Edition. Prentice Hall, United States.

B. Bing, 2002. *Wireless Local Area Networks: The New Wireless Revolution*, 1st Edition. John Wiley & Sons, Inc., New York.

Bakshi, B., Krishna, P., Vaidya, N., Pradhan, D., 1997. *Improving Performance of TCP over Wireless Networks*. In: *ICDCS '97: Proceedings of the 17th International Conference on Distributed Computing Systems (ICDCS '97)*. IEEE Computer Society, Washington, DC, USA, pp. 365–373.

Balakrishnan, M., Sadasivan, M., 2007. *Mobile Interactive Game Interworking in IMS*. White Paper. http://www.infosys.com/offerings/engineering-services/product-engineering/white-papers/Documents/mobile-gaming-paper.pdf.

Chan, P. M. L., Sheriff, R. E., Hu, Y. F., Conforto, P., Tocci, C., 2001. Mobility management incorporating fuzzy logic for a heterogeneous IP environment. *IEEE Communications Magazine* **39** (12), 42–51.

Chang, P., May, B. W., 1996. Adaptive Fuzzy Power Control for CDMA Mobile Radio Systems. *IEEE Transactions on Vehicular Technology* **45** (2), 225–236.

Chee, K., David, J., 1989. Packet Data Transmission Over Mobile Radio Channels. *IEEE Trans. on Vehicular Technology* **38**, 95–101.

Chien, C., Srivastava, M. B., Jain, R., Lettieri, P., Aggarwal, V., Sternowski, R., 1999. Adaptive Radio for Multimedia Wireless Links. *IEEE Journal on Selected Area in Communications* **17**, 793–813.

Driankov, D., Hellendoorn, H., Reinfark, M., 1994. *An Introduction to Fuzzy Control*, 2nd Edition. Springer-Verlag, New York.

Frantti, T., 2005. Cascaded Fuzzy Congestion Controller for TCP/IP Traffic. *Journal of Advanced Computational Intelligence and Intelligent Informatics* **9** (2).

Frantti, T., 2006. Multiphase transfer of control signal for adaptive power control in CDMA systems. *Control Engineering Practice,* Elsevier Science Vol 14/5, 489–501.

Frantti, T., Jutila, M., 2009. Embedded Fuzzy Expert System for Adaptive Weighted Fair Queueing. *Expert Systems with Applications*, Elsevier Science Vol. 36, No. 8, 11390–11397.

Frantti, T., Kallio, S., 2004. Expert System for Gesture Recognition in Terminal's User Interface. *Expert Systems with Applications* **26** (2).

Frantti, T., Mahonen, P., 2001a. Fuzzy Logic Based Forecasting Model. *Engineering Applications of Artificial Intelligence* **14**(2), 189–201.

Frantti, T., Mahonen, P., 2001b. *Fuzzy Reasoning in WCDMA Radio Resource Functions. Advances in Computational Intelligence and Learning, Methods and Applications* . Kluwer Academic Publishers.

Frantti, T., Majanen, M., 2010. *Internet Traffic Shaping in WLANs by Packet Size Control* .

Frantti, T., Majanen, M., Sukuvaara, T., 2010. Delay Based Packet Size Control in Wireless Local Area Networks. In: *ICUFN 2010 The Second International Conference on Ubiquitous and Future Networks, June 16-18, 2010, Jeju Island, Korea. Invited paper.* Jeju Island, Korea.

Giupponi, L., Agusti, R., Perez-Romero, J., Roig, O. S., 2008. A novel approach for joint radio resource management based on fuzzy neural methodology. *IEEE transactions on vehicular technology* **57** (3).

Habetha, J., Walke, B., 2002. Fuzzy Rule-Based Mobility and Load Management for Self-Organizing Wireless Networks. *International Journal of Wireless Information Networks* **9** (2), 119–140.

Jammeh, E., Fleury, M., Ghanbari, M., 2007. Fuzzy Logic Congestion Control of Transcoded Video Streaming without Packet Loss Feedback. *IEEE TRANS. on Circuits and Systems for Video Technology* .

Juuso, E., 1992. Linguistic Equations Framework for Adaptive Expert Systems. In: Stephenson, J. (Ed.), Modelling and Simulation 1992, Proceedings of the 1992 European Simulation Multiconference. pp. 99–103.

Juuso, E. K., 1993. Linguistic Simulation in Production Control. In: Pooley, R., Zobel, R. (Eds.), *UKSS'93 Conference of the United Kingdom Simulation Society* . Keswick, UK, pp. 34–38.

Kang, Q., Wang, J., Meng, X., 2009. Tcp vegas-like expert-controlled multicast congestion control algorithm for wireless networks. In: International Conference on Artificial Intelligence and Computational Intelligence. Vol. 4. *IEEE Computer Society*, Los Alamitos, CA, USA, pp. 50–54.

Koomey, J. G., 2010. *Outperforming Moore's Law* . IEEE Spectrum March 2010, 68.

Korhonen, J., Wang, Y., 2005. Effect of Packet Size on Loss Rate and Delay in Wireless Links. In: *Proceedings of the 2005 IEEE Conference on Wireless Communications and Networking,* vol. 3. IEEE Communications Society, New Orleans, LA USA, pp. 1608–1613.

Kwon, O., Yoo, K., Suh, E., 2005. UbiDSS: a proactive intelligent decision support system as an expert system deploying ubiquitous computing technologies. *Expert Systems with Applications* **28**, 149–161.

Lettieri, P., Srivastava, M. B., 1998. Adaptive Frame Length Control for Improve Wireless Link Range and Energy Efficiency. In: *Proceeding of the IEEE INFOCOM'98*. IEEE communications Society, San Francisco, USA, pp. 564–571.

Leung, K. K., McNair, B., Cimini, L., Winters, J. H., 2002. Outdoor IEEE 802.11 Cellular Networks: MAC Protocol Design and Performance. In: *Proc. of the IEEE International Conference on Communications 2002 (ICC 2002)*, Vol. 1. pp. 595–599.

Li, T., Ni, Q., 2005. Performance Analysis of the IEEE 802.11e Block ACK Scheme in a Noisy Channel. In: *Proc. IEEE BroadNets05*. pp. 551–557.

Li, Y. F., Lau, F., 1989. Development of Fuzzy Algorithm for Servo Systems. *IEEE Control Systems Magazine* **9** (3), 65–72.

Patel, A., McDermott, G., Mulvihill, C., 1989. *Integrating network management and artificial intelligence*. In: Integrated Network Management I.

Sankarasubramaniam, Y., Akyildiz, I., McLaughlin, S., 2003. Energy Efficiency Based Packet Size Optimization in Wireless Sensor Networks. In: *Proceedings of the First IEEE International Workshop on Sensor Network Protocols and Applications, 2003*. IEEE Communications Society, Anchorage, Alaska, USA, pp. 1–8.

Shen, X., Mark, J. W., Ye, J., 2000. User mobility profile prediction: An adaptive fuzzy inference approach. *Wireless Network* **6**, 363–374.

Sheu, S.-T., Lee, Y.-H., Chen, M.-H., Yu, Y.-C., Huang, Y.-C., 2000. PLFC: The Packet Length Fuzzy Controller to Improve the Performance of WLAN Under the Interference of Microwave Oven. In: *Global Telecommunications Conference, 2000. GLOBECOM '00*. IEEE. Volume: 3. IEEE Communications Society, San Francisco, USA, pp. 1427–1431.

Smadi, M., Szabados, B., 2006. Error-recovery Service for the IEEE 802.11b Protocol. *IEEE Transactions on Instrumentation and Measurement* **55**, 1377–1382.

Steinder, M., Sethi, A. S., 2004. A survey of fault localization techniques in computer networks. *Science of Computer Programming* **53**.

Thomas, R. W., Friend, D. H., DaSilva, L. A., MacKenzie, A. B., 2006. Cognitive Networks: Adaptation and Learning to Achieve End-to-End Performance Objectives. *IEEE Communications Magazine*, 51–57.

Wu, J., Djemame, K., 2003. An expert-system-based structure for active queue management. In: *Proceedings of the Second International Conference on Machine Learning and Cybernetics*, Xi'an, 2-5 November 2003. Xi'an, China, pp. 824–829.

Younis, M., Farrag, O., D'Amico, W., 2009. Packet Size Pptimization for Increased Throughput in Multi-Level Security Wireless Networks. In: *Military Communications Conference, 2009. MILCOM 2009.* IEEE Communications Society, Boston, USA, pp. 1–7.

Zadeh, L., 1965. Fuzzy Sets. *Information and Control* **8**, 338 – 353.

Reviewed by Prof. Kauko Leiviskä, University of Oulu, Finland.

Reviewed by Prof. Yoshito Tobe, Tokyo Denki University, Japan.

In: Expert System Software
Editors: Jason M. Segura and Albert C. Reiter

ISBN: 978-1-61209-114-3
© 2012 Nova Science Publishers, Inc.

Chapter 7

AN ENHANCED APPROACH FOR DEVELOPING AN EXPERT SYSTEM FOR FUND RAISING MANAGEMENT

Luca Barzanti[*] *and Marcello Mastroleo*[†]
Department of Mathematics for Economic and Social Sciences,
University of Bologna, Italy

Abstract

In social economy a great attention is devoted to non profit organizations, whose mission's fulfillment is strongly related to the success of fund raising strategies. Then a decision support system for optimizing them is very useful. Using associations donors database a fuzzy expert system has been developed, which is able to suggest the best strategies with respect to donors profiles. This system integrates the profiles with a model for historical information evaluation and operative rules suggested by experts in the field and related literature. There are however many little and medium size organizations which don't own or efficiently mange the donors database. In these cases another approach has been proposed, which is able to individuate the most promising raising strategies on the basis of the features of the association. The profile factors of a non profit association are widely explored and hierarchically organized in a decision tree, in order to effectively employ the Choquet integral methodology, which is recommended in these kind of multi-criteria decision problems.

In the present contribution, some extensions are developed in order to enhance the first approach. In particular an integration with the second methodology is proposed, by substituting some fuzzy components with a hierarchic organization of the knowledge, that allows to use also in this context the Choquet integral, with an improvement of the tuning process and of the computational effort required. Moreover a wide analysis of donors features is performed; the donors interests evolution is managed, allowing a more precise characterization of the donors profile; an *utility function* approach is developed as extension of the expected gift model; new elements in the management process are modeled. The results obtained in a real operational context show the effectiveness of the proposed improvements.

[*]E-mail address: luca.barzanti@unibo.it
[†]E-mail address: marcello.mastroleo@unibo.it

Keywords: social economy, fund raising management, expert systems engineering, mathematical modeling, utility functions.

1. Introduction

The world of non profit organizations (NPO) is very varied, for spheres, features and dimensions. Some associations are involved in medical problems and persons diseases, others in environmental conservation, or in every kind of social causes, or in education, ... There are foundation so as mutual companies, multi national organizations and territorial associations.

Despite these radical differences, any NPO has the need to sustain itself so to be able to pursue its mission and the only way to do it is seeking for funds. That's way fund raising management is at the core of any successful organization.

Anyway not all organizations, especially the middle and lower-sized ones, own the internal resources to face fund raising complexity so they have to import from outside the knowledge by means of extern consultants. In fact even the simple use of a DB support to handle contacts is not so diffused.

There is an actual gap between organizations, fund raisers and support systems. Organizations need to raise funds, fund raisers have the knowhow in terms of both operational knowledge and econometric data (see for example [10, 22]) but they can not handle the complexity of a deep record by record analysis of DB's records, and the supports as presented in [14] are not capable to cover this distance since their use is limited as a just data containing tools.

The need of a better use of informatics tools to cover the distance between organizations, knowledge and data was early analyzed in [2, 16], then a first knowledge based approach to fund raising was showed in [3] which culminates in the work [4] where the presented fuzzy decision support system [12, 13, 21, 24, 25, 26] was capable to suggest the best strategy to pursue in order to rise the desired economic objective.

The expert system in [4] looks at several aspects of a donor which are considered influent to evaluate his attitude to give (see the related operational literature [1, 11, 17]) like his interests, his social network and his personal profile. This deep analysis of a donor is used to decide whether or not to include him in the campaign's target list *de facto* realizing what a practitioner can not. An "intelligent" record analysis is motivated by the fund raisers' claim that the success of a campaign is heavily (in the order of the 70-80%) determined by a right choice of its target (see [20], p.191).

The system presented in the present contribution, even if it is rooted in the work [4], represents the effort to overcome the limitation of a rule based approach to knowledge by reaching a mathematical model of the process behind that knowledge. The substitution of fuzzy rules with a non additive measure based approach, like in [5], was possible thanks to the constant feedback given by the collaboration with a top Italian NPO working in the humanitarian field.

The reader can find in Section 2. an overview of the fund raising process coded into the new system, which is instead introduced in Section 3.. The new modeling approach is then delineated from Section 4. where the donor is analyzed in all his features from the interests he has in the campaign contents to the empirical probability he gives to a particular good cause. The details about the new system go on in Section 5. with the selection of the campaign's target which is refined by the usage of a suitable class of compound utility functions instead of just looking at the expected gift. Section 6. describes the last part of the system's computational flow which is about the comparison among different strategies; here a conformity to a gift range chart measure is introduced, so to obtain a performance measure which works on a finer clustering of target than just big or small donors as done in the aforementioned work. Finally, Section 7. shows some results of the new system and Section 8. drafts some of its possible evolutions.

2. Overview of Fund Raising Management

The fund raising management aims to motivate donors, so they will continue to support the organization at increasingly higher levels over time. Since donors are the aim of fund raising, they have to be cultivated, as fund raisers use to say. Cultivating a donor is a time process where firstly the potential donor is selected according to heuristics that match personal interests to NPO's working area and then the donor's motivation is increased together with the amount of his donations. In this Section the process of cultivating a donor will be summarized introducing the common accepted metaphor of the giving pyramid (also known as fund raising pyramid) and the so called gift range chart which induce a clustering of donors accordingly to their giving potential at a specific time.

2.1. The Giving Pyramid

The Giving Pyramid (see Figure 1) is a commonly used model to envision the time evolution of donors (see [20], Section 4). Starting by the entry level strategies, where the aim is to attract new donors, the pyramid describes how they should be cultivated in order to increase over time the fidelity to the organization's mission and so their donations.

This chart is a pyramid since only few donors emerge from the pool of one level to the next one, nevertheless the potential of their donation increases thus is realized Paretian equilibrium in which the 80% of the total donations amount is provided by just the 20% of the donors. Let we analyze the pyramid in details emphasizing the characteristics that differentiate each of its levels so to easily understand in Section 5. how to detect who is plausibly ready to jump to from one level to the next one.

The Ground: At the ground of the Pyramid there are all the people that the NPO can contact for the first time. Usually NPO's buy or rent[1] people records from providers. These providers merge and filter personal data so to profile people according to their interest, for example having an annual subscription to a magazine denotes the interest in the magazine topics. Providers have access to all this kind of personal data and can select records of people whose interests better fit the NPO characteristics and features.

---

[1]The way personal record are distributed is matter of privacy laws. Those are different from one country to another; for example, in Italy, which has stricter policies on privacy that Anglo-Saxon countries, the property of records is owned by providers which can rent them for a one time use only. The NPO can then add to its DB only the records of those people which actually donate.

Figure 1. The giving pyramid chart.

Clearly attracting new donors is fundamental for fund raising management but, at the same time, it is the most expansive task since the percentage of people which positively respond is very low together with their average donation. Thus in the ground level the key point is to learn the right profile of people to contact so to reach as earlier as possible the equity point in which donations cover campaign costs. The mechanism to extrapolate donor's interests is the topic of Subsection 4.1..

Pyramid Level 1: The base of the pyramid is the entry level of a donor into the organization program. It is characterized by the large pool of first-time donors.

Pyramid Level 2: Each donor which renews his first donation with a new one automatically rises to the second level of the fund raising pyramid. The problem of detecting who is most plausible to jump to this level is not very interesting form a modeling point of view since the common practice is to "always" contact for a second donation who rises in level 1. Anyway the common characteristic of these donors is that they are just starting to hear about the organization. Thus they randomly respond to gift requests and they will jump to the next level as much they are constant and present.

Pyramid Level 3: This level is composed by all those donors which renounce to the freedom of giving when they want and subscribe a time scheduled sponsorship program. By subscribing such kind of program, donors implicitly say that they are not afraid to give repeatedly when the organization needs and at the same time they start to look at their future into the organization's life.

Pyramid Level 4: In this level there are all those donors which strongly identify themselves with the focus of the organization and which have recognized that giving to the organization is a priority in their life.

Pyramid Level 5: At the top of the pyramid there are the planned gifts as bequests or endowments. Donors at this level want to assign a substantial share of their wealth to the organization since they realized that the organization has resonance in their life. Doing so they are trying to make the difference by establishing an enduring legacy.

2.2. The Gift Range Chart

While the giving pyramid describes and delineates the possible time evolution of a donor, the gift range chart induces a cluster of donors according to their capability to give. The starting point is the economic goal G that the organization wants to achieve in the campaign, then n different gift ranges r_i are delineated so to guarantee a sort of psychological differentiation among them, in this way there is an objective visible difference in being in a class or in its upper one. This psychological differentiation roots in the return of image that the donor has and it became substantial in the higher ranges of donations which are populated by donors in the higher level of the giving pyramid. As an actual example can be considered the economic return that a corporate company working in the food field has in supporting the United Nations World Food Programme (WFP). Doing so the corporation can sell an added values together with its products, it sells the idea that "if you buy my products you give the possibility to have a meal to all those people that can not". While this example involves world scale organizations, the psychological mechanism remains true even in smaller context like the business man who wants to be visible into its community.

After G is allocated among the n levels, these have to be populated by a sufficient number n_i of donation in order to achieve the desired economic goal for each range, *i.e.* $G_i = n_i \cdot r_i$. Using statistical considerations is then possible to have an idea of how many donors have to be contacted for each level to obtain the n_i donations.

Table 1. Example of a Gift Range Chart to raise 10.000 dollars

i	r_i	n_i	Prospects required	Subtotal	Cumulative total	Cumulative %
5	1.000,00	2	6	2.000,00	2.000,00	20%
4	500,00	5	35	2.500,00	4.500,00	45%
3	250,00	10	70	2.500,00	7.000,00	70%
2	100,00	20	200	2.000,00	9.000,00	90%
1	< 100,00	20	1000	1.000,00	**10.000,00**	**100%**

Given a gift range chart, the campaign sustainability is proportional to the ability that the organization has to fill its levels from the top one to the bottom one, because any extra donation in the level i can cover missed donations in lower levels by realizing a sort of waterfall effect. Clearly, higher motivated donors correspond to higher r_i, this is why the number of prospects is inverse proportional to r_i, nevertheless the number of major donors is usually of the order of few units, thus the need of lower levels to achieve G.

3.   Expert System Overview

The knowledge of the life cycle of an organization is a primary subject in order to better understand the modeling choices made within the system; so it is important to classify campaigns according to the role they play in the organization's expansion.

As previously said, each organization has to finance itself and the efficient coordination of fund raising campaigns is the way they do it. The two charts presented above are thought by fund raisers to find the good way for an organization to survive, but at this point to be more concrete is important because, for the sake of efficiency, nothing is left to chance and there is a tough planning behind fund raising management that the system has to capture.

There are different *objectives* that campaigns could pursue, namely *preservation*, *expansion*, *specific* and *emergency*. The first category is represented by all those campaigns which aim to cultivate the actual donors; the most representative typology is the annual campaign, *i.e.* the annual request of donation that the organization addresses to its donors. In the second category there are all those campaigns which aim is to rise the pyramid level of donors together with their donation's amounts or to acquire new donors so to populate the first pyramid level. Specific campaigns instead point to a particular target of donors and usually aim to gratify them with a present or with a "thank you" letter. The last category includes campaigns which face humanitarian or environmental emergencies, like the first aid after a calamity. Emergency campaigns have usually a return more in terms of image than monetary in the sense that no part of the acquired funds is going to be used to sustain the preservation of the organization.

The objective induce a classification of campaigns according to their importance in the organization's life. By looking an organization as a social organism, objectives ensure its survival so, in order of importance, it has to preserve itself, to look for expansion possibilities and to consolidate itself facing specific problems.

Nevertheless there are other variables that influence a campaign. In fact, campaigns can be also differentiated according to their *type* which is the set of means used to meet donors attention. The type could be a *letter*, a *phone call*, a *door to door*, a *face to face*, an *SMS*, an *email* or the participation to an *event*.

Another differentiation is made in terms of *content*, indicating by this the specification of the interests that the campaign involves, like *"poverty"*, *"childhood"*, *"developing countries"*, ... and the *period* chosen to do the campaign, namely one of the four seasons or the main Christian festivities, *i.e.* Christmas and Easter.

Each campaign can be so described in term of its *objective*, *type* and *content*. Any campaign specification in these terms is called *strategy* and the system's first aim is to analyze the practicability of each strategy to pursue the prefixed economic *goal*.

3.1.   Expert System Structure

The system, which is summarized in Figure 2, is an evolution of what in [4] and represents part of the evolution from a fuzzy rules based system to a mathematically modeled fund raising management. While the flow of computation is closer to the earlier version, each

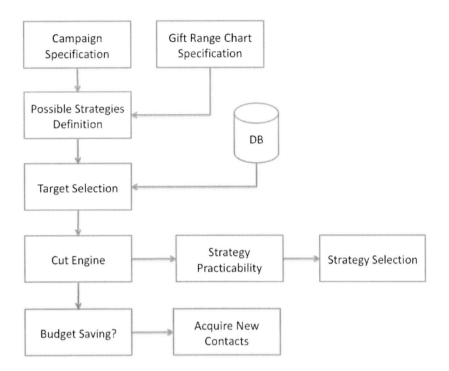

Figure 2. Expert system graphical representation.

block has been substituted with a new one which lies on a mathematical model for that particular task. Substantial is the work behind the target selection, which is the topic of Sections 4. and 5..

The system starts its computation with the specification of some campaign properties as input, like the content, the economic goal, the available budget plus some constrains about its type and objective; then it generates the possible strategies to pursue. A gift range chart is also required as additional input with respect to the earlier version of the system. The chart can be defined by the fundraiser or automatically generated by the system, and its usage constitutes an improvement for the analysis of the practicability of a strategy as described in Section 6..

Due to computational needs the system is equipped with a knowledge rule based module that has the specific aim to reduce the space of all possible strategies by using basic fund raising rules to select compatible terms. For example Christmas is well known to be the best period of the year to seek for donations so, when it is possible, an expansion campaign should be scheduled reflecting this collective attitude. Another example is the need to involve big donors into the organization, so the only type of action which is practicable to them is the *face to face*.

Once the system selects the strategies which fit the basic fund raising rules, the problem is to find the best target of donors to address them. This is the task solved by the target selection block which is the topic of the next two Sections. The resulting target list is cut by the cut engine to fit the available budget and then the practicability of the strategy is evaluated according to a prefixed gift range chart. The list of all strategies which are able to return at least the budget is then outputted to the fund raiser which can now choose the suitable one. Notice that last selection is left to the fund raiser; this is the spirit of a decision support tool like this system aims to be.

4. Donor Analysis

After exposing the fund raising management process in Section 2. and the main structure of the system in Section 3., here we will present all the new tools developed for the Decision Support System, so providing the ability to cultivate donors through time and according to their potential.

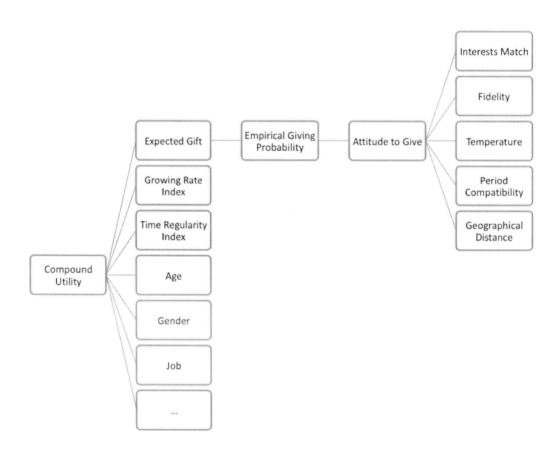

Figure 3. Workflow of the compound utility model.

Figure 3 represent the work flow to calculate the compound utility that the organization has if it contacts a specific donor. This section starts with the analysis of the interests match mechanism and it goes on until the evaluation of the empirical giving probability. The selection of donors using compound utility functions is the topic of Section 5..

4.1. Understanding Donor's Interests

Understanding who is interested to give to an organization or to one of its campaigns is the first step in order to fish donors in the right spot and according to fund raisers it constitutes the 70-80% of a campaign's success.

In [4] the space of all interests Ω^I was organized in categories which show affinities among interests, like *"Sport"*, *"Music"*, *"Business"*, *"Hobby"*, ... Each category was then refined in sub-categories and so on until single interests were reached. The number of levels to climb in order to find the common root of the interest I_1 and the interest I_2 was then proposed as a measure of distance between the two interests.

As it is, this methodology has a main drawback: the update of the donor's interests is not possible, so the system does not capture the evolution of them over time which is a peculiarity of the relationship between donors and organizations (see for example [23] for a discussion about the lifetime value of a donor).

To encompass this, the problem needs to be approached from a different point of view. Instead of giving a well structured space of knowledge about interests, the new model looks at the feedbacks given by donors, *i.e.* the amount of their donations, together with the knowledge that the fund raiser puts in organizing the campaign by means of degrees of the interests involved in it.

While the amount of a donation is clearly understandable, the degree of an interest needs a bit of extra explanation. Each campaign aims to give a contribution in solving a specific problem but two campaigns can be focused on different aspects of it so, while they share the same interests, each of them can differ in weight and the fund raiser has the knowledge to assign weights rightly.

As an example let we suppose that the fund raiser assigns to the current campaign the interests *"Health"*, *"Childhood"* and *"Developing Countries"* with a degree of 0.3, 0.1 and 0.6 respectively. He then searches for new records of people interested in at least one of them by querying personal data providers. Among the selected records there is Alice who responds by giving her first donation of $50,00. Now Alice enters in the first level of the giving pyramid and together with her donation she let the organization know that she shares the same interests of the campaign with the same degree. After a while the fund raiser organizes a new campaign which involves *"Developing Countries"* with degree 0.3 and *"Food"* with degree 0.7 and Alice donates $30,00 to this new campaign. Now the organization acquire new knowledge about what Alice's interests are. This new information can be merged with the previous ones by means of the normalized donation amounts.

More precisely, if there are n campaigns, $W_i(j)$ is the weight of the j-th interest in the i-th campaign and d_i^k is the donation of the k-th donor to the i-th campaign, then the **degree of interest of the donor k in j** is calculated as

$$I_k(j) = \frac{\sum_{i=1}^{n} W_i(j) \cdot d_i^k}{\sum_{i=1}^{n} d_i^k}, \tag{1}$$

where the denominator is the total amount of the donations of the donor k. Notice that, for any fixed k, $I_k(j)$ can be interpreted as the observed k-th donor's probability distribution over the space of all interests Ω^I and the weights $W_i(j)$, that the fund raiser assigns to the i-th campaign, are also a probability measure among Ω^I.

$I_k(j)$ is updated each time the donor k gives a positive feedback to the organization. The choice to exclude negative ones is done according to the principle that, if k donates he is clearly interested in the campaign, but the contrary is not necessarily true and so a negative feedback can not be considered as a clear statement about his interests.

Within this model, the comparison between the interests of a donor and the ones related to a campaign is done by a measure of similarity among them. This is a more rigorous setting from a logical point of view than what done in [4], since the notion of similarity between two profiles of interests is not dependent on the way the knowledge about Ω^I is organized, *i.e.* the way categories are organized, which instead is the root of the distance between interests used before.

A straight forward starting point to reach the notion of similarity S is the famous *Jensen–Shannon divergence* (see for example [18]) that, in our notation, is

$$JS(I_k, W_i) = \frac{1}{2} \cdot \sum_{j \in \Omega} I_k(j) \log\left(\frac{I_k(j)}{M(j)}\right) + \frac{1}{2} \cdot \sum_{j \in \Omega} I_k(j) \log\left(\frac{W_i(j)}{M(j)}\right), \qquad (2)$$

where the logarithms are in base 2, $\overline{\Omega} \subset \Omega$ is the union of the supports of I_k and W_i, *i.e.* $\overline{\Omega} = \{j \in \Omega^I | I_k(j) + W_I(j) > 0\}$, and $M(j) = \frac{1}{2} \cdot I_k(j) + \frac{1}{2} \cdot W_i(j)$ for all $j \in \overline{\Omega}$.

Recalling that $JS(I, W)$ is symmetric and it is always a number between 0, if and only if $I = W$, and 1, if and only if the supports of I and W have no intersection, $S(I, W)$ is then defined as

$$S(I, W) = 1 - JS(I, W). \qquad (3)$$

Returning to the example of Alice, Table 2 shows the resulting degree of her interest. Let we now suppose that the fund raiser is organizing two new campaigns, C_1 involving *"Childhood"* and *"Developing Countries"* with degrees W_1 equals to 0.5 for both and C_2 involving *"Childhood"*, *"Developing Countries"* and *"Food"* with degrees W_2 equals to 0.25, 0.5 and 0.25 respectively. If he is concerned about which campaign better fits Alice's interests, all he has to do is to check the similarity between their weights and what he knows about Alice. After few calculation he discover that $S(I_A, W_1) = 0.9088$ and $S(I_A, W_2) = 0.9657$ so it is better to inform Alice about C_2 than C_1.

Table 2. Alice's degree of interest after her two donations

Interest j	w_1^j	d_1^A	w_2^j	d_2^A	$I_A(j)$
Health	0.3	\$50,00			3/16
Childhood	0.1	\$50,00			1/16
Dev. Countries	0.6	\$50,00	0.3	30,00	39/80
Food			0.7	30,00	21/80

Two useful properties that S inherits from JS are that

1. given a set of donors D, the problem of finding W^* that maximizes the global similarity

$$S(I_D, W) = \sum_{k \in D} S(I_k, W)$$

   is well posed;

2. it is possible to cluster donors with respect to the similarity of their interests.

The first property is a direct consequence of the fact that the square root of JS is a norm over the space of probability distributions on Ω^I and the second one is a consequence of the first property.

Moreover the knowledge of W^* helps the copywriting organization of the campaign, once some donors are selected as its target using the procedure in Section 5.. In fact, W^* gives information on which message is better to emphasize so to touch the feeling of as much donors as possible.

4.2.   Estimating Donor's Features

While the interest in a good cause is an important motivating force for people to donate, it is not the only one. The evaluation of donor's attitude to give needs a wider knowledge about him that just his interests.

Factors other than interests those, according to the fund raising literature (see for example [1, 11, 17] and [6] for a specific study for the Italian case), have an influence to a positive response of donor d are listed below together with the indices the system uses to evaluate their degree. Each index, associated to a factor, is built to be bounded in $[0, 1]$, where 0 means total absence of the factor and 1 is the total presence of it.

In what follows d is meant as the array of all donor's records. In details, a donor is summarized as $d \equiv (G, a)$ where G is the list of all his gifts, including their amounts g_i and their dates t_i, and a is the geographical coordinates of his address.

Fidelity: $\mathcal{F}$ is a measure of how much the donor is faithful to the organization's acts by looking at his donations. It is expressed in terms of total amount of gifts $\tilde{g} = \sum g_i$, years elapsed since his first donation t_0, *i.e.* the time he enters into the fund raising pyramid, and the percentage of positive given feedback p. The term p is an improvement with respect to what done before, and it is added to better compare donors which were differently exhorted. The index $\mathcal{F}$ is then calculated as

$$\mathcal{F}(p, \tilde{g}, t_0) = \frac{1}{1 + e^{-p \cdot \frac{\tilde{g}}{t_0} + \bar{G}}},$$

where $p \cdot \frac{\tilde{g}}{t_0}$ is the empirical expected gift on annual base and $\bar{G}$ is the average annual gift that the organization wants to obtain. Notice that the parameter $\bar{G}$ relativizes the fidelity degree of a donor to what the organization considers to be the discriminating value between a high and a low fidelity degree.

Temperature: $\mathcal{T}_\lambda$ is referred to the time t elapsed by the donor's last donation. According to the temperature, donors are divided into three main lists, namely *hot, cold* and *lapsed* donors. Usually in the first list there are all those donors whose last donation was done within the last year. A donor is in the second list if he lastly donates more than one and less than two years ago. Finally lapsed donors are all the others. Hot donors are usually more incline to give than cold donors and there is a positive correlation between hotness and fidelity. Lapsed donors instead are usually contacted once then if they do not donate again, they are considered as lost and deleted form the organization's targets. Temperature policies depend on the organization's fund raising behavior. There are organizations which prefer to involve donors on a monthly based schedule, others those prefer a less frequent solicitation like on quarterly base. Putting all together

$$\mathcal{T}_\lambda(t) = e^{-\frac{t}{\lambda}},$$

where the parameter λ has to be chosen to meet the different organization's policies.

Period: People are more incline to give differently over the year according to their economic possibilities during it. For example Christmas is averagely a better period to ask for donation than summer. Since a person is mostly inclined to donate if the campaign's period fits his habitual tendency, then the index $\mathcal{P}$ measures the affinity between the period the campaign is programmed and the distribution over time of donor's gifts. To evaluate $\mathcal{P}$, the year is divided into six main periods, namely the four seasons plus *Christmas* and *Easter*, where the last two are separately considered due to the effect showed by religious festivity on people behavior. $\mathcal{P}$ is then calculated as the similarity S (see Equation 3) between the relative frequencies of donor's gifts over the six periods f_g and the specific period of the campaign, meant as the certain distribution $\mathbf{1}_p$ so

$$\mathcal{P}(f_g, \mathbf{1}_p) = 1 - JS(f_g, \mathbf{1}_p) = \frac{1 + f_c(p) - f_g(p) \cdot \log\left(\frac{2f_g(p)}{1+f_g(p)}\right) - \log\left(\frac{2}{1+f_c(p)}\right)}{2},$$

where $f_g(p)$ is the relative frequency for the period p of donor's gifts and the last equality is a consequence of the Jensen-Shannon divergence. By definition $\mathcal{P}(f_g, \mathbf{1}_p) = 1$ if and only if $f_g(p) = 1$ and $\mathcal{P}(f_g, \mathbf{1}_p) \to 0$ as $f_g(p) \to 0^+$.

Geographical distance: $\mathcal{D}$ is built by the distance between donor address a and the place where his money will bring a contribution a_0. This distance is an important aspect especially for campaigns with a local relevance. While on national or international campaigns donors usually perceive the importance of their gifts, if the campaign's implications involve only a certain urban area, like ensuring the survival of the theater in a city, donors that are outside the relevance radius of the campaign are not incline to give something to it. $\mathcal{D}$ is then calculated according to

$$\mathcal{D}(a, a_0) = \frac{1}{h(a, a_0) + 1},$$

where $h(\cdot, \cdot)$ is the geographical distance between two points on earth by means of their parallels and meridians coordinates.

These indices, together with the similarity of interests S, can be divided in two groups. The first one is composed by the $\mathcal{F}$ and $\mathcal{T}_\lambda$ which only depend on the donor historical records, and all the others which measure a compatibility between the donor and the specific campaign's profile.

4.3. Evaluating Donor's Giving Attitude

Within the system the above components are aggregated to produce the donor's giving attitude $\mathcal{A}$ as a measure of how most likely the organization should expect a positive response of the donor. The ability to evaluate the feeling of donors about a campaign is a key point to select them rightly and so to contain expenses without sacrificing performance.

The above indices are a refinement of the related ones of the system in [4], which uses fuzzy rules to compute $\mathcal{A}$. Here a different approach based on non additive measures, like [5] does in a different context, is presented.

Both ways can be opportunely tuned to output similar results, nevertheless they have different peculiarities which could state the difference in the operative context. In particular fuzzy rules offer an understandable interpretation of their behavior thanks to the their easy linguistic interpretation but, to have an expressive discrimination among inputs, surfaces those are not phase of transition shaped is important to obtain. Despite its simplicity of interpretation, to make smooth a fuzzy system requires an adequate number of linguistic terms for each of its variables and this makes hard the expert's tasks of calibration.

On the other side non additive measures are less readable but they allow the expert to reason only on extremal situation, where each index takes value 0 or 1, then they smoothly interpolate what is in between thus reducing the complexity of expert's work.

The easiest way to compute $\mathcal{A}$ is by means of a convex combination between the above indices, formally

$$\mathcal{A}_w(I) = w \cdot I,$$

where w is the vector of weights and $I \equiv (\mathcal{F}, \mathcal{T}, \mathcal{S}, \mathcal{P}, \mathcal{D})$ is the indices vector.

Several experts are requested to express their weights w_i according to their experience and then the problem is to merge all their evaluations in a coherent way, *i.e.* without loosing information.

Each weights assessment w_i can be interpreted as a probability distribution that the expert gives on the space of events Ω partitioned by the five indices, *i.e.* by looking at the truth values of the following events:

1. F = *"The donor is faithful to the organization"*;

2. T = *"The temperature of donor is high"*;

3. S = *"Donor's interests match the campaign's ones"*;

4. P = *"The period is compatible with the donor profile"*;

5. D = *"The donor is close to the geographical relevance of the campaign"*;

Furthermore $I(d,c)$ is a normalized stochastic variable on Ω and the resulting $\mathcal{A}_{w_i}(I)$ is its expected value according to the probability w_i. By this, to merge several w_i, the need is to extend the framework of probabilities to the one of capacities (see for example [7]) and then to consider the Choquet integral in place of the expected values.

Briefly, a capacity μ is an uncertainty measure satisfying the following two axioms:

1. $\mu(\emptyset) = 0$ and $\mu(\Omega) = 1$;

2. $\mu(A \vee B) \geq \max(\mu(A), \mu(B))$ for all A and B incompatible events;

in particular μ can fail to be additive as a probability does. Remarkable is the deep connection between capacities and convex combinations of probability measures (see for example [8, 9, 15, 19]). In fact each capacity is, depending to its properties, the lower or the upper envelope of a particular convex space of probabilities and, on the contrary, given a certain number of probability measures, the space of their convex combinations gives rise to a unique couple of capacity measures which embodies that convex space.

So all the experts evaluations w_i can be aggregated by means of the lower and upper capacities which embody the space of all their convex combinations, building so the lower and upper attitude to give measures $\mathcal{A}_*$ and $\mathcal{A}^*$, with

$$\mathcal{A}_*(X) = \inf_{w \in \mathcal{W}} \mathcal{A}_w(X),$$

$$\mathcal{A}^*(X) = \sup_{w \in \mathcal{W}} \mathcal{A}_w(X),$$

for all $X \in \{0,1\}^5$, where $\mathcal{W}$ is the set of all the convex combinations of w_i's. These two measures $\mathcal{A}_*$ and $\mathcal{A}^*$ are the "nutshell" of $\mathcal{W}$, implying that no information about experts knowledge goes lost.

Table 3 reports the calculation of $\mathcal{A}_*$ and $\mathcal{A}^*$ according to the different weights profiles given by three different experts who were requested to express their weights thinking at a campaign of national relevance, *i.e.*

$$w_1 = (0.3, 0.2, 0.4, 0.1, 0.0),$$

$$w_2 = (0.2, 0.4, 0.2, 0.1, 0.1)$$

and

$$w_3 = (0.3, 0.3, 0.2, 0.15, 0.05).$$

As can be seen the first profile gives no weight to $\mathcal{D}$ and considers important $\mathcal{S}$ and $\mathcal{F}$, the second one looks at the temperature $\mathcal{T}$ as the predominant component and the last one is something in between except for a tiny accent on $\mathcal{P}$.

By looking at Table 3, for all $X \in \{0,1\}^5$, $\mathcal{A}^*(X)$ is clearly equals to $1 - \mathcal{A}_*(X^c)$ where X^c has ones in place of X zeros and vice versa. This is the duality relation which links the lower and upper envelope of a convex class of probabilities.

Once the lower and the upper envelopes of experts weights are calculated, the attitude to give of a donor d to a certain campaign c is given by the Choquet integrals of $I(d,c) \in [0,1]^5$ with respect to $\mathcal{A}_*$ and $\mathcal{A}^*$, meaning them as the lower and the upper Choquet integrals associated to the experts knowledge w_i, $i = 1, 2, 3$.

Formally let I_i be the i-th entry of the I vector, σ_i, with $i \in \{1,2,3,4,5\}$, be a permutation of I entries that makes its entries increasing and let X_i, with $i \in \{1,2,3,4\}$, be the support of the event $\{I \geq I_{\sigma_i}\}$, then the two Choquet integrals are:

$$\mathcal{A}_*(I) = I_{\sigma_1} + \sum_{i=2}^{5} (I_{\sigma_i} - I_{\sigma_{i-1}}) \cdot \mathcal{A}_*(X_{i-1});$$

Table 3. $\mathcal{A}_*$ **and** $\mathcal{A}^*$ **resulting from** w_1, w_2 **and** w_3

$\mathcal{F}$	$\mathcal{T}_\lambda$	$\mathcal{S}$	$\mathcal{P}$	$\mathcal{D}$	$\mathcal{A}_{c_1}$	$\mathcal{A}_{c_2}$	$\mathcal{A}_{c_3}$	$\mathcal{A}_*$	$\mathcal{A}^*$
0	0	0	0	0	0	0	0	0	0
0	0	0	0	1	0	0.1	0.05	0	0.1
0	0	0	1	0	0.1	0.1	0.15	0.1	0.15
0	0	0	1	1	0.1	0.2	0.2	0.1	0.2
0	0	1	0	0	0.4	0.2	0.2	0.2	0.4
0	0	1	0	1	0.4	0.3	0.25	0.25	0.4
0	0	1	1	0	0.5	0.3	0.35	0.3	0.5
0	0	1	1	1	0.5	0.4	0.4	0.4	0.5
0	1	0	0	0	0.2	0.4	0.3	0.2	0.4
0	1	0	0	1	0.2	0.5	0.35	0.2	0.5
0	1	0	1	0	0.3	0.5	0.45	0.3	0.5
0	1	0	1	1	0.3	0.6	0.5	0.3	0.6
0	1	1	0	0	0.6	0.6	0.5	0.5	0.6
0	1	1	0	1	0.6	0.7	0.55	0.55	0.7
0	1	1	1	0	0.7	0.7	0.65	0.65	0.7
0	1	1	1	1	0.7	0.8	0.7	0.7	0.8
1	0	0	0	0	0.3	0.2	0.3	0.2	0.3
1	0	0	0	1	0.3	0.3	0.35	0.3	0.35
1	0	0	1	0	0.4	0.3	0.45	0.3	0.45
1	0	0	1	1	0.4	0.4	0.5	0.4	0.5
1	0	1	0	0	0.7	0.4	0.5	0.4	0.7
1	0	1	0	1	0.7	0.5	0.55	0.5	0.7
1	0	1	1	0	0.8	0.5	0.65	0.5	0.8
1	0	1	1	1	0.8	0.6	0.7	0.6	0.8
1	1	0	0	0	0.5	0.6	0.6	0.5	0.6
1	1	0	0	1	0.5	0.7	0.65	0.5	0.7
1	1	0	1	0	0.6	0.7	0.75	0.6	0.75
1	1	0	1	1	0.6	0.8	0.8	0.6	0.8
1	1	1	0	0	0.9	0.8	0.8	0.8	0.9
1	1	1	0	1	0.9	0.9	0.85	0.85	0.9
1	1	1	1	0	1	0.9	0.95	0.9	1
1	1	1	1	1	1	1	1	1	1

$$\mathcal{A}^*(I) = I_{\sigma_1} + \sum_{i=2}^{5}(I_{\sigma_i} - I_{\sigma_{i-1}}) \cdot \mathcal{A}^*(X_{i-1}) = I_{\sigma_1} + \sum_{i=2}^{5}(I_{\sigma_i} - I_{\sigma_{i-1}}) \cdot (1 - \mathcal{A}_*(X_{i-1}^c)).$$

By the properties of upper and lower measures the following relation is true for all $I \in [0,1]^5$

$$\mathcal{A}_*(I) \leq \mathcal{A}^*(I),$$

and these two values are the interval bounds of all the expected values of I which is possible to obtain by a convex combination of the weights w_1, w_2 and w_3. As a numerical example if a donor scores $I(d,c) = (0.1, 0.7, 0.9, 1.0, 1.0)$, his $\mathcal{A}_*(I(d,c))$ and $\mathcal{A}^*(I(d,c))$ are respectively 0.61 and 0.7; this means that for every value $a \in [0.61, 0.7]$, $w_a \in \mathcal{W}$ exists such that $w_a \cdot I(d,c) = a$.

Finally the empirical probability of giving $p_g(d,c)$ of a donor d to a campaign c can be derived from the interval $A = [\mathcal{A}_*(I(d,c)), \mathcal{A}^*(I(d,c))]$ by using a *ranking structure*.

4.4. Ranking Donors

A ranking structure is a partition of the interval $[0, 1]$, within $\mathcal{A}_*$ and $\mathcal{A}^*$ take values, such that an empirical probability to give is associated to each of its intervals. These probabilities can be a priori assessed by an expert or derived by the historical performances of the campaigns. The system uses a partition of $[0, 1]$ in five different range classes as reported in Table 4.

Table 4. Structure of donors' rank classes with their empirical probability of giving p

Name	min	max	p
R_5	0.95	1	0.8
R_4	0.85	0.95	0.65
R_3	0.65	0.85	0.5
R_2	0.4	0.65	0.3
R_1	0	0.4	0.01

The empirical probability that a donor d gives to a campaign c according to a range structure is then calculated as

$$p(d,c) = \frac{\sum_{i=1}^{5} p_i \cdot \mu(A_i)}{\mu(A)}$$

where p_i is the probability associated to the i-th range, $\mu([a, b]) = b - a$ is the length of the interval $[a, b]$, $A = [\mathcal{A}_*(I(d,c)), \mathcal{A}^*(I(d,c))]$ and $A_i = A \cap R_i$ for $i \in \{1, 2, 3, 4, 5\}$.

The surface of p in $[0, 1]^2$ is showed in Figure 4(a), as numerical example; if $A = [0.61, 0.7]$, as above, its associated p is equal to 0.411.

Within the system, the ranking structure is used to match between the giving attitude model and the actual results. As previously mentioned, the number of ranking classes R_i, their widths and the associated p_i can be set a priori by experts or inferred by the organization's DB; in fact, the task of building a ranking structure is nothing more than a statistical analysis of the distribution of donations varying the giving attitude index.

Moreover several ranking structure can be used to evaluate different situations. For example, if the organization acts on two different kind of problems one of which is considered as controversial (*i.e.* alcoholism, prostitution, drugs addiction, ...) then the probabilities of giving associated to them could not be the same. Since in general persons are reluctant to

Table 5. Structure of donors' rank classes with their empirical probability of giving p in the case of a controversial cause

Name	min	max	p
R_5	0.95	1	0.9
R_4	0.85	0.95	0.8
R_3	0.65	0.85	0.3
R_2	0.4	0.65	0.1
R_1	0	0.4	0.01

give to controversial causes but, if they do, they are really firm in their belief, it is clear that to handle both situations at the same way is misleading.

The ranking structure of a controversial cause is expressed in Table 5 while the p surface is in Figure 4(b).

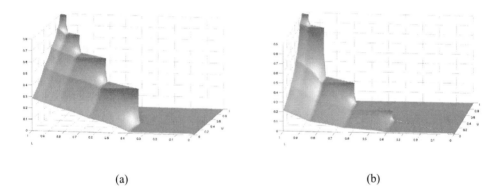

(a)   (b)

Figure 4. Probability of giving according to the range structure R_i, $i = \{1,2,3,4,5\}$, where $L = \mathcal{A}_*(d,c)$ and $U = \mathcal{A}^*(d,c)$ for a not controversial cause (a) and for a controversial one (b).

5. Donor's Selection

Usually each campaign is constrained to a maximum budget B which can be spent to contact people in seeking for donations, so if f_c is the unitary cost to contact a person in the campaign c the organization can contact at most

$$N_c = \frac{B}{f_c}$$

different potential donors. Thus choosing the right potential donors is a fundamental task in planning a fund raising campaign since it will maximize the return of spending B.

The approach proposed in [4] consists in preferring who can potentially give more and most probably to the campaign c, in other words donors d_i's are selected in accord to their expected gift

$$E(d_i,c) = p(d_i,c) \cdot \overline{G}(d_i)$$

which is the product of donor's empirical probability of giving to the campaign $p(d_i,c)$ times donor's average gift $\overline{G}(d_i)$.

Notice that this method is consistent with the gift range chart since it fills up donors lists from major to minor ones. Donor's giving attitude is important to detect potential motivation nevertheless by itself is a static tool.

Here we propose a more sophisticated approach which consists in select specific targets of donors to perform specific action on them, like for example leading donors to climb the fund raising pyramid or starting to build a future scenario which is a long time optimal strategy but it could seem to be a not remarkable strategy in the short time. In order to do so, it is necessary to extend an expected gift approach to a model based on utility functions.

5.1. Detecting Who Is Ready to Jump

The following indices can be used to predict who is presumably ready to jump from a level to the next one in the giving pyramid. These indices are built involving different variables than the used to evaluate the giving attitude; this is consistent with the aim to extend the functionality of the system.

Growing Rate of Donations: The index $G(d)$ measures the growing factor of the gifts of donor d. To evaluate it, donation amounts g_i and their times t_i are expressed by the exponential growing model

$$g(t) = g_0 \cdot e^{\alpha(d) \cdot (t-t_0)}$$

where the right parameter $\alpha(d)$ is obtained by a regression. Once $\alpha(d)$ is found, by looking at the number n of d's donations, $G(s)$ is set to

$$G(d) = \begin{cases} e^{\alpha(d)} & \text{if } n > 1, \\ 1 & \text{otherwise.} \end{cases}$$

The interpretation of G is clear: if $G > 1$ then the amount of donations is increasing over time, else if $G = 1$ the donor is constant, otherwise, when $0 \leq G < 1$, his donations have a decreasing tendency.

Time Regularity: The index $R(d)$ detects when a donor's gifts amounts have over time a similar behavior to a time scheduled sponsorship program. If so, he should be less reluctant to subscribe it and to jump consequently over the base of the fund raising pyramid. To evaluate $R(d)$, donor's past gifts amounts are grouped using a time structure similar to the one used to evaluate the period index $\mathcal{P}$. The resulting amounts a_g are then normalized and $R(d)$ is given by the similarity between a_g and the normalized amount of gifts of the sponsorship program a_p, so

$$R(d) = \mathcal{S}(a_g, a_p) = 1 - JS(a_g, a_p).$$

The index is a positive number which in 0 express a complete incompatibility between donor's giving habits and the sponsorship program, while there is a perfect match in 1.

The detection of who is ready to reach the top of the pyramid has not been investigated since at this level everything relays on relationships. At this stage donors are involved in the everyday life of the organization and detecting the genuinely of a relationship is out of the decision support system aims.

5.2. Donors Selection by Compound Utility Functions

Here we discuss about the root of the Figure 3, *i.e.* how to aggregate the different presented indices so to modulate the preference among donors to suite organization specific aims.

The system presented in [4] only uses the expected gift to prefer among donors, so the list of persons to contact is filled starting by the one who should be incline to give more and most probably and then going down. Here this criterion is extended by introducing other parameters to tune the preference in a very specific way.

In general we assume that the organization wants to differentiate its actions by looking at k different criteria u_i like the expected gift, the predisposition to give a regular donation and other features which do not necessarily positively influence neither the probability of giving or the amount of the donation, but which have a strategical mean for other reasons. An example is the organization's desire to find young donors which clearly are less incline to donate considerably, but their youth ensures a long time relationship.

A normalized vector of k weights e is defined according to the relevance the organization wants to attribute to each criterion C_i, the compound utility U_e is then evaluated as

$$U_e(u_1, u_2, \ldots, u_k) = u_1^{e_1} \cdot u_2^{e_2} \cdot \ldots \cdot u_k^{e_k}.$$

Figure 5 shows the surfaces that the utility, which is compound by expected gift E_g and regularity index R, assumes varying the coefficients e_i. In particular the sub figure (a) shows the case in which the whole weight is given to E_g thus showing that the utility approach to donor selection is a proper generalization of the one presented in [4].

Differently to the selection made by only looking at the expected gift, the list of donors obtained by means of compound utility functions is non necessarily consistent with the gift range chart. Nevertheless quantifying this inconsistence is a straight forward approach to the analysis of campaign's practicability.

6. Strategies Analysis

Once the system finds for each strategy profile c_i the right target by scanning the organization's DB of donors, the problem is to have a valid comparison methodology among the different ability that each strategy has to raise the campaign's goal G.

Clearly the first value to look at is the total expected gift $\bar{G}(c)$, which is the performance that the system associates to the particular profile. Anyway, by itself this value is not representative of the whole risk behind the strategy. In fact even if two strategies output similar expected gifts, they usually have not the same power to collect that gift.

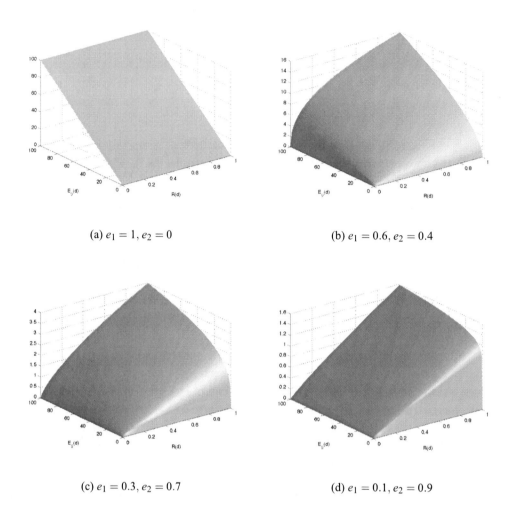

(a) $e_1 = 1, e_2 = 0$ (b) $e_1 = 0.6, e_2 = 0.4$

(c) $e_1 = 0.3, e_2 = 0.7$ (d) $e_1 = 0.1, e_2 = 0.9$

Figure 5. Compound utility $U_e(E_g(d), R(d))$ of expected gift $E_g(d)$ and regularity index $R(d)$, varying their respective weights e_1 and e_2.

6.1. Practicability Index and Strategy Comparison

The method chosen to evaluate the practicability of a strategy c is rooted in the common accepted idea that the Paretian ratio of gift range chart's levels confers to it good hedging properties thanks to the aforementioned waterfall effect.

The stating point is to have a gift range chart for the economic goal G that the organization wants to raise. This could be drafted by the fund raiser according to his experience or automatically generated by the system. For simplicity let we refer to the one in Table 1. There are so five levels L_i each one with an economic goal of $G_i = r_i \cdot n_i$; the organization has to raise 10.000 dollars and we assume it has a budget $B = 2.000$ dollars to invest.

Let we see how the procedure works in details. Each time the donor's selection part of the system runs with a campaign modality c_j and a budget B; it returns a list $D(c_j, B)$ of donors decreasingly sorted by their utility and whose length N_j is determined by the budget constraint.

The output list of donors $D(c_j, B)$ is then rearranged by means of the past average gift $\bar{G}(d)$, for each $d \in D(c_j, B)$. In this way each donor d is collocated in the right level of the chart L_i; let $\{D^i(c_j, B)\}_{i=1,...,5}$ be the resulting partition of $D(c_j, B)$.

To respect the Paretian structure of the chart, each of its level L_i is coupled with a weight l_i. The weights choice for a five levels chart is

$$l_1 = \tfrac{1}{32}, l_2 = \tfrac{1}{16}, l_3 = \tfrac{5}{32}, l_4 = \tfrac{5}{16} \text{ and } l_5 = \tfrac{7}{16}.$$

Notice how the repartition of weight gives more importance to the higher levels than to the lower ones. Finally the practicability of c_j is determined by

$$P(c_j) = \sum_{i=1}^{5} l_i \cdot \frac{E(D^i(c_j, B))}{G_i},$$

where $E(D^i(c_j, B)) = \sum_{d \in D^i(c_j, B)} E(d, c_j)$ is the expected gift for the whole level i.

The practicability index $P(c_j)$ measures the capacity that each $D^i(c_j, B)$ has to cover the level's economic targets G_i, so an index value close to 0 reveals that c_j is impracticable, or too risky, to raise T and the higher is the value the lower is the risk to fail in rising the expected gift $\bar{G}(c_j)$. An important value is 1 which denotes a good cover of each L_i and if the index is above 1 it means that c_j overfills T.

The system automatically discards all those strategies which fail to rise at least the budget B and returns the list of all the others c_j together with the associated couple $(\bar{G}(c_j), P(c_j))$ composed by the total expected gift and the practicability index.

Finally, the task to choose the strategy to pursue is left to the fundraiser with the recommendation to ponder between expected return and associated risk.

7.   Computational Results

Several tests have been conducted to evaluate the system's behavior. The results of each test have been subjected by the judgment of an expert fundraiser which validates them. Each test was conducted by using a synthetic DB of donors which is randomly built according to the scenario under examination. The following two tests are reported in order to show the effectiveness of the system in two different significant scenarios.

Both example show how the new modeling conveys expressivity to the system. In particular, in [4] target donors where clustered in only two groups, big and small donors. Big donor is everyone whose expected gift is grater then the $2,5\%$ of the economic goal and small donors are all the others. Here, the use of a gift range chart, which induce a finer partition of the target, helps to better comprehend system's results.

Both examples show a positive correlation between the practicability index P and the expected gift $\bar{G}$, but this is not always the case especially if the gift range chart does not reflect the effective organization capabilities.

7.1. Example 1

In this example the capability of a young organization to rise $10.000, 00 is tested. The organization was born less than two years ago and has a small DB of 11731 donors. The organization has a local relevance and its work is in helping homeless and disadvantaged people by providing them meals. While the greatest part of the funds for its daily sustainment is provided by parishes in the neighborhood, for exceptional needs, like renewing its equipments, it has the necessity to rise funds on its own.

The parameters of the simulation are set in Table 6 and the gift range chart associated to the campaign is presented in Table 7. The results given by the system are showed in Table 8. It is possible to notice that the winning strategy outperforms the campaign's economic goal and while its lower levels are less populated than other strategies, the upper ones are not.

Table 6. Parameters of Example 1

Budget:	$2.000,00
Interests:	("Homeless", "Charity", "Meals")
Degree:	(0.3, 0.2, 0.5)
Period:	Winter
Type:	unset
Objective:	expansion
Compound Utility:	weight 1 to the expected gift

Table 7. Gift Range Chart of Example 1

i	r_i	n_i	Prospects required	Subtotal	Cumulative total	Cumulative %
5	1.000,00	2	6	2.000,00	2.000,00	20%
4	500,00	5	35	2.500,00	4.500,00	45%
3	200,00	10	70	2.000,00	6.500,00	65%
2	50,00	40	200	2.000,00	8.500,00	85%
1	< 50,00	30	3500	1.500,00	**10.000,00**	**100%**

7.2. Example 2

In this example an expansion campaign of a middle-sized organization is analyzed. The organization wants to lead donors at the second level of the fund raising pyramid to the next one where they should subscribe a quarterly donation of $25, 00 to sustain a family in Sierra Leone. The organization works in Africa since the last 20 years, it has a solid fund raising management at its back and its DB consists of 57302 donors.

The parameters of the simulation are set in Table 9 and the gift range chart associated to the campaign is showed in Table 10. Notice that in this kind of campaigns the economic goal

Table 8. Result of Example 1 (L, Letter; T, Telephone call; LT, Letter and Telephone call; LL Letter and Leaflet)

	Strategy 1	Strategy 2	Strategy 3	Strategy 4
Type	LT	LL	L	L
n_1	3123	2988	4543	4867
n_2	401	371	389	385
n_3	71	68	80	75
n_4	22	23	17	10
n_5	7	6	4	3
G_1	1.561,50	956,16	2.044,35	2.092,81
G_2	4.460,32	3.754,52	3.734,40	3.195,50
G_3	1.569,10	1.585,76	1.476,00	1.457,25
G_4	2.023,56	2.026,76	1.535,27	905,40
G_5	2.317,84	1.929,30	1.200,40	825,33
G	**11.932,32**	10.252,50	9.990,42	8.476,29
P	**1,0545**	0,9365	0,7291	0,5510

has not the same meaning as in the previous example since the amount does not correspond to what the organization needs but it is just what the organization thinks to rise. The results given by the system are presented in Table 11. Strategies are sorted in descending order from the most suitable to the less one. Analyzing the results, the best strategy outperforms the economic goal and its practicability index is greater than one, meaning it is practicable. Notice that in the last strategy the lowest P does not correspond to the lowest G.

Table 9. Parameters of Example 2

Budget:	$10.000,00
Interests:	*("Family", "Poverty", "Developing Countries", "Food")*
Degree:	(0.5, 0.3, 0.1, 0,1)
Period:	*unset*
Type:	Letter
Objective:	expansion
Compound Utility:	Expected Gift, 0.4; Time Regularity Index, 0.6

8.   Conclusion

An expert system capable to suggest the right strategy to adopt in fund raising management is presented. This system constitutes an evolution of what was in the literature both in terms of capacity to model the problem and in flexibility. In particular a better understanding of

Table 10. Gift Range Chart of Example 2

i	r_i	n_i	Prospects required	Subtotal	Cumulative total	Cumulative %
5	1.000,00	2	6	2.000,00	2.000,00	2%
4	500,00	6	45	3.000,00	5.000,00	10%
3	200,00	50	110	10.000,00	15.000,00	30%
2	50,00	200	440	10.000,00	25.000,00	50%
1	< 50,00	500	2.500	25.000,00	**50.000,00**	**100%**

Table 11. Result of Example 2

	Strategy 1	Strategy 2	Strategy 3	Strategy 4
Period	Christmas	Autumn	Easter	Winter
n_1	5382	5182	4822	6762
n_2	562	511	475	417
n_3	121	115	92	82
n_4	32	23	18	16
n_5	4	2	2	1
G_1	28.040,22	21.919,86	18.082,50	30.699,48
G_2	14.119,13	11.814,32	13.110,00	8.048,10
G_3	11.023,10	11.306,80	7.493,40	5.857,26
G_4	3.871,36	2.302,76	1.805,58	1.608,64
G_5	1.564,48	683,10	606,20	340,11
G	**58.618,29**	48.026,84	41.097,68	46.553,59
P	**1,0410**	0,6672	0,5423	0,4222

the donor's interests, the use of non additive measures and the compound utility based approach to target selection give to this system the possibility to handle strategies in a finer way. Therefore these improvements lead to a more suitable and sharp analysis of the fundraising management.

A possible extension is the substitution of the rule based technique to generate the strategies to explore with a non additive measures approach; also the possibility to spread strategies over time could be an interesting further topic.

Acknowledgments

We are grateful to Dr. Davide Saletti for his active role in the connection with the real operational context.

References

[1] J. Andreoni. (2005). Philanthropy, in LA. Gerard-Varet, SC. Kolm and J. Ythier (eds), *Handbook of giving, reciprocity and altruism* , North Holland, Amsterdam.

[2] L. Barzanti and L. Pieressa. (2006). Technological solutions for fund raising management: a comparative analysis, Facoltà di Economia, University of Bologna, Sede di Forlì, *Working Paper CLEONP*, n. 30.

[3] L. Barzanti, N. Dragoni, A. Degli Esposti and M. Gaspari. (2007). *Decision making in fund raising management: a knowledge based approach,* in R. Ellis, T. Allen and M. Petridis (eds), Applications and Innovations in Intelligent Systems XV, (pp. 189-201) Springer.

[4] L. Barzanti, M. Gaspari and D. Saletti. (2009). Modelling decision making in fund raising management by a fuzzy knowledge system, *Expert Systems with Applications,* **36** (5), 9466-9478.

[5] L.Barzanti and S.Giove. *A decision support system for fund raising based on the Choquet integral methodology,* submitted.

[6] L. Cappellari, P. Ghinetti and G. Turati. *On time and money donations*, Università Cattolica di Milano, Quaderni dell'Istituto di Economia dell'Impresa e del Lavoro.

[7] G. Choquet. (1954). Theory of capacities, *Annales de l'Institut Fourier*, 5, 131-295.

[8] A. P. Dempster. (1967). Lower and Upper probabilities induced by a multivalued mapping, Annales of Mathematical Statistics, 38, 325-339.

[9] A. P. Dempster. (1968). A generalization of Bayessian inference, *The Royal Stat. Soc. B,* **50**, 205-247.

[10] J. Duffy, J. Ochs and L. Vesterlund. (2007). Giving little by little: Dynamic voluntary contribution games, *Journal of Public Economics,* **91**(9), 1708-1730.

[11] B. Duncan. (1999). Modeling charitable contributions of time and money, *Journal of Public Economics* **72**, 213-242.

[12] J. Durkin. (1994). *Expert System Design and Development,* Prentice Hall, Englewood Cliffs, NJ.

[13] G. Feng. (2006). A survey on analysis and design of model based fuzzy control systems, *IEEE Trans. Fuzzy Systems,* **14**(5), 676-697.

[14] P. Flory. (2001). *Building a fundraising database using your PC* , DSC, London.

[15] J. Y. Halpern. (2003). *Reasoning About Uncertainty,* The MIT Press.

[16] J. Kercheville and J. Kercheville. (2003). *The effective use of technology in nonprofits* , in E. Tempel (eds), Hank Rosso's achieving excellence in fund raising, (pp. 366-379) John Wiley & Sons.

[17] L. Lee, JA. Piliavin and VR. Call. (1999). Giving time, blood and money: similarities and differences, *Social Psychological Quarterly,* **62**(3), 276-290.

[18] Lin, J. (1991). Divergence measures based on the shannon entropy. *IEEE Transactions on Information Theory,* **37**(1), 145-151.

[19] M. Mastroleo. (2009). *Evidence Theory in a Coherent Setting*, PhD Thesis, University of Perugia.

[20] V. Melandri. (2004). *Fundraising course materials,* D.U. Press, Bologna, (in Italian).

[21] M. Mendel, (1995). Fuzzy logic systems for engineering: A tutorial, *Proc. IEEE*, vol. 83, (pp.345-377).

[22] SP. Nudd. (2003). Thinking strategically about information, in E. Tempel (eds.), *Hank Rosso's Achieving excellence in fund raising,* (pp. 349-365), John Wiley & Sons.

[23] A. Sargeant, (2001). Using Donor Lifetime Value to Inform Fundraising Strategy, *Nonprofit Management & Leadership*, John Wiley & Sons Inc, 12(1), 25-38

[24] ES. Sazonov, P. Klinkhachorn, HVS. GangaRao, and UB. Halabe. (2002). Fuzzy logic expert system for automated damage detection from changes in strain energy mode shapes, *Non-Destructive Testing and Evaluation*, Taylor & Francis Publishing, 18(1), 1-17.

[25] M. Sugeno. (1999). On stability of fuzzy systems expressed by fuzzy rules with singleton consequences. *IEEE Transactions Fuzzy Systems,* **7**(2), 201-223.

[26] GL. Zadeh. (1965). *Fuzzy sets, Information and Control,* **8**, 338-353.

In: Expert System Software

Editors: Jason M. Segura and Albert C. Reiter

ISBN: 978-1-61209-114-3

© 2012 Nova Science Publishers, Inc.

Chapter 8

ALGEBRAIC APPROACHES TO THE DEVELOPMENT OF RULE BASED EXPERT SYSTEMS

A. Hernando[1],* *E. Roanes-Lozano*[2],† *and L. M. Laita*[3],‡

[1]Depto. de Sistemas Inteligentes Aplicados,
Universidad Politécnica de Madrid, Spain
[2]Depto. de Algebra,
Universidad Complutense de Madrid, Spain
[3]Depto. de Inteligencia Artificial,
Universidad Politécnica de Madrid, Spain

Abstract

Based on previous mathematical results, questions related to consistence and tautological consequence in rule based expert systems can be translated into algebraic terms. Different algebraic approaches can be obtained depending the representation paradigm used. In this Chapter we will describe these algebraic approaches and show how to take advantage of them to implement easily different rule based expert systems. Mastering logic and computer algebra techniques is not required, as the Chapter should be suitable for unacquainted readers.

1. Introduction

Expert systems are computational programs on a certain domain which try to simulate the decisions that human experts on this domain would take. In the last years, much research has been focused on developing both techniques for representing the human knowledge in a computer and techniques for reasoning automatically.

An interesting way for representing knowledge in a rule based expert system (RBES) is based on propositional logic, under which, the issue about the knowledge inference is completely related to the concept of tautological consequence. Besides, by means of a

---

*E-mail address: ahernando@eui.upm.es

†E-mail address: eroanes@mat.ucm.es

‡E-mail address: laita@fi.upm.es

mathematical result [16] based on previous works [1, 4, 8, 10], this issue can be translated to an algebraic problem involving calculating certain Groebner bases [2]. In this way, RBES based on propositional logic may be very easily implemented by means of a computer algebra system like CoCoA [3, 15] or Maple [17]. Making use of this result, different RBES have been so far developed in the last recent years [11, 12, 14, 18].

The "Concept-Attribute-Value" paradigm [13] provides another way for representing knowledge in RBES which presents some advantages over propositional logic. Recently, we have obtained a similar mathematical result [6] which let us implement a RBES based on "Concept-Attribute-Value" paradigm by means of computer algebra systems.

In this paper, we will summarize and compare the different algebraic approaches for implementing RBES on computer algebra systems.

2. Overview of RBES Implemented on Computer Algebra Systems

2.1. Representation Formalism

Expert systems are computational programs composed by these three elements:

Input: The input of an expert system is concerned with the information related to the environment of the expert system. Since environment may change, this information is also subject to change as times goes by. The information related to the input will be denoted by $\mathcal{I}$.

Output: The output of an expert system is concerned with the information deducted by the expert system which will be useful for performing actions in the environment. The information related to the output will be denoted by $\mathcal{O}$.

Knowledge-Base: The knowledge-base of the expert system is concerned with the information contained in the system, which is used along with the input of the expert system to infer the output of the system. This knowledge is usually described by means of rules. That is to say, knowledge with the form "if some conditions related to the input hold, then it is required to take a particular action". In this element, it is possible to find different knowledge informing for example that it is impossible that two conditions hold at the same time. This kind of knowledge is usually named as "integrity constraints". The information related to the knowledge base will be denoted by $\mathcal{K}$.

In order to develop programs able to simulate the knowledge of human experts, AI researches have managed to developed different representation paradigms able to specify formally this kind of knowledge. In this Chapter, RBES uses different variables $X_1, ..., X_m$ to specify a particular state of the input and the output of the RBES. Depending on the representation paradigm, variables may take different possible values. We will consider different kinds of variables:

Input variables: Variables which describe the input of the RBES. That is to say, variables which describe the environment of the RBES.

Output variables: Variables which describe the possible actions or consequents that the RBES system deducts.

Auxiliary variables: Variables which are necessary to specify the knowledge-base of the RBES.

A state, S, is a possible situation on which each variable takes a value. Given a state S and a variable X, the expression $S(X)$ denotes the value that the variable X takes in the state S.

As we will see in next sections, the information related to the input, output and the knowledge-base is defined through formulae. For each representation paradigm, we define formally the concept of formula. The set of formulae in a particular representation paradigm is denoted by $\mathcal{C}$. Input and output are usually constrained to a specific kind of formulae which limits the possible values of the input and output variables. While the input and output formulae change depending the environment of the RBES, the formulae describing the knowledge-base keep invariable.

Formulae can hold or not in a particular state. For each representation paradigm, we define formally when a formula A holds in a state S. Output formulae are deducted from the formulae in the input and the knowledge-base. The question of determining which formulae are deducted is formally defined as follows:

Definition 1. A formula B is deducted by the RBES if and only if for every state S on which the formula $A \in \mathcal{K} \cup \mathcal{I}$ holds in the state S, the formula B also holds in the state S.

Example 1. Let us consider a RBES which supervises the safety operation of a car engine.

The input in this RBES shows the state of a car engine. In order to describe this input, we need, for instance, information related to the outside temperature, the engine temperature, or the level of coolant liquid.

The output in this RBES shows the actions that a car driver should take. One of them could be the advice that the car must be stopped immediately.

The knowledge base in this RBES describes knowledge about how the input and output are related. This knowledge may be represented by rules as the following:

> "If both the outside and engine temperature are high and the level of coolant
> liquid is low, then the car must be stopped immediately".

2.2. Algebraic Model

Thanks to different mathematical results, we will see in this Chapter how some RBES can be implemented in computer algebra systems. These mathematical results are based on translating every possible formula describing knowledge, $\mathcal{C}$, into polynomials of a ring $\mathcal{A}$ through a function $\varphi : \mathcal{C} \rightarrow \mathcal{A}$. As we will see in the next sections, different polynomial rings, $\mathcal{A}$, and functions φ are defined depending on the representation paradigm used to specify the knowledge of the RBES.

An important concept related to polynomial rings is the concept of (polynonial) ideal. The ideal generated by a set of elements $e_1, ..., e_n$ (denoted by the expression $\langle e_1, ..., e_n \rangle$), is a subset of elements of $\mathcal{A}$ which includes the elements $e_1, ..., e_n$ and fulfills some properties[1]. Two ideals can be "summed" resulting in a new ideal[2]. As we will see in next sections, we will consider the following ideals whose formal definition depends on the representation paradigm:

Ideal J: Ideal defined in the polynomial ring $\mathbb{Z}_q[x_1, ..., x_m]$ (where q depends on the representation paradigm)[3] required to define the ring $\mathcal{A}$ on which formulae are represented. Once defined the ideal J, the ring $\mathcal{A}$ is defined as the residue class ring[4] $\mathcal{A} = \mathbb{Z}_q[x_1, ..., x_m]/J$.

Ideal I: Ideal (of $\mathcal{A}$) related to the input of the RBES.

Ideal K: Ideal (of $\mathcal{A}$) related to the knowledge-base of the RBES.

Ideals play an important role since the question of determining if a RBES deducts a formula can be translated to the algebraic problem of determining if a polynomial belongs to an ideal. Indeed, as we will see in the next sections, a formula A can be deducted by the RBES, if and only if a polynomial p, related to the formula A belongs to the ideal $I + K$ (of $\mathcal{A}$). That is to say:

$$A \in \mathcal{O} \Leftrightarrow p \in I + K$$

This algebraic problem is solved by means of the concept of Groebner bases and normal forms [2]. Although these concepts are enough complex to be defined formally here (see [5] for an introduction to computer algebra), it is enough to know that the normal form of a polynomial, p, modulo an ideal $I + K$ (which is denoted by $\mathrm{NF}(p, I + K)$) is another polynomial and that the following holds:

$$p \in I + K \Leftrightarrow \mathrm{NF}(p, I + K) = 0$$

3. RBES Based on Boolean Propositional Logic

3.1. Representation Formalism

A RBES based on Boolean propositional logic uses Boolean variables $X_1, ..., X_m$ in order to specify a particular state of the input and output of the RBES. Each variable may take either the value $true$ or the value $false$.

The knowledge-base of this kind of RBES is described by means of Boolean propositional formulae. These propositional formulae are described by means of the well-known Boolean logic connectives $\neg, \wedge, \vee, \rightarrow$ according to the following definition.

Definition 2. A formula A is defined recursively as follows:

---

[1] An ideal is very special kind of subring: it satisfies that any element of the subring multiplied by any element of the ring belongs to the subring

[2] The minimum ideal containing the union of the two given ideals.

[3] The polynomial variables $x_1, ..., x_m$ correspond to the logical variables $X_1, ..., X_m$.

[4] The idea behind a residue class ring modulo an ideal is that all elements of the ideal vanish in the new structure.

- X_i where X_i is a variable,

- $\neg B$ where B is a formula,

- $B \vee C$ where B and C are formulae,

- $B \wedge C$ where B and C are formulae,

- $B \rightarrow C$ where B and C are formulae.

We will use $\mathcal{C}$ to denote the set of formulae. Boolean propositional rules are the most natural formulae to enunciate the knowledge-based of RBES. Rules are formulae with the form:

$$(A_1 \wedge ... \wedge A_r) \rightarrow (B_1 \vee ... \vee B_s)$$

where each formula $A_1, ..., A_r, B_1, ..., B_s$ is either a variable or the negation of a variable.

A state, S, is a possible situation on which each variable takes either the value $true$ or the value $false$. Given a state S and a variable X, the expression $S(X)$ denotes the value that the variable X takes in the state S. According to the following definition, we can determine whether a formula A holds or not in a particular state S.

Definition 3. Let A be a formula. Let S be a state. The formula A holds in the state S if and only if:

Case i): A is X_i where X_i is a variable:

$$A \text{ holds in } S \Leftrightarrow S(X_i) \text{ is true.}$$

Case ii): A is $\neg B$ where B is a formula:

$$A \text{ holds in } S \Leftrightarrow B \text{ does not hold in } S.$$

Case iii): A is $B \vee C$ where B and C are formulae:

$$A \text{ holds in } S \Leftrightarrow \text{ either } B \text{ holds in } S \text{ or } C \text{ holds in } S.$$

Case iv): A is $B \wedge C$ where B and C are formulae:

$$A \text{ holds in } S \Leftrightarrow B \text{ holds in } S \text{ and } C \text{ holds in } S.$$

Case v): A is $B \rightarrow C$ where B and C are formulae:

$$A \text{ holds in } S \Leftrightarrow \text{ the formula } \neg B \vee C \text{ holds in } S.$$

By means of formulae we describe the input, the output and the knowledge-base of a RBES.

Input: The input is a set of formulae with the form X or $\neg X$ where X is an input variable describing the environment of the RBES. While the formula X in the input represents that the input variable X takes the value $true$, the formula $\neg X$ represents that the output variable X takes the value $false$. Naturally, the set of formulae embodied the input of the RBES changes depending the environment of the RBES (which describes the input of the RBES). The symbol $\mathcal{I}$ denotes the set of formulae representing the input of the RBES.

Knowledge-base: The knowledge-base is a finite set of formulae. Unlike the input, these formulae are static and keep the same as time goes by. The symbol $\mathcal{K}$ denotes the set of formulae representing the knowledge-base of the RBES.

Output: The output is a set of formulae with the form X or $\neg X$ where X is an output variable. These formulae are deducted by the RBES by means of the formulae related to the input and the knowledge-base. Like the input, a formula X represents that the output variable X takes the value $true$ and the formula $\neg X$ represents that the variable X takes the value $false$. Obviously, this set of formulae changes depending the input of the RBES. The symbol $\mathcal{O}$ denotes the set of formulae representing the output of the RBES.

Example 2. In relation to the example described previously, we will consider the following variables:

Input Variables: The input in this RBES shows the state of a car engine (this may be considered as the illuminated dashboard gauge lights and, perhaps, a visual inspection of the engine compartment). In order to describe the input, several input variables will be used. Some of them could be the following:

T_1: "The outside temperature is high"

T_2: "The outside temperature is normal"

T_3: "The outside temperature is low"

E_1: "The engine temperature is high"

E_2: "The engine temperature is normal"

E_3: "The engine temperature is low"

C_1: "The level of coolant liquid is high"

C_2: "The level of coolant liquid is normal"

C_3: "The level of coolant liquid is low".

Output Variables: The output in this RBES shows the actions that a car driver should take. In order to describe the output, other different variables are used. One of them could be the following:

S: "The car must be stopped immediately"

Auxiliary Variables: In this example, we will not consider any auxiliary variable.

In relation to the knowledge-base of this RBES, we consider the following:

Integrity Constraints: We take into account the following integrity constrains related to the input variables.

- The outside temperature can take only one of the values "high", "normal", or "low":
  $IC1 : T_1 \vee T_2 \vee T_3$
  $IC2 : \neg(T_1 \wedge T_2)$
  $IC3 : \neg(T_1 \wedge T_3)$
  $IC4 : \neg(T_2 \wedge T_3)$

- The engine temperature can take only one of the values "high", "normal", or "low".
  $IC5 : E_1 \vee E_2 \vee E_3$
  $IC6 : \neg(E_1 \wedge E_2)$
  $IC7 : \neg(E_1 \wedge E_3)$
  $IC8 : \neg(E_2 \wedge E_3)$

- The level of coolant liquid can take only one of the values "high", "normal", or "low".
  $IC9 : C_1 \vee C_2 \vee C_3$
  $IC10 : \neg(C_1 \wedge C_2)$
  $IC11 : \neg(C_1 \wedge C_3)$
  $IC12 : \neg(C_2 \wedge C_3)$

Rules: We consider the following rule connecting input variables to the output variable:

> "If both the outside and engine temperature are high and the level of coolant liquid is low, then the car must be stopped immediately".

Formally in propositional logic:

$$R : T_1 \wedge E_1 \wedge C3 \rightarrow S$$

Consequently, the knowledge-base of the RBES is:

$$\mathcal{K} = \{R, IC1, IC2, IC3, IC4, IC5, IC6, IC7, IC8, IC9,$$
$$IC10, IC11, IC12\}$$

Let us consider that both the outside and engine temperature is high and the level of coolant liquid is low. That is to say, we have that $\mathcal{I} = \{T1, E1, C3\}$. In this case, we have that $\mathcal{K} \cup \mathcal{I} \models S$ and consequently, the RBES outputs S (namely, the car must be stopped immediately).

3.2. Algebraic Model

The problem of determining if a formula can be deducted from others can be dealt algebraically. Indeed, by representing every formula in $\mathcal{C}$ as a Boolean polynomial, we can transform the problem of determining if a formula can be deducted from others into an algebraic problem.

First of all, we will consider how the formulae are translated into Boolean polynomials. We need to define the ideal J in $\mathbb{Z}_2[x_1, ..., x_m]$:

$$J = \langle x_1^2 + x_1, ..., x_m^2 + x_m \rangle$$

Once defined the ideal J, formulae are transformed into an element of the ring $\mathcal{A} = \mathbb{Z}_2[x_1, ..., x_m]/J$ by means of the following function:

Definition 4. We define recursively the function $\varphi : \mathcal{C} \longrightarrow \mathcal{A}$ as follows:

Case i): A is X_i where X_i is a variable:

$$\varphi(A) = \varphi(X_i) = x_i$$

Case ii): A is $\neg B$ where B is a formula:

$$\varphi(A) = \varphi(\neg B) = 1 + \varphi(B)$$

Case iii): A is $B \wedge C$ where B and C are formulae:

$$\varphi(A) = \varphi(B \wedge C) = \varphi(B) \cdot \varphi(C)$$

Case iv): A is $B \vee C$ where B and C are formulae:

$$\varphi(A) = \varphi(B \vee C) = \varphi(B) + \varphi(C) + \varphi(B) \cdot \varphi(C)$$

Case v): A is $B \rightarrow C$ where B and C are formulae:

$$\varphi(A) = \varphi(B \rightarrow C) = 1 + \varphi(B) + \varphi(B) \cdot \varphi(C)$$

In relation to RBES based on Boolean propositional logic, we will consider the following ideals:

Ideal J: Ideal required to define the ring $\mathcal{A}$ on which formulae are represented.

$$J = \langle x_1^2 + x_1, ..., x_m^2 + x_m \rangle$$

Ideal I: Ideal related to the input of the RBES.

$$I = \langle \varphi(\neg A_i) | A_i \in \mathcal{I} \rangle$$

Ideal K: Ideal related to the knowledge-base of the RBES.

$$K = \langle \varphi(\neg A_i) | A_i \in \mathcal{K} \rangle$$

Once translated the formulae into polynomials, we can deal algebraically the question of determining if a formula can be deducted by the RBES.

Theorem 1. A formula B can be deducted by the RBES if and only if:

$$\varphi(\neg B) \in I + K$$

This theorem may be also rewritten in the following way:

Theorem 2. Let X_i be an output variable.

- $S(X_i)$ is $true \Leftrightarrow \mathrm{NF}(x_i, I + J + K) = 1$

- $S(X_i)$ is $false \Leftrightarrow \mathrm{NF}(x_i, I + J + K) = 0$.

This last theorem is specially useful since we can find the value of output variables calculating the normal form of a polynomial modulo an ideal (which can be computed by computer algebra systems).

3.3. Implementation in Computer Algebra Systems

Next, we will show how RBES based on propositional logic may be easily implemented through mathematical software. We will stand out a recent special software "Polybori" [9] specialized on Boolean rings on which calculations is highly speed.

3.3.1. General Computer Algebra System: CoCoA

In this section, we will use the computer algebra system named CoCoA [3, 15] in order to show how a RBES can be implemented in a computer algebra system.

First of all, we need to specify the ring on which formulae will be translated. In the example considered in the previous section, the ring will be defined in CoCoA as follows:

```
A::=Z/(2)[t[1..3],e[1..3],c[1..3],s];
USE A;
MEMORY.J:=Ideal(t[1]^2+t[1], t[2]^2+t[2], t[3]^2+t[3],
                e[1]^2+e[1], e[2]^2+e[2], e[3]^2+e[3],
                c[1]^2+c[1], c[2]^2+c[3], c[3]^2+c[3],
                s^2+s);
```

We define also the Boolean logic connectives according to the definition of φ. In Co-CoA syntax[5]:

```
NEG(M):=NF(M+1,MEMORY.J);
Y(M,N):= NF(M*N, MEMORY.J);
O(M,N):= NF(M+N+M*N, MEMORY.J);
IMP(M,N):= NF(1+M+M*N,MEMORY.J);
```

---

[5]O and Y have been chosen to represent OR and AND, respectively (OR and AND are reserved words in CoCoA). NEG and IMP represent negation and conditional, respectively.

Next, we will define the knowledge-base of the RBES. Here we will show the commands required to define it for the example described above.

```
IC1:=O(O(t[1],t[2]),t[3]);
IC2:=NEG(Y(t[1],t[2]));
IC3:=NEG(Y(t[1],t[3]));
IC4:=NEG(Y(t[2],t[3]));
IC5:=O(O(e[1],e[2]),e[3]);
IC6:=NEG(Y(e[1],e[2]));
IC7:=NEG(Y(e[1],e[3]));
IC8:=NEG(Y(e[2],e[3]));
IC9:=O(O(c[1],c[2]),c[3]);
IC10:=NEG(Y(c[1],c[2]));
IC11:=NEG(Y(c[1],c[3]));
IC12:=NEG(Y(c[2],c[3]));
R:=IMP(Y(Y(t[1],e[1]),c[3]),s);

MEMORY.K:=Ideal(NEG(R),NEG(IC1),NEG(IC2),NEG(IC3),
                NEG(IC4),NEG(IC5),NEG(IC6),
                NEG(IC7),NEG(IC8),NEG(IC9),
                NEG(IC10),NEG(IC11),
                NEG(IC12));
```

Let us consider that both the outside and engine temperature is high and the level of coolant liquid is low (that is to say, $\mathcal{I} = \{T1, E1, C3\}$). In this case, the input is:

```
MEMORY.I:=Ideal(NEG(t[1]),NEG(e[1]),NEG(c[3]));
```

We could find out the value of the output variable S inferred by the RBES by means of the following:

```
NF(s,MEMORY.I+MEMORY.J+MEMORY.K);
```

CoCoA responds the following:

```
1
```

That is to say, we have that the RBES infers that the car must be stopped immediately.

3.3.2. PolyBoRi

PolyBoRi [9] is a recent library on C++ specialized on Boolean polynomials which involves high speed on calculations over this kind of polynomials. The use of PolyBoRi instead of a general computer algebra system involves two main advantages: on the one hand, the implementation of RBES based on Boolean propositional logic in PolyBoRi is simpler than in a general computer algebra system; on the other hand, these RBES run faster in PoliBoRi than in a general computer algebra system. Consequently, it is very interesting to implement a RBES based on propositional logic in PoliBoRi.

However PolyBoRi is only a library on C++, and not a computer algebra system, so it makes harder the implementation of RBES. Nevertheless, it is available an interface for Python which makes easier the implementation of RBES.

4.   The "Concept-Attribute-Value" Paradigm

4.1.   Representation Formalism

An expert system based on the "Concept-Attribute-Value" paradigm uses different variables $X_1, ..., X_m$ in order to specify a particular state of the input and output of the expert system. Each variable may take a subset of possible values $V = \{v_1, ..., v_n\}$.

Formulae in this representation paradigm is defined as follows:

Definition 5. A formula A is defined recursively as follows:

- $X_i = v$ where X_i is a variable and v is a possible value of X_i,

- $X_i = X_j$ where X_i and X_j are variables,

- $\neg A$ where A is a formula,

- $A_1 \vee A_2$ where A_1, A_2 are formulae,

- $A_1 \wedge A_2$ where A_1, A_2 are formulae,

- $A_1 \rightarrow A_2$ where A_1, A_2 are formulae.

We will use $\mathcal{C}$ to denote the set of formulae. Rules are the most natural formulae to enunciate the knowledge-based of expert systems. Rules are formulae with the form:

$$(A_1 \wedge ... \wedge A_r) \rightarrow (B_1 \vee ... \vee B_s)$$

where each formula $A_1, ..., A_r, B_1, ..., B_s$ is either a formula with the form $(X_i = X_j)$, $\neg(X_i = X_j)$, $(X_i = v)$ or $\neg(X_i = v)$ where X_i, X_j are variables, and v is a possible value of the variable X_i.

According to the following definition, we can determine whether a formula A holds or not in a particular state S.

Definition 6. Let A be a formula. Let S be a state. The formula A holds in the state S if and only if:

Case i): A is $X_i = v$ where X_i is a variable and v is a possible value of X_i:

$$A \text{ holds in } S \Leftrightarrow S(X_i) = v$$

Case ii): A is $X_i = X_j$ where X_i and X_j are variables:

$$A \text{ holds in } S \Leftrightarrow S(X_i) = S(X_j)$$

Case iii): A is $\neg B$ where B is a formula:

$$A \text{ holds in } S \Leftrightarrow B \text{ does not hold in } S$$

Case iv): $A \equiv B \vee C$ where B and C are formulae:

$$A \text{ holds in } S \Leftrightarrow \text{ either } B \text{ holds in } S \text{ or } C \text{ holds in } S$$

Case v): $A \equiv B \wedge C$ where B and C are formulae:

$$A \text{ holds in } S \Leftrightarrow B \text{ holds in } S \text{ and } C \text{ holds in } S$$

Case vi): $A \equiv B \rightarrow C$ where B and C are formulae:

$$A \text{ holds in } S \Leftrightarrow \text{ the formula } \neg B \vee C \text{ holds in } S.$$

By means of formulae we describe the input, the output and the knowledge-base of a RBES.

Input: The input is a set of formulae with the form $(X = v)$ where X is an input variable and v is a possible value of X. The symbol $\mathcal{I}$ denotes the set of formulae representing the input of the RBES.

Knowledge-base: The knowledge-base is a finite set of formulae. Unlike the input, these formulae are static and keep the same as time goes by. As usual, the symbol $\mathcal{K}$ denotes the set of formulae representing the knowledge-base of the RBES.

Output: The output is a set of formulae with the form $(X = v)$ where X is an output variable and v a possible value of X. These formulae are deducted by the RBES by means of the formulae related to the input and the knowledge-base. The symbol $\mathcal{O}$ denotes the set of formulae representing the output of the RBES.

Example 3. We will use the example described previously. We will consider the following variables:

Input Variables The input in this RBES shows the state of a car engine. In order to describe the input, several input variables will be used. Some of them could be the following:

> T: "The outside temperature". This variable may take the possible values $\{low, normal, high\}$.
>
> E: "The engine temperature". This variable may take the possible values $\{low, normal, high\}$.
>
> C: "The level of coolant liquid". This variable may take the possible values $\{low, normal, high\}$.

Output Variables The output in this RBES shows the actions that a car driver should take. In order to describe the output, other different variables are used. One of them could be the following:

S: "The car must be stopped immediately". This variable may take the possible values $\{true, false\}$.

Auxiliary Variables In this example, we do not consider any auxiliary variable.

In relation to the knowledge-base of this RBES, we consider the following:

Integrity Constraints In this representation paradigm, integrity constraints are not required to be defined since they are taken into account implicitly in this representation paradigm.

Rules We consider the following rule connecting input variables to the output variable:

"If both the outside and engine temperature are high and the level of coolant liquid is low, then the car must be stopped immediately".

Formally:
$$R : (T = high) \wedge (E = high) \wedge (C = low) \rightarrow (S = true)$$

Consequently, the knowledge-base of the RBES is:

$$\mathcal{K} = \{R\}$$

4.2. Algebraic Model

The problem of determining if a formula can be deducted from others can be dealt algebraically [6].

Let p be a prime integer greater or equal that the number of possible values which may take any variable. First of all, we need to codify the possible values of the variables. That is to say, we need to define a function, ϕ, between the possible values of the variables and $\{0, ... p - 1\}$:

$$\phi : V \longrightarrow \{0, ..., p - 1\}$$

Obviously, given two possible values of a same variable, $v, w \in V$, the function ϕ must fulfill that $\phi(v) \neq \phi(w)$.

Given a variable X_i, which may take a possible value $\{v_1, ..., v_n\}$, we define a polynomial r_i associated to it:

$$r_i = (x - \phi(v_1)) \cdot (x - \phi(v_2)) \cdot ... \cdot (x - \phi(v_n))$$

The ideal J on $\mathbb{Z}_p[x_1, ..., x_m]$ is defined as follows:

$$J = \langle r_1, ..., r_m \rangle$$

Once defined the ideal J, formulae are transformed into an element of the ring $\mathcal{A} = \mathbb{Z}_p[x_1, ..., x_m]/J$ by means of the following function:

Definition 7. We define recursively the function $\varphi : \mathcal{C} \longrightarrow \mathcal{A}$ as follows:

Case i): A is $X_i = v$ where X_i is a variable and v a possible value of X_i:

$$\varphi(A) = \varphi(X_i = v) = x_i - v$$

Case ii): A is $X_i = X_j$ where X_i and X_j are variables:

$$\varphi(A) = \varphi(X_i = X_j) = x_i - x_j$$

Case iii) A is $\neg B$ where B is a formula:

$$\varphi(A) = \varphi(\neg B) = \varphi(B)^{p-1} - 1$$

Case iv): A is $B \vee C$ where B and C are formulae:

$$\varphi(A) = \varphi(B \vee C) = \varphi(B) \cdot \varphi(C)$$

Case v): A is $B \wedge C$ where B and C are formulae:

$$\varphi(A) = \varphi(B \wedge C) = \varphi(\neg(\neg B \vee \neg C)))$$

Case vi): A is $B \rightarrow C$ where B and C are formulae:

$$\varphi(A) = \varphi(B \rightarrow C) = \varphi(\neg B \vee C)$$

The translation of a rule, $(A_1 \wedge ... \wedge A_r) \rightarrow (B_1 \vee ... \vee B_s)$, is especially simple:

$$\varphi((A_1 \wedge ... \wedge A_r) \rightarrow (B_1 \vee ... \vee B_s)) = \varphi(\neg A_1) \cdot ... \cdot \varphi(\neg A_r) \cdot \varphi(B_1) ... \cdot \varphi(B_s)$$

Once translated the formulae into polynomials, we can deal algebraically the question of determining if a formula can be deducted. We consider the following ideals:

Ideal J: Ideal required to define the ring $\mathcal{A}$ on which formulae are represented.

Ideal I: Ideal related to the input of the RBES:

$$I = \langle \varphi(A_i) | A_i \in \mathcal{I} \rangle$$

Ideal K: Ideal related to the knowledge-base of the RBES:

$$K = \langle \varphi(A_i) | A_i \in \mathcal{K} \rangle$$

Once translated the formulae into polynomials, we can deal algebraically the question of determining if a formula can be deducted by the RBES.

Theorem 3. A formula B can be deducted by the RBES if and only if

$$\varphi(B) \in I + K$$

This theorem may be also rewritten in the following way:

Theorem 4. Let X_i be an output variable and v a possible value of X_i.

$$S(X_i) = v \Leftrightarrow \text{NF}(x_i, I + J + K) = \phi(v)$$

This last theorem is specially useful since we can find the value of output variables calculating the normal form of a polynomial modulo an ideal (which can be computed by computer algebra systems).

4.3.   Implementation in Computer Algebra Systems

In this section, we will use the computer algebra system CoCoA in order to show how a RBES can be implemented in a computer algebra system. We will use the example considered above.

First of all, we codify the possible values of variables on natural numbers.

$\phi(LOW) = 0$;
$\phi(NORMAL) = 1$;
$\phi(HIGH) = 2$;
$\phi(FALSE) = 0$;
$\phi(TRUE) = 1$;

As may be seen, in this example $p = 3$. Now, we can specify the ring on which formulae will be translated. The ring will be defined in CoCoA as follows:

```
A::=Z/(3)[t,e,c,s];
USE A;
LOW:=0;
NORMAL:=1;
HIGH:=2;
FALSE:=0;
TRUE:=1;

MEMORY.J:=Ideal((t-HIGH)*(t-NORMAL)*(t-LOW),
                (e-HIGH)*(e-NORMAL)*(e-LOW),
                (c-HIGH)*(c-NORMAL)*(c-LOW),
                (s-TRUE)*(s-FALSE));
```

We will define also the connectives according to the definition of φ. In CoCoA syntax:

```
NEG(M):=NF(M^2-1,MEMORY.J);
O(M,N):= NF(M*N, MEMORY.J);
Y(M,N):= NEG(O(NEG(M),NEG(N)));
IMP(M,N):= O(NEG(M),N);
```

Next, we will define the knowledge-base of the RBES. Here we will show the commands required to define knowledge-base of the RBES:

```
R:=IMP(Y(Y((t-HIGH),(e-HIGH)),c-LOW),s-TRUE);
MEMORY.K:=Ideal(NEG(R));
```

Let us consider that both the outside and engine temperature is high and the level of coolant liquid is low (that is to say, $\mathcal{I} = \{T = HIGH, E = HIGH, C = LOW\}$). In CoCoA syntax:

```
MEMORY.I:=Ideal(t-HIGH,e-HIGH,c-LOW);
```

We could find out the value of the output variable S inferred by the RBES by means of the following:

```
NF(s,MEMORY.J+MEMORY.I+MEMORY.K);
```

CoCoA responds the following:

```
1
```

That is to say, we have that the RBES infers that the car must be stopped immediately.

5. RBES Based on Multivalued Propositional Logic

The multivalued propositional logic may be used to represent uncertainty on the knowledge.

5.1. Representation Formalism

In multivalued propositional logic, variables $X_1, ... X_m$ may take different truth degrees. The possible truth values will be denoted by natural numbers from 0 to $q-1$, where 0 stands, as usual, for "false" and $q - 1$ for "true". Logics have built different multivalued propositional logic with different truth degrees. Each logic not only extends differently the Boolean connectives $\wedge$, $\vee$, $\neg$, $\rightarrow$ but also define different new connectives. Each unary connective, f_u (respectively binary connective, f_b), has associated a function $F_u : \{0, ..., q-1\} \longrightarrow \{0, ..., q-1\}$ (respectively a function $F_b : \{0, ..., q-1\} \times \{0, ..., q-1\} \longrightarrow \{0, ..., q-1\}$).

Formulae are defined on multivalued propositional logic as follows:

Definition 8. A formula A is defined recursively as follows:

- X_i where X_i is a variable.

- $f_u(B)$ where B is a formula and f_u is a unary connective of the logic.

- $f_b(B, C)$ where B and C are formulae, and f_b is a binary connective of the logic.

We will use C to denote the set of formulae. We will term as a state, S, a possible situation on which each variable takes a degree value between 0 and $q - 1$. Given a state S and a variable X, the expression $S(X)$ denotes the value that the variable X takes in the state S. Given a formula A and a state S, the expression $S(A)$ denotes a value between 0 and $q - 1$ associated to the formula A in the state S:

Definition 9. Let A be a formula. Let S be a state. $S(A)$ is defined as follows:

Case i): A is X_i where X_i is a variable:

$$S(A) = S(X_i)$$

Case ii): A is $f_u(B)$ where B is a formula and f_u a unary connective associated to the function $F_u : \{0, ..., q-1\} \rightarrow \{0, ..., q-1\}$:

$$S(A) = F_u(S(B))$$

Case iii): A is $f_b(B, C)$ where B and C are formulae:

$$S(A) = F_b(S(B), S(C))$$

Definition 10. Let A be a formula and let S be a state. The formula A holds in S if and only if $S(A) = q - 1$

By means of formulae we describe the input, the output and the knowledge-base of a RBES.

Input: The input is a set of formulae with the form X or $f_u(X)$ where X is an input variable and f_u is a unary connective. The symbol $\mathcal{I}$ denotes the set of formulae representing the input of the RBES.

Knowledge-base: The knowledge-base is a finite set of formulae. The symbol $\mathcal{K}$ denotes the set of formulae representing the knowledge-base of the RBES.

Output: The output is a set of formulae with the form X or $f_u(X)$ where X is an output variable. The symbol $\mathcal{O}$ denotes the set of formulae representing the output of the RBES.

5.2. Algebraic Model

The problem of determining if a formula can be deducted from others can be dealt algebraically when q is a prime[6].

First of all, we will consider how the formulae are translated into polynomials. First of all, we need to define the following ideal J in $\mathbb{Z}_q[x_1, ..., x_m]$:

$$J = \langle x_1^q - x_1, ..., x_m^q - x_m \rangle$$

Once defined the ideal J, formulae are transformed into an element of the ring $\mathcal{A} = \mathbb{Z}_q[x_1, ..., x_m]/J$ by means of the following function:

Definition 11. We define recursively the function $\varphi : \mathcal{C} \longrightarrow \mathcal{A}$ as follows:

Case i): A is X_i where X_i is a variable:

$$\varphi(A) = \varphi(X_i) = x_i$$

Case ii): A is $f_u(B)$ where B is a formula:

$$\varphi(A) = p_u(\varphi(B))$$

where $p_u(x)$ is a polynomial which fulfills that for every truth degree, v, between 0 and $q - 1$, we have that $p_u(v) = f_u(v)$.

---

[6]This result was extended in [7] when q is a power of a prime.

Case iii): A is $f_b(B, C)$ where B and C are formulae.

$$\varphi(A) = p_b(\varphi(B))$$

where $p_b(x, y)$ is a polynomial which fulfills that for every v, w between 0 and $q - 1$, we have that $p_u(v, w) = f_u(v, w)$:

In relation to RBES, we will consider the following ideals:

Ideal J: Ideal required to define the ring $\mathcal{A}$ on which formulae are represented.

$$J = \langle x_1^q + x_1, ..., x_m^q + x_m \rangle$$

Ideal I: Ideal related to the input of the RBES.

$$I = \langle q - 1 - \varphi(A_i) | A_i \in \mathcal{I} \rangle$$

Ideal K: Ideal related to the knowledge-base of the RBES.

$$K = \langle q - 1 - \varphi(A_i) | A_i \in \mathcal{K} \rangle$$

Once translated the formulae into polynomials, we can deal algebraically the question of determining if a formula can be deducted by the RBES.

Theorem 5. A formula B can be deducted by the RBES if and only if:

$$q - 1 - \varphi(B) \in I + K$$

This theorem may be also rewritten in the following way:

Theorem 6. A formula B can be deducted by the RBES if and only if

$$\mathrm{NF}(\varphi(B), I + J + K) = q - 1$$

6.   Comparison of the Models

In this Chapter, we have considered different representation paradigms for implementing RBES on computer algebra systems. Each representation paradigm has advantages and drawbacks. The most suitable paradigm depends on the specific application and therefore, it must be chosen depending on each particular case.

While the representation paradigm based on Boolean propositional logic and the "Concept-Attribute-Value" paradigm cannot manage uncertainty in the knowledge, the representation paradigm based on multivalued propositional logic can manage it. However, the algebraic model based on multivalued propositional logic involves very slow calculations and it is not suitable when implementing large RBES.

When a RBES does not require to manage uncertainty, then the "Concept-Attribute-Value" paradigm and the paradigm based on Boolean propositional logic can be used to represent knowledge. Both paradigms are equivalent in the sense that every RBES represented under one paradigm can be represented under the other paradigm. The 'Concept-Attribute-Value' presents the advantage over Boolean propositional logic that involves generally lower number of variables and lower number of formulae in the knowledge-base (the reader may observe the example used in this Chapter) which makes the RBES smaller. However RBES implemented on propositional logic can be implemented on the specialized computer algebra system, "PolyBoRi", which performs calculations very fast. In general, we have observed that when a RBES deals with a great number of variables which may take a great number of possible values, the "Concept-Attribute-Value" paradigm is more suitable than Boolean propositional logic. Otherwise, when a great number of variables only can take two possible values, Boolean propositional logic provides better performance.

7. Conclusions

In this paper, we have described and compared different algebraic approaches for modeling RBES: Boolean propositional logic; the "Concept-Attribute-Value" paradigm; and multivalued propositional logic. Each paradigm presents advantages and drawbacks and the choose of the most suitable paradigm depends on the specific application.

Acknowledgment

This work was partially supported by the research projects TIN2009-07901 (Ministerio de Educacin y Ciencia, Spain) and UCM2008-910563 (UCM - BSCH Gr. 58/08, Spain / Research Group ACEIA).

References

[1] J. A. Alonso, E. Briales: Lógicas Polivalentes y Bases de Gröbner. In: C. Martin, ed.: *Actas del V Congreso de Lenguajes Naturales y Lenguajes Formales.* University of Seville, Seville (1995) 307-315.

[2] B. Buchberger: Bruno Buchberger's PhD thesis 1965: An algorithm for finding the basis elementals of the residue class ring of a zero dimensional polynomial ideal. *Journal of Symbolic Computation* **41**/3-4 (2006) 475-511.

[3] A. Capani, G. Niesi: *CoCoA User's Manual.* Dept. Mathematics, Univ. of Genova, 1996.

[4] J. Chazarain, A. Riscos, J. A. Alonso, E. Briales: Multivalued Logic and Gröbner Bases with Applications to Modal Logic. *Journal of Symbolic Computation* **11** (1991) 181-194.

[5] D. Cox, J. Little, D. O'Shea: Ideals, Varieties, and Algorithms. *An Introduction to Computational Algebraic Geometry and Commutative Algebra* , Springer, New York, 1992.

[6] A. Hernando: A New Algebraic Model for Implementing Expert Systems Represented Under the 'Concept-Attribute-Value' paradigm. *Mathematics and Computers in Simulation* (accepted for publication) DOI:10.1016/j.matcom.2010.06.020.

[7] A. Hernando, E. Roanes-Lozano, L. M. Laita: A Polynomial Model for Logics with a Prime Power Number of Truth Values. *Journal of Automated Reasoning* (accepted for publication) DOI: 10.1007/s10817-010-9191-0.

[8] J. Hsiang: Refutational Theorem Proving using Term-Rewriting Systems. *Artificial Intelligence* **25** (1985) 255-300.

[9] M. Brickenstein, A. Dreyer: PolyBoRi: PolyBoRi: A framework for Gröbner-basis computations with Boolean polynomials, *Journal of Symbolic Computation* **44/9** (2009) 1326–1345.

[10] D. Kapur, P. Narendran: An Equational Approach to Theorem Proving in First-Order Predicate Calculus. In: *Proceedings of the 9th International Joint Conference on Artificial Intelligence (IJCAI-85)*, vol. 2 (1985) 1146-1153.

[11] L. M. Laita, E. Roanes-Lozano, V. Maojo, L. de Ledesma, L. Laita: An Expert System for Managing Medical Appropriateness Criteria Based on Computer Algebra Techniques. *Computers and Mathematics with Applications* **51/5** (2000) 473–481.

[12] M. Lourdes Jiménez, J. M. Santamaría, R. Barchino, L. Laita, L. M. Laita, L. A. González, A. Asenjo: Knowledge representation for diagnosis of care problems through an expert system: Model of the auto-care deficit situations, *Expert System with Applications* **34** (2008) 2847–2857.

[13] M. Minsky: A Framework for Representing Knowledge, MIT-AI Laboratory Memo 306 (1974)

[14] C. Pérez-Carretero, L. M. Laita, E. Roanes-Lozano, L. Lázaro, J. González-Cajal, L. Laita: A Logic and Computer Algebra-Based Expert System for Diagnosis of Anorexia. *Mathematics and Computers in Simulation* **58** (2002) 183–202.

[15] D. Perkinson, (2000). CoCoA 4.0 online help (electronic file acompanying CoCoA v.4.0).

[16] E. Roanes-Lozano, L. M. Laita and E. Roanes-Macías, A Polynomial Model for Multivalued Logics with a Touch of Algebraic Geometry and Computer Algebra. *Mathematics and Computers in Simulation* **45/1** (1998) 83–99.

[17] E. Roanes-Lozano, L. M. Laita and E. Roanes-Macías, A Groebner bases based many-valued modal logic implementation in Maple. In: S. Autexier et al. (eds.) AISC / Calculemus / MKM 2008. *Lecture Notes in Artificial Intelligence* **5144**, Springer, Berlin (2008) 170-183.

[18] C. Rodríguez-Solano, L. M. Laita, E. Roanes Lozano, L. López Corral, L. Laita, A Computational System for Diagnosis of Depressive Situations. *Expert System with Applications* **31** (2006) 47–55.

In: Expert System Software
Editors: Jason M. Segura and Albert C. Reiter

ISBN: 978-1-61209-114-3
© 2012 Nova Science Publishers, Inc.

Chapter 9

"A PRACTICAL OVERVIEW OF EXPERT SYSTEMS IN TELECOMMUNICATION NETWORKS, MEDICINE AND POWER SUPPLIES"

I. Monedero, A. Martín, J. M. Elena, J. I. Guerrero, F. Biscarri and C. León

Electronic Technology Department, University of Seville, Spain

INTRODUCTION

Expert systems are being applied with success in multiple fields like engineering, medicine, geology, chemistry, etc., for the realization of diverse tasks (interpretation, prediction, diagnosis, design, planning, instruction, control, etc.). Some of these applications in these fields include:

- Inside engineering: The management and design of Telecommunication Networks.
- Inside medicine: Disease Detection.
- Inside power supplies: Fraud Detection.

In this chapter, we will give an overview of the applications of Expert Systems in these fields. On the other hand, we will describe case studies of real problems solved in diverse projects carried out by the authors, explaining, from the experience of the authors, how to deal with such problems. The projects that will be described are the following ones:

- An expert system for the management of an ionospheric communication.
- An expert system for an efficient network management.
- An expert system for automatic routing of a HFC telecommunication network.
- An expert system for the diagnosis of stomach disorders.
- An expert system for the detection of frauds in a power supply.

All these expert systems have been developed by the group of authors in the Electronic Technology Department of the University of Seville (Spain).

INSIDE ENGINEERING: THE MANAGEMENT AND DESIGN OF TELECOMMUNICATION NETWORKS

As a result of the great evolution, which has taken place in telecommunications due to the advances produced by new technologies, it is possible to access information rapidly, especially nowadays with the use of communication networks such as the Internet. Telecommunication networks have evolved in time to satisfy the demands of different telecommunication services, which day by day require greater bandwidth and a better quality of service. Network technology has increased in complexity, generating the need for a better administration of the resources of these systems, which has favored the associated evolution of network management.

Expert systems may also be applied to the field of telecommunication networks, because many of the previously enumerated tasks are carried out in these networks. In addition, these tasks require specialized knowledge and, therefore, an expert system can help with the automation process.

Figure 1 schematically shows the different application domains of expert systems related to telecommunication networks [1][2]:

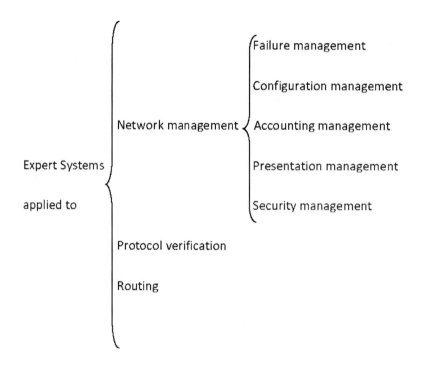

Figure 1. Expert systems in telecommunication networks.

The efficiency of the tasks of operation and maintenance of current telecommunication networks largely depends on the degree of co-operation between the management system and the human operators. The management system plays a very important part, informing on possible anomalies and executing the commands of control.

The different tasks involved in this management and for which currently exist commercial expert systems, are:

- Failure management. This task refers to the group of functions related to network management, which are necessary for the detection, diagnosis, recovery and correction of shortcomings of the elements that form a telecommunication network. Examples include Max & Opti-Max (an expert administrator of telephony line maintenance developed by NYNEX) [3], Trouble Locator (an intelligent system developed by Pacific Bell for locating failures at the physical level of a local telephony network) [4], ANSWER (Expert system developed by AT&T and in charge of supervising their 4ESS switches) and Scout (developed by AT&T for identifying persistent failures in the network) [5].
- Configuration management. This function helps the administrator to exercise control on the configuration of the components of the network. Changes in the configuration are carried out to eliminate congestions, to isolate shortcomings or to make changes, which the users need. Examples of expert systems supporting configuration management include ECXpert (detection and reparation of failures, developed by Lucent Technologies) [5], ACE (an expert system developed by AT&T for helping in the detection and diagnosis of failures in cables) [6] and NEMESYS (also developed by AT&T for avoiding network congestions) [5].
- Accounting management. This function allows us to determine and locate positions and costs for the use of the resources of the network, e.g. APRI (also developed by AT&T for forecasting the probability of falling into new debts) [7].
- Presentation management. This task helps the network administrators to monitor and evaluate the benefits of the system. Example expert systems for presentation management are Net/Advisor & NetCommand (for monitoring the state of the network in real time) [5].
- Security management. This function helps the network administrators manage the services that provide protection in the access to the communication resources. Examples of expert systems related to security management include EXSYS (a set of expert systems developed by Pacific Bell which executes on an AT&T 3B2/600 computer for supervising the Loop Maintenance Operating System from a server) [5].

In addition, there are other expert systems such as NetHELP (which provides assistance for user trouble shooting) and ExSim (assistance in the process of routing a network) applied to other fields [5], enumerated in Figure 1.

There is an especially interesting yet less investigated field for the application of expert systems to the world of telecommunication networks: Systems applied to assist during the tasks of network design. Within the design process, the use of knowledge-based systems is of particular interest for the topological design of the network. Among these tasks are:

- The choice of the type of transmission: Transmission by physical support (cable, microstrip, wave-guided) and/or transmission by radio (electromagnetic waves).
- The layout of the network: On radio networks it would be necessary to establish the layout depending on the type of communication (bidirectional or omni-directional) and signal propagation and interference characteristics. On cable networks, this task comprises the process of wiring.
- Placement of the network elements: Establishment and localization of the different nodes and necessary elements in order to obtain the suitable signal level (splitters, amplifiers, etc).

Especially the latter two tasks require the work of experts who apply various design rules and their empiric knowledge. Because of the great number of limitations of the physical media, these tasks are especially complex in cable networks.

On the other hand, due to the very particular characteristics of the design rules for each network, as well as due to the high complexity of the application of the knowledge, the development and commercial use of expert systems for cable network design is still not very widely extended. Thus, the currently existing approaches mainly focus on research [8][9][10]. In some cases of paper [8], the design is only partial; others [9][10] are limited to the design of local networks.

INSIDE MEDICINE: DETECTION OF DISEASE

The main advantage of expert systems in medicine [11][12] lies in making decisions in diseases with complex diagnoses [13][14]. These expert systems facilitate the work of doctors while producing an increase in productivity. Another benefit occurs when confirming a suspected diagnosis.

In order to realize an adequate diagnosis the doctor has a great amount of knowledge about the signs and symptoms of diseases. Thus, his/her expertise lies in the ability to relate the status of a patient with descriptions provided by the texts. The doctor determines what symptoms and signs are present and matches their meaning with the absent ones and the disease with which he thinks that it is. The greater your ability to combine their knowledge with actual observations, the more accurate is his/her technique of diagnosis. The limiting factors are the ability to remember things organized, to correlate the observed cases with the pattern of existing data and apply this knowledge when the data are incomplete or not well adapted to the previous cases. The first two factors are the main advantage of computers; on the other hand, the latest factor is the strong point of human experts. If a computer system can replace the sharpness of the statistical analysis, its higher powers to organize data could enable it to emulate in some degree the doctor's expertise. It is intended that the expert system is capable of approaching the diagnosis and help in management issues.

Expert systems have the capacity to learn, understand and be understood, to develop alternative hypotheses to resolve conflicts and to justify their conclusions. They have advantages such as handling a large amount of information and being useful in medical education because they are developed thorough a study of the representation and reasoning of medical knowledge. In order to solve problems, expert systems are based on methods that derive their results by reasoning from knowledge about the specific topic previously entered into the system, in contrast with conventional systems that solve problems through algorithms or fixed repetitive processes, scheduled in advance and expect the same type of input data to process and generate the response. Expert systems are able to provide an explanation of the procedure followed to arrive at a solution, justifying the steps used in the process of deduction. Finally, expert systems can increase their knowledge base by adding more data. Among the drawbacks and disadvantages of expert systems we have to include the high cost of design and that its realization requires a highly specialized staff with sophisticated technology during a relative long time and long periods of testing to prove its reliability, especially when the system handles large volumes of information. Also an inappropriate use can have a negative impact on the relation between doctor and patient.

Since the early seventies diverse expert systems applied to medicine have been developed. For instance, the CASNET [15] is an expert system for diagnosis and management of glaucoma, the MYCIN [15] for diagnosis and treatment of infectious diseases, or the DIALOG-INTERNIST (today called Caduceus) to make a differential diagnosis in the broad context of internal medicine. A more recent approach is ONCOCIN [16], which is focused on the topic of chemotherapy of patients with lymphoma.

On the other hand, many other applications with well defined roles and goals in different medical specialties have been developed. Each of these expert systems has a specific way of representing medical knowledge and of performing the logical reasoning to reach a conclusion and support it. The development of expert systems in medicine has received contributions from non-medical programs but which led to new ideas, among them the DENDRAL, META-DENDRAL and PROSPECTOR [15].

INSIDE POWER SUPPLIES: FRAUD DETECTION

The application of expert systems to power utilities covers a wide spectrum of applications. They are applied in power energy production, transport, distribution and consumption. In some works [17][18] a series of categories very similar among themselves are proposed. These categories allow classifying functionalities of the expert systems in power systems applications:

- Alarm processing [19].
- Fault diagnosis or Technical losses diagnosis [20].
- Steady-state security and dynamic security assessment [21].
- Remedial controls [22].
- Restoration [23].
- Environments for operational aids [24].
- Substation monitoring and control [25].
- Maintenance scheduling [26].
- Expert System development methods and tools [27].

Smart Grids and remote management allow new research and application fields:

- Management of communication networks in power distribution networks [28][29].
- Management of electric vehicle or Vehicle-to-Grid (V2G) technology [30].

Normally, the current expert systems could be classified in more than one of these categories, because they aren't perfectly delimited and some expert systems have several functionalities.

In addition, customers' consumption is very important for power distribution companies. The non-technical losses are the main problem of the power distribution companies, because they cannot be forecasted as the technical losses. The techniques and technologies used on non-technical losses detection and classification are very similar to the ones used in other research fields, as for example: credit card fraud, intrusion detection, communication network fraud, etc.

The work [31] uses rough sets for fraud detection in electrical energy consumers. The technique used is based in the treatment of incomplete information about consumption. The success of this one is of 20 %. On the other hand, the work [32] uses a Radial Basis Function (RBF) neural network. This method uses a matrix of 12 columns and n rows (according to the annual evolution of each of the variable on monthly periods) as input of the neural network.

In some cases, such as the work [33], the neural network is used to predict electrical energy consumption using the seasonal ARIMA model and MAPE (Media Absolute Percentage Error) index to compare the efficiency with other methods. But in this case, the demand forecasting is made over several customers. In the works [31] and [32] the detection is applied individually in each customer. In the same way [33], the work [34] uses a Multi Layer Perceptron (MLP) which processes information about customer consumption taken from ANOVA.

The work [35] combines a Support Vector Machine (SVM) and customers' consumption that has registered 25 months of consumption. In addition, the work [36] improves the results using genetic algorithms and the customers' consumption obtained through electronic-Customer Information Billing System (e-CIBS).

AN EXPERT SYSTEM FOR THE MANAGEMENT OF AN IONOSPHERIC COMMUNICATION: ICARO

Introduction

The use of the ionized layer that surrounds the earth, the ionosphere, as a medium for the accomplishment of long distance radio communications is increasing, as a consequence of the appearance of HF band radio sets joining high technical specifications with low cost and great availability. Added characteristics are high portability, due to its limited weight, and a great independence of other external communications systems as satellites or repeaters.

Contrariwise, the variable behavior of the ionospheric conditions and the increasing number of radio stations using the same portion of the radio electric spectrum makes frequently necessary to be an expert radio operator in order to establish the wished communication. This factor, that raises notably the cost of the radio communications system, makes it especially attractive to adopt an expert system control strategy.

The ionosphere is the name applied to parts of the upper atmosphere of the earth containing free ions in adequate quantity to affect the propagation of electromagnetic waves [37].

The ionosphere is structured in several layers called D, E, F1 and F2, with different radio wave reflecting properties. Because of these differences, the receiving station may get the information by several different paths from the transmitting station, as can be appreciated in Figure 2.

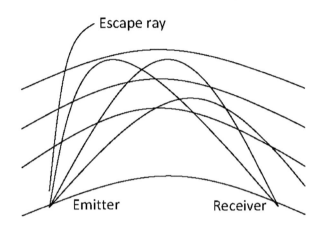

Figure 2. Different ionospheric paths.

The most characteristic properties of the ionosphere as a communications channel are the long term variation, as the sun activity varies with a periodicity of approximately eleven years, the medium term variation, because the sun activity varies with the season of the year and finally the short term variation, that manifest the strong dependency between the hour of the day and the geographical coordinates of the stations intended to link.

It is also necessary to consider the influence of other, different variables such as the distance between radio stations, transmission power and the type of antennas, one of the link quality's most determinant factors. The noise and previous occupation in the frequency that is wished to use are frequently the radio communication's most limiting factors.

All these limiting factors imply that the radio operators must possess a great experience in the managing of their radio stations and a deep knowledge of all the elements implicated in the radio communication process.

The problem of the lack of expert operators is attempting to be solved through a new generation of radio communications equipment, capable of creating and maintaining automatic radio links, the HF ALE RADIOS (High Frequency Automatic Link Establishment Radios). There actually exist several federal standards (FS-1045A, FS-1046, FS-1047, FS-1048, FS-1049, FS-1050, FS-1051 and FS-1052) within the Federal Communication Standards Program for the U.S.A. National Communications Systems [38] [39].

These standards determine that an ALE radio communication set automatically selects the best available channel based on link quality data stored in memory, establishes and confirms the links upon operator command, transfers data, does error checking, and relays messages.

Objective

The system (which was named ICARO) was conceived in order to facilitate the use of the long distance radio communications in the HF band to non-expert radio operators. It presents a user interface simple and effective and establishes a virtual link between the stations wishing to be communicated.

As can be seen in Figure 3, it is realized with common elements generally present in any radio station: a transmitter receiver in HF, also denominated a transceiver, with its antenna and power supply and a personal computer. It is necessary to add a TNC (Terminal Node Controller) or controller for digital communications, in order to separate the error control function from the frequency managing function made in the PC computer. The TNC also includes a multimode radio-modem and is an accessible element at an attainable cost. The HF transceiver, TNC, modem and keyboard are the required elements in a digital communications HF station. Just adding a personal computer running the ICARO program to a digital radio station determines its full automation, so near to the ALE Radio standards as complete can be made the rules set of the expert system that govern it.

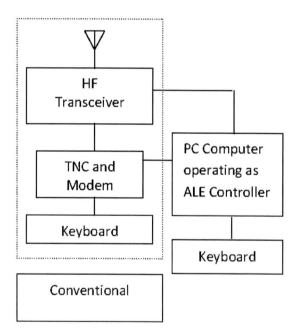

Figure 3. ICARO Radio System.

The expert system uses different sources of data:

- Embedded data from an ionospheric forecast program. Usually these programs need to know [40] the location of transmitting and receiving stations, antenna types, time, day or month in the year, transmitter power, available frequency set, man-made noise level or ITU-R noise mode and SSN (Solar Spot Number) index, related with the solar activity. Given these inputs, the program habitually generates the HF path distance and great circle path bearings from site to site, the best usable frequency for each hour and the corresponding ray-path elevation angle, the received signal power, total noise power and signal/noise ratio.

- Information about propagation acquired by listening to automatically identified radio stations with known geographic coordinates. The system is in a continuous listening of a set of radio stations with frequency and geographic coordinates perfectly known. Every time a station is heard, the time, frequency and identification data are saved in a database register.

- Data from link quality analysis made in an automatic way when the stations are not required to do any other specific duty. If allowed by the radio operator, the system tries to connect to the previously listened radio stations that have radio transmission capacity. Provided the connection is made, a link quality analysis is realized, by the method of taking account of the time spent in transmitting successfully a determined amount of text.

The final objective of the system ICARO is to obtain automated digital communications following the basic behavior of ALE radio equipment but with a low cost, in contraposition to other systems in those which is intended the total integration of the calculation and radio communications capacity in a unique radio set. This last solution leads to expensive equipment of a very exclusive use, which makes difficult its employment in applications where the low level of utilization does not justify the high investment to accomplish.

Architecture

The forecast program proceeds from the ITU-R (International Telecommunications Union Radio Section). This program applies the ITU-R HF Propagation Prediction Method based on the ITU-R P533-5 recommendation [41]. It generates a file containing the everyday best frequency utilizable to communicate two geographic points over the earth's surface. These frequencies belong to a frequency set previously determined for this type of digital communication.

The expert systems kernel is CLIPS (C Language Integrated Production System) from the NASA's Lyndon B. Johnson Space Center. This kernel provides a tool for handling a wide variety of knowledge with sup-port for three different programming paradigms: 1) Rule-based programming that allows knowledge to be presented as heuristics, or "rules of thumb", which specify a set of actions to be performed for a given situation. 2) Object oriented programming, allowing complex systems to be modeled as modular components, which can be easily reused to model other systems or to create new components. 3) Procedural programming possibilities, similar to the capabilities found in languages such as Java, Pascal, Ada or Lisp.

The rules that govern the expert system come from humane expert radio operators in the field of the HF ionospheric communications. These rules act on the transmitter-receiver to establish and maintain a digital link through an ionospheric channel.

A configuration program requests to the operator for the own station initial data and puts all the information in a database. This program will ask for the identification and geographic coordinates of the own station and identification call and geographic coordinates of the network stations and control stations, the type of antenna, etc. The configuration program will also ask for the identification calls and geographic coordinates of the network radio stations and control radio stations.

After the initial configuration process, the operator executes the ICARO principal program and the expert system creates the object's classes [BEST_ FREQUENCY] and [HEARD_STATION] and runs the forecasting program with successive entries, one for every network radio station. For each available frequency indicated by the forecasting program, an object of the [BEST_FREQUENCY] class will be instantiated with the attributes time and data of predicted connection, predicted best frequency and IRS Identification.

Later the expert system initiates the scanning process that tries to hear the network and control radio stations. The scanning process will be effectuated over the frequencies predicted by the propagation-forecast program, situated as an attribute in the objects belonging to the [BEST_FREQUENCY) class and establishing a short connection in order to perform a link quality analysis if the radio operator previously enabled this operation. Every time one of the expected radio stations is listened to, an object of [HEARD_STATION] class will be instantiated, containing all the link attributes.

If authorized by the operator, the system will send periodically auto identification calls that, acting as a beacon, facilitate its localization by the other network stations. These calls will be emitted in the stand-by and scanning intervals of operation.

If the operator wishes to connect with a determinate radio station the system will consider itself as the ISS (Information Sending Station) and the other radio station as the IRS (Information Receiving Station). Also, it will ask the operator for the identification of the station desired to connect and will initiate the ionospheric forecasting program that will determinate the best frequencies, from the available frequency set, in order to establish the link.

The Expert System Rules

With all precedent information the expert system evaluates the possibility of establishing the solicited connection, applying an adequate set of rules. Samples of these rules are:

1. Look for any object of the [HEARD_STATION] class with an attribute of station identity corresponding to the desired station and the attribute of time corresponding to the desired transmission hour. If it is found, initiate the connection in the transmission frequency and at the hour indicated in the corresponding object attributes.

2. If there is not an object with the desired station identity and time attributes, or if it exists but the connection fails, look for any object of the [HEARD_STATION] class representing a control station with the attributes near the desired station and the wished transmission hour. If it is found, initiate the connection in the transmission frequency and at the hour indicated in the corresponding object attributes.

3. After a previously determined period of time without getting connected, look for objects of the [BEST FREQUENCY] class with the desired time and identity attributes. If it is found send a connect-request call with the transmission frequency and at the hour indicated in the corresponding object attributes.

As can be observed the rules test the attribute values of the instantiated objects, triggering different actions in case of positive results in the comparison.

The rules elaboration was based in the sequence of operations that a human radio operator habitually follows. This knowledge comes from twenty written forms and ten personal interviews where expert radio operators tell his/her own experiences. After a trial period, a document with the behavior of the system was sent to the radio operators. Their appreciation and comments were used to evaluate, and modify, the rules set.

AN EXPERT SYSTEM FOR AN EFFICIENT NETWORK MANAGEMENT

Introduction

This system focuses on a framework and a language for formalizing knowledge management descriptions and combining them with existing Guidelines for the Definition of Managed Object definitions (GDMO). It was used as an extension of GDMO standard with the following goals: facilitate the normalization and integration of the knowledge base of expert system into resources specifications, allow developers to specify the storage location and the update method of intelligent management, and provide a way to specify complex management.

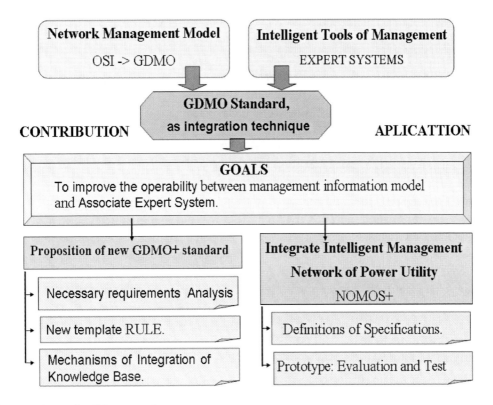

Figure 4. Synopsis of the research.

First, the current management models are analyzed for its evolution and the applications of the expert systems in the network management. The normalization of the knowledge management necessary to administrate the resources that exist in the networks independently from the builder of the management resources is carried out. So, syntactically uniformed normalization of intelligence applied to the management was observed. In the design the new standard called Integrated Management Expert System was used that employs both managed model and AI reasoning techniques for the intelligent management of heterogeneous networks. This technique integrates the Expert System within the Management Information Base. The advantage is that a large problem can be broken down into smaller and manageable sub-problems/modules. For this goal a new property named RULE has been added, which gathers important aspects of the facts and the knowledge base of the embedded expert system. Secondary and in order to show the viability of own proposal, a practical demonstration was performed in which the information and the management knowledge are unified in a unique specification, Figure 4.

Management Models

A management model provides a common understanding between communicating processes in a heterogeneous environment, serves as the basis for a precise specification of network services and protocols and constitutes a vendor-independent concept. At the moment there are two main management models for computer communication:

- Internet: A structured and standardized approach to Internet management. This uses the Simple Network Management protocol.
- The term Open System Interconnection (OSI) systems management actually refers to a collection of standards for network management that include a management service and protocol and the definition of a database and associated concepts: Common Management Information Protocol (CMIP), Systems Management Functions and a Management Information Model.

The fundamental function within OSI systems management is the exchange of management information between two entities: the managing system (the manager or requestor) and the managed system (the agent or responder) by means of a protocol CMIP [42]. The description of management information has two aspects. First, a Structure of Management Information (SMI) defines the logical constitution of management information and how it is identified and described. Second, the Management Information Base (MIB), which is specified using the SMI, defines the actual objects to be managed. The MIB is a conceptual repository of management information. It is an abstract view of all the objects in the network than can be managed [43].

Within the OSI management framework, the specification language GDMO has been established as a means to describe logical or physical resources [44]. GDMO has been standardized by ITU and is now widely used to specify interfaces between different components of the TMN [45]. This specification language allows network object designers and manager/agent implementers to communicate designs and build upon existing designs.

The language is used to define the structure and some of the relationships between managed objects. GDMO is organized into templates, which are standard formats used in the definition of a particular aspect of the object, with rules for how these templates refer to each other. A complete object definition is a combination of interrelated templates. There are nine of these templates: Managed object class, Package, Behavior, Attribute, Attribute group, Action, Notification, Parameter and Name binding [46].

GDMO Standard Extension

The elements that at the moment form the GDMO standard do not make a reference to the knowledge base of an expert system. To answer these questions, it will be necessary to make changes on the template of the GDMO standard. In this section it is described how to accommodate the intelligent management requirements. To achieve this goal the new extension GDMO+ was used. This extension presents a new element RULE, which defines the knowledge base of the management expert system. This template groups the knowledge base supplied by an expert in a specific management dominion. It allows the storage of the management knowledge in the definition of the resources that form the system to be managed. The standard, which was studied, contained the singular template RULE and its relations to other templates, Figure 5.

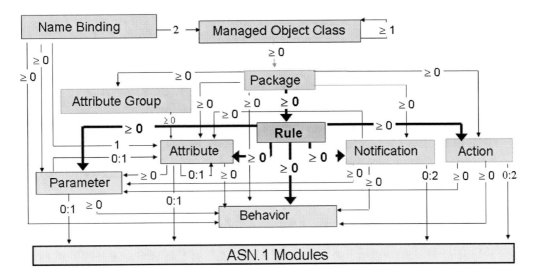

Figure 5. Relations between GDMO+ standard templates.

Two relationships are essential for the inclusion of knowledge in the component definition of the network: Managed Object Class and Package template. In the standard GDMO+, both templates have the new property RULES.

This template is used to define the different kinds of objects that exist in the system. The definition of a managed Object Class is made uniformly in the standard template, eliminating the confusion that may result when different persons define objects of different forms. This way it is ensured that the classes and the management expert rules defined in system A can be easily interpreted in system B [47].

```
<class-label> MANAGED OBJECT CLASS
[DERIVED FROM <class-label> [,<class-label>]*;]
[CHARACTERIZED BY <package-label> [,<package-label]*;]
[CONDITIONAL PACKAGES
 <package-label> PRESENT IF condition;
,<package-label>] PRESENT IF condition]*;]
REGISTERED AS object-identifier;
```

DERIVED FROM plays a very important role when determining the inheritance relations that make it possible to reutilize specific characteristics in others classes of managed objects. In addition, a great advantage is the reusability of the object classes and therefore of the expert rules which are defined. This template also can contain packages and conditional packages, including the clauses CHARACTERIZED BY and CONDITIONAL PACKAGES.

This template is used to define a package that contains a combination of many characteristics of a managed object class: behaviors, attributes, groups of attributes, operations, notifications, parameters, behavior and notifications. In addition to these properties a new property was added called RULES, which contains all the specifications of the knowledge base for the expert system [48]. Next definition shows the elements of a package template, in which it is possible to observe the new property RULES.

```
<package-label> PACKAGE
[BEHAVIOUR <behaviour-label> [,<behaviour-label>]*;]
[ATTRIBUTES <attribute-label> propertylist [,<parameter-label>]*
[,<attribute-label> propertylist [,<parameter-label>]*]*;]
[ATTRIBUTE GROUPS <group-label> [<attribute-label>]*
[<group-label> [<attribute-label>]*]* ;]
[ACTIONS <action-label> [<parameter-label>]*
[<action-label> [<parameter-label>]*]* ;
[NOTIFICATIONS <notification-label> [<parameter-label>]*
[<notification-label> [<parameter-label>]*]* ;]
[RULES <rule-label> [,<rule-label>]*;]
REGISTERED AS object-identifier;
```

All the properties, which were defined in the package, would be included later in the Managed Object Class Template, where the package is incorporated. Furthermore a same package can be referenced by more than one class of managed objects. Like the rest of the other properties defined in a package, the property RULES need a corresponding associated template.

Expert Rule Template

There are a number of different knowledge representation techniques for structuring knowledge in an expert system. The three most widely used techniques are expert rules, semantic nets and frames [49]. This system was designed with expert rules. Knowledge is represented in production rules or simply rules. Rules are expressed as IF-THEN statements, which are relatively simple, very powerful, as well as very natural to represent expert knowledge. A major feature of a rule-based system is its modularity and modifiability, which allow for incremental improvement and fine-tuning of the system with virtually no degradation of performance [50].

In the standard GDMO+ the template RULE permits the normalised definition of the specifications of the expert rule to which it is related. This template allows a particular managed object class to have properties that provide a normalised knowledge of a management dominion. The structure of the RULE template is shown here:

```
<rule-label> RULE
[PRIORITY <priority> ;]
[BEHAVIOUR <behaviour-label> [,<behaviour-label>]*;]
[IF occurred-event-pattern [,occurred-event-pattern]*]
[THEN sentence [, sentence]* ;]
REGISTERED AS object-identifier;
```

The first element in a template definition is headed. It consists of two sections:

- <rule-label>: This is the name of the management expert rule. Rule definitions must have a unique characterizing name.
- RULE: A key word indicates the type of template, in our case a definition template and the specifications for the management expert rule.

After the head the following elements compose a normalized definition of an expert rule:

- BEHAVIOUR: This construct is used to extend the semantics of previously defined templates. It describes the behavior of the rule. This element is common to the other templates of the GDMO standard.
- PRIORITY: This represents the priority of the rule, that is, the order in which competing rules will be executed.
- IF: It contains all the events that must be true to activate a rule. Those events must be defined in the Notification template. The occurrence of these events is necessary for the activation of the rule and the execution of their associated actions. It is possible to add a logical condition that will be applied on the events occurred or their parameters.
- THEN: This gives details of the operations performed when the rule is executed. These are actions and diagnoses that the management platform makes as an answer to network events occurred. Those operations must be previously defined in the Action template.
- REGISTERED AS is an object-identifier: A clause identifies the location of the expert rule on the ISO Registration Tree. The identifier is compulsory.

Case of Study

To show the viability of our proposal, the study and building of a management expert system was carried out, so that the corresponding knowledge base begins to belong to the normalized proprieties information defined by the managed resources. It was provided a rule-based expert system applied to the fault diagnosis in telecommunication system of a power utility. The communications systems employed to implement the integrated intelligent management prototype belongs to the SEVILLANA-ENDESA a major Spanish power utility, Figure 6.

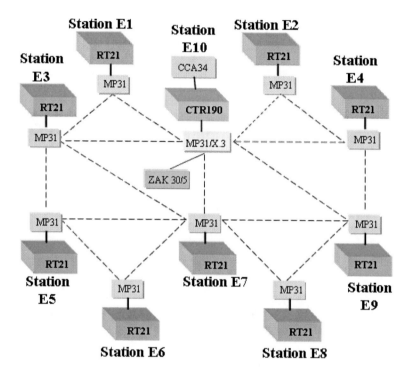

Figure 6. Power Company Network.

Before management and control of that network was based on another expert system called NOMOS also developed by the Electronic Technology Department in the University of Seville [51]. This tool understands transceivers and multiplex equipment. Afterwards an extension of this expert system was presented that integrated the knowledge base and the resources definition into a unique specification. The characteristic of the employed resources and the expert knowledge base use unique specifications. The architecture of this expert management system is based on the principle of the standard GDMO+. To define these specifications, the syntax and rules investigated in GDMO+ standard are used. The knowledge base of this system is integrated in the specifications of the resources using for that purpose our GDMO+ proposal. These new specifications contain management information of managed resources and include also the set of expert rules that provides the knowledge base of the expert system.

The following example is an expert rule named transmissionError, which takes charge of detecting failures in the data transmission module of the transceiver equipment.

transmissionError RULE
PRIORITY 4;
BEHAVIOUR transmissionErrorBehaviour;
IF (?date ?time1 ?local 7_TX_C2 ?remote ALARM)
(?date ?time2 ?local 7_TX_C2 ?remote ALARM & : (<(ABS(? ?time1 ?time2)) 1.00))
THEN ("Severity:" PRIORITY),
("Diagnostic: " It damages in the modulate transmission", ?local),
("Recommendation "Revision transceiver");
REGISTERED AS {nm-rule 2);

AN EXPERT SYSTEM FOR THE DESIGN OF AN HFC TELECOMMUNICATION NETWORKS: DATACAB

Introduction

A typical cable network, which covers a medium-sized city, consists of an HFC (Hybrid Fiber Coax) network, which is made up of an optical fiber network and its continuation into a coax network. Potentially, a parallel telephony network is deployed [52][53].

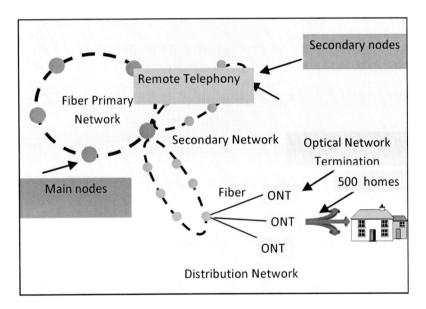

Figure 7. The HFC network to be designed

The cable network structure supports cable television, Internet access and telephony services and it is represented in Figure 7. The structure of the network depends on each country and operator, but typically a fiber optic network is made up of a head-end connected to a primary network, which contains a number of primary nodes, for example servicing between 30.000 and 90.000 homes each. These main nodes are connected to a network of several secondary nodes (secondary networks), each of which typically serves around 10.000 homes. In general, the secondary nodes also contain an RTC (Remote Telephony Center). The tertiary networks (distribution networks) connect to the secondary node and end in ONTs (Optical Network Terminations), which are connected to a Coax Network. This Coax Network finally distributes the signal to the subscribers.

In the design of an HFC network the layout of the first, secondary and distribution fiber networks are normally easy to carry out because the location of their elements depends on the availability of adequate premises. Thus, the part of the network, which particularly requires a deep expert knowledge during design, is the coax network.

When a human designer carries out a coax network design he, in many cases, is only guided by his expert knowledge and intuition, and very basic support tools. The designer works this way: with the help of a specific software which reads and represents the geographical information from a GIS he begins the layout at the ONT (Optical Network Termination) progressively placing the cables and elements and carrying out the calculation of the signal level. If at some point it is not possible to reach the desired level signal on a particular connection with the layout in process, the designer has to redesign all or a part of the layout. Following this commonly used approach, the average time of producing a finished design for an ONT zone of around 500 connections is around 8 hours.

Objective

Datacab is the name of an expert system, which was designed and implemented based on rules for the automatic design of an HFC telecommunication network and which works in an integrated manner with a GIS.

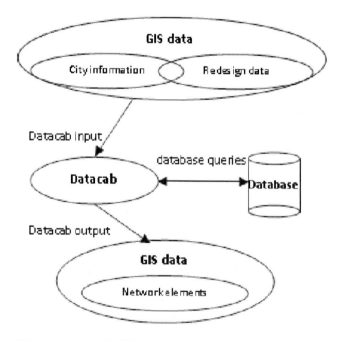

Figure 8. Datacab's interaction with GIS.

The great advantage of the proposed expert system approach is the great reduction of human workforce needed for the design of HFC networks. With Datacab, instead of doing the designs himself, the human expert only has to verify the different designs generated by Datacab. Another important advantage is its adaptability, being possible to easily modify the knowledge base if the design criteria change; and its high integration, working as add-on software to the existing GIS. Finally, similar to other expert systems, the developed system can be used to train new staff.

The GIS into which integrated Datacab is GE SmallWorld [54], a powerful commercial geographical information system with special deployment in the areas of distribution networks like water, electricity, gas, and telecommunication networks.

Datacab performs the design of the HFC network through the phases represented in Figure 8.

- Phase 1: Datacab processes the geographical information corresponding to the zone to be designed, adding it to its knowledge base. The input data of the different elements of the zone with their location and all redesign information (i.e. possible access to accommodations, previous channel locations, non-permitted façades, etc.) is obtained from the GIS.
- Phase 2: By means of a graph representation of the GIS elements of the zone and the mechanisms of application of the knowledge, Datacab carries out the necessary calculations to achieve an optimal solution for the cable network design. Previously, a database access is realized in order to obtain the different parameters, such as the degree of attenuation of the cables or the gain of the available amplifiers for the different commercial network elements typically installed by the HFC operator.
- Phase 3: Datacab processes the obtained information, generates the network design based on the rule database and provides the GIS with the geographical information of the elements belonging to the cable network.

Rule-Based System

When the geographic information is read from the GIS, each element of the zone, like a street or a building, is converted into an object of the class diagram and a connected graph is generated. The designed algorithm was based on Kruskal's algorithm [55], which selects the edges sorted by cost avoiding cycles in the layout. Kruskal's algorithm selects the lowest cost edge in each one of the iterations, as long as it does not generate any cycles.

Note that when a human expert carries out the design of a network, the radio frequency elements are placed at the same time as the layout is determined, which resembles more the second algorithm. However, this approach was discarded because of its higher system requirements and because the first algorithm proved to result in similarly good design results.

The difference between Kruskal's algorithm and our algorithm lies in the dynamic characteristics of the latter one. While the edge cost in Kruskal's algorithm does not depend on the previously selected edges, in our algorithm the cost will be allowed to vary.

Two kinds of edge cost are distinguished in the algorithm:

–   Static cost: the static cost of a certain edge is defined as the cost which does not depend on the previously selected edges for the layout by the algorithm, i.e., the cost which is independent of the state of the layout such as the longitude of a certain street and the necessary cable to cover it.

–   Dynamic cost: the dynamic cost is defined as the cost which at the same point depends on the previously selected edges for the layout; i.e., the cost which is related to the state of the layout as, for example, the cost of a crossing between a placed cable and another cable (the company tries to avoid such cases).

On the other hand, the previous costs are determined by a priority number, which was defined for the firing of each one of the rules. Thus, if the firing of two rules at the same point was possible, the one with the higher priority would be fired and therefore it would get assigned a lowest cost.

Once the layout is achieved, the network elements are placed by means of a group of rules, which calculates the signal levels corresponding to each one of the nodes of the layout. They thus determine the elements of amplification due to the calculated attenuation in order to provide the subscriber with the right signal levels.

These rules call methods belonging to the different radio frequency objects, which are derived from the class radio-frequency. There are two especially useful methods of signal level calculation:

–   Regressive signal-level calculation. This method calculates regressively the level of signal at a certain object. Therefore, it calculates the signal level belonging to an element and all the elements connected from it until the ONT.

–   Progressive signal-level calculation. This method calculates progressively the level of signal at an object. Thus, it calculates the signal level belonging to an element and all the elements connected from it until the different points of connection in which it is involved.

The knowledge data is represented in the form of if-then rules, or, to put it another way, of rules made up of premises and conclusions to which a salience mechanism was added in order to provide them with a priority order. This system of reasoning has been chosen instead of, for example, other kinds of reasoning, such as one based on cases, because the design of an HFC network is based on rules and on the experience of the experts.

There are five main groups of rules in our system:

–   Rules of initialization (R1): a group of rules that carry out the pre-processing of the information of the streets from the GIS, converting this data into DataCab information. In addition, they carry out a series of previously necessary calculations for the execution of the algorithm.

–   Rules of sorting of edges by static cost (R2): a group of rules which carries out a sorting by static cost of the different streets of the zone. This group of rules comprises the rules for the division of zones, e.g., from 500 homes into 4 zones of about 125 homes.

- Rules of sorting by dynamic cost and selection of edges (R3): these rules sort by dynamic cost the different streets of the zone. In addition, this group contains the necessary rules to select from the previous order the edges necessary for the layout.
- Rules of location of elements (R4): a group of rules belonging to the placement of the different necessary radio frequency elements for the correct wiring of the zone. By firing these rules, which calculate the signal level at each node, the different RF elements (i.e. amplifiers, closets, etc.) are located. If it is not possible to locate the elements, it is necessary to go back and fire the next group of rules.
- Rules of generation of the output data toward the GIS (R5): these rules generate the files with the necessary GIS information for the specification of the different elements belonging to the resulting layout, as well as their corresponding parameters.

Firstly, Datacab is initialized and the GIS data are read by means of firing the group R1 of rules. Later, the ordering of the several edges is carried out by means of the groups R2 and R3 of rules. The ordering from dynamic sorting generates a layout. The elements are placed and the signal calculations are carried out by means of the R3 group. If it is possible to reach the desired level signal with the generated layout from the previous phase, the design is considered good and the GIS data generated. Otherwise, another static order is forced and therefore another layout designed.

The total number of rules is 147. Table 1 shows some examples of rules for each group. The table contains 4 columns with information for each of the rules. The first column indicates the phase in which the rule is fired, the second one contains the name of the rule; the third one shows the priority in the firing, with a lower number meaning a lower priority, and, finally, in the last column a brief description of the rule is given.

Table 1. Some rules of each group

	RULE	P.	DESCRIPTION
R1	CONV1	900	Converts the facts obtained in the reading of the file into Datacab objects
R1	CONV2	800	Completes the attributes of the objects created by rule CONV1.
R1	R1-R2	-1	Carries out the additional steps from phase R1 to phase R2.
R2	ONT	900	Selects the edges that reach the ONT.
R2	FAÇ	700	Selects the edges that represent cable preferably over façade versus cable through tubes.
R2	LNG	100	Sorts the edges by length of cable.
R2	DIV	900	Separates the streets belonging to each zone of 125 homes.
R3	CIC	900	Detects cycles in the layout.
R3	AVN	800	Selects edges belonging to main streets.
R3	PRN	900	Pruning of the non-necessary edges for the layout.
R3	ADJ	600	Selects the edges adjacent to the currently selected edges.
R4	CABZ1	900	Places the wiring of the first 125-home zone.
R4	CONN2	700	Places a splitter with one input port and three output ports.
R4	AMP	600	Places the necessary amplifiers for the layout.
R4	R4-R5	-1	Carries out the step from phase R4 into phase R5.
R5	CONV	900	Converts the objects generated by Datacab into GIS information

An Example Use

For this example, a zone of the city of Seville, Spain, was selected. More precisely, a node which is placed at Llerena Street, in the center zone of Seville and which connects 370 points.

Thus, the design of a zone by means of Datacab includes the follow stages:

1. A technician obtains the re-design information of the zone by means of a visit to the zone, which must include e.g. possible access to accommodations, previous channel locations, non-permitted façades, etc. The duration of this stage is 2 hours.
2. The previous information is introduced into the GIS. The duration of this stage is around 3 hours.
3. The GIS generates the gis.out file. The duration of the stage is 28 seconds.
4. Datacab reads the gis.out file and obtains the gis.in file (with the design of the zone) in 1 hour and 23 minutes by means of the execution of the following stages:
   – For each element read from the gis.out file, an object is generated.
   – The properties of the object related to the technical characteristics of the different elements for the design (such as the degree of attenuation of the cables or the gain of amplifiers) are filled in from the database of elements.
   – Datacab fires the 5 groups of rules (R1-5); 125 rules are fired and the result is a design, which includes 350 design elements. The cable structure of the design is shown in Figure 9.
5. The GIS reads the generated gis.in file relating to the design and stores the corresponding information. The duration of this process is 1 minute and 20 seconds.
6. The design is validated and approved by a human expert. The time of this validation is 42 minutes.

Figure 9. A layout generated by Datacab.

This zone was also designed by a human expert without the use of Datacab. In the human design, the stages 2, 3, 5 and 6 were not considered and stage 4 was replaced by a human design, which took around 7 hours.

Therefore, once calculated the total design time for both cases by means of Datacab for all design phases was around 7 hours as opposed to around 10 hours of the human expert, which means a 30% time saving. Besides in the Datacab design the above-mentioned stage 2 made it possible to store the re-designing information in GIS for future uses. The deployment costs of the elements like cable meters, splitters, amplifiers, etc. placed by Datacab and the human design were similar.

AN EXPERT SYSTEM FOR THE DIAGNOSIS OF DIGESTIVE DISORDERS: SEDDIC

Introduction

Diarrhea affects all ages and races, and nowadays it is an important cause of morbidity and mortality worldwide. Infectious diarrhea is the main cause of infant mortality in developing countries. Each year more than 5 million children in the first year of life die due to this cause. Diarrheal diseases are also a considerable socioeconomic problem causing great absenteeism.

Diarrhea is a sign that reveals a pathophysiological alteration of one or more functions of the intestine (secretion, digestion, absorption and motility) and which ultimately indicates a disorder of intestinal transport of water and electrolytes. Diarrhea is defined as increased volume, fluidity or frequency of bowel movements in relation to bowel habits of each individual. Since 60-75% of stool weight for the water, diarrhea is mainly due to excessive fecal water.

Chronic diarrhea is a situation in which there is a greater fecal excretion of 200 grams per day for a period exceeding 2 weeks.

With the aim of diagnosing diarrhea, doctors begin with a diagnostic approach aimed to rule out causes of easy diagnosis or, at least, to guide the diarrheal syndromic and identified three possible starting points: steatorrhea (excessive fat loss in the feces), watery diarrhea, or a colonic disease.

Objective

There are hundreds of cases that can cause chronic diarrhea (from a poorly administered medication to a possible tumor). A large number of them are easily diagnosed and require few additional tests. But, on the other hand, it is extremely difficult to know the exact etiology in a substantial number of cases. This causes medical professionals to encounter many problems in order to make a diagnosis of high reliability.

Among all the documentation the reference point is situated on the main scheme (Figure 10) of the disease developed by Dr. Laso in his book: "Differential Diagnosis in Internal Medicine." [1].

SEDDIC is an expert system, which aims to help the specialist in digestive diseases in the diagnosis of chronic diarrhea.

Rule-Based System

The previously shown scheme covered perfectly the needs of our expert system, in which the facts would store most of the symptoms and patient data, firing them a set of rules for the increased likelihood of some diagnoses (there is a maximum recall saying that no medical diagnosis can be considered 100% accurate) or the discarding of others.

Thus, the knowledge acquisition was structured in a sequential way, trying to imitate the behavior of the physician in his/her medical consultation. This procedure distinguishes the following phases:

- Collection of symptoms and physical examination: In this first phase, the expert system asks about the existence or not of different symptoms related to characteristics of diarrhea syndrome (frequent stools, diarrhea processing time, volume of feces, etc.) and the outcome of the physical examination of the patient carried out by the doctor.
- Collection of early diagnosis: SEDDIC processes the results of the previous step (patient data, symptoms and physical examination), firing a first set of production rules, which obtains a number of possible diagnoses. The result of this phase is a set of diagnoses along with a corresponding degree of safety. This degree of certainty or probability ranges from 0 to 5, depending on the number of symptoms associated with a disease suffered by the patient.
- Grouping of diagnoses by symptoms: The work of restructuring carried out internally by SEDDIC aims to bring together, from the previously obtained set of diagnoses, those that use the common symptoms. Once this task is carried out the knowledge is prepared to be displayed to the user.
- Display of preliminary results: The system shows the first conclusions as possible diagnoses. In the case that any one of the diagnoses is of a high reliability (4 or 5 of probability in the designed scale), the doctor is informed and given the option to terminate consultation or continue with the same process of diagnosis oriented to another alternative.
- First analysis: At this point, it is requested the results of a series of tests and additional examinations on the patient, including blood, urine, stool, and rectal examination. If the patient does not have these results, the consultation will continue with it later.
- Obtaining the second diagnosis: Using data from the analysis requested by SEDDIC, a set of additional diagnoses is generated, following the same procedure as in the first phase in the case that some diagnoses were of high reliability.
- Decision on the diagnostic tree: Once you get the result of the consultation on this point, without a clear diagnosis or without it being accepted by the physician, a decision is taken for any of the three main routes of diagnosis: steatorrhea, diarrhea of colonic origin or chronic watery diarrhea. Once a diagnosis is chosen (the

selection will be calculated with the percentage of symptoms suffered by patients in each one) and checking that it was not taken before, the system will trigger the analysis to that route.

- Route of steatorrheic, colonic or aqueous diarrhea: Once the diagnosis is oriented towards one of these three cases, the system turns on to their analysis and, following the guidance and knowledge relative to the treatment of this disease, it requests the results of other analyses and the corresponding route through the feature tree.
- Route of dark diarrheic process: In the case that SEDDIC arrives to this phase and it dies not have a main diagnosis, it will discuss a possible dark diarrhea and the possible conclusions are obtained with the set of all data.

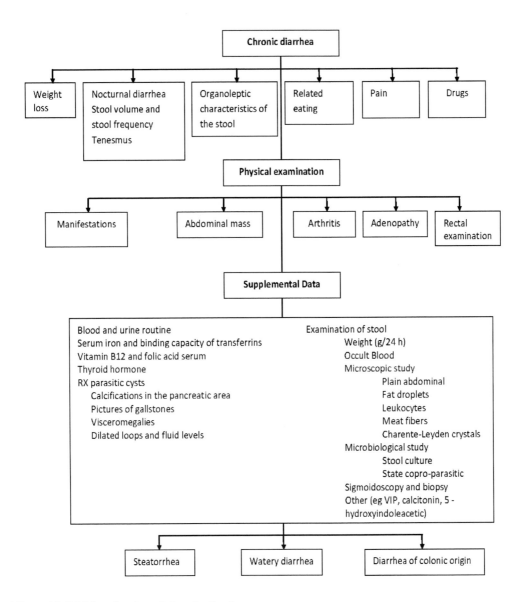

Figure 10. Initial evaluation of chronic diarrhea.

Finally, the language CLIPS was later used for programming tasks and to generate the system. Later, the tests for verification and validation of the system were carried out.

Tests and Conclusions

The first of two essential tasks in the assessment of any expert system was carried out by conducting multiple tests (see Table 2) in which abnormalities were corrected in the knowledge kernel of SEDDIC.

Table 2. Verification of the system

SYMPTONS	TEST 1	TEST 2	TEST 3
Duration	14	7	21
Frequent bowel movements	Yes	No	No
Weight loss	No	Yes	No
Stool volume	Normal	Abundant	Abundant
Appearance of stools	Paste	Solid	Liquid
Blood	No	No	No
Mucus or pus	Yes	Yes	No
Nocturnal diarrhea	No	Yes	No
Laxative Drugs	No	No	No
Diarrhea after eating	No	Yes	No
Pain	Yes	No	No
Tenesmus	No	Yes	No
Hyperpigmentation	Yes	No	No
Telangiectasias	No	Yes	Yes
Eczematous lesions look	No	Yes	No
Dermatitis herpetiformis	Yes	No	No
Oral thrush	No	Yes	Yes
Pioestomatitis vegetans	No	Yes	No
Lower extremity nodules	Yes	No	No
Septal panniculitis	No	Yes	Yes
Streptococcal infections	Yes	No	No
Pyoderma gangrenosum	No	Yes	No
Sweet Syndrome	No	Yes	Yes
Splenomegaly	No	Yes	No
Hepatomegaly	Yes	No	No
Left quadrant mass	Yes	No	No
Right quadrant mass	Yes	No	No
Arthritis	No	Yes	No
Lymphadenopathy	No	Yes	Yes
Fistulas	No	Yes	No
Perianal abscess	Yes	No	Yes

The validation of the system was carried out with the collaboration of Dr. Ovidio Belda Laguna of the Hospital Universitario Virgen del Rocío (Seville – Spain).

AN EXPERT SYSTEM FOR THE DETECTION OF FRAUDS IN A POWER SUPPLY

Introduction

Mainly, the utilities present two classes of incidents relative to the losses of energy:

–   Technical losses. These losses are produced in the distribution stage. In the power distribution companies, they correspond with energy losses related with: wire warming (Joule Effect), distribution facility blemishes and natural reasons.
–   Non-technical losses. Faults and/or manipulations on the installation that induce the total or partial absence or modification of the consumption on the company side. If the company cannot control the consumption correctly it is not possible to invoice the utility and, therefore, an economic loss is produced. The most common are:
    1.   Anomaly. They are produced by breakdowns or mistakes by the company installation technical personnel or by deterioration of the equipment.
    2.   Frauds. Manipulations illegally realized by clients in their installations, with the objective of modifying the amount registered on the meter.

Currently, non-technical losses cannot be forecasted easily. However, technical losses can be forecasted because utility distribution network is continuously monitored.

Utility distribution companies have a lot of information about clients' facilities and their utility consumption. In case of power utilities, there are a lot of customers in low voltage, because the domestic supplies normally have a low voltage. The control of these customers is realized by two methods:

–   Telemeasuring. Usually, in customers with high power connection, the facility has a MODEM. It is used to transmit different information about a customer's facility: consumption, phasors, etc. This information can be used to make a better power supply decision or to make a better detection of non-technical loss.
–   Manual measuring. Normally, in customers with low contracted power, the information about a facility is provided by a company employee, who gets around the client location and manually takes the information. This information can be collected monthly or bi-monthly. Company employees gather information about consumption, but, sometimes, they provide additional information about a client's facility using comments, which can be added in the company databases.

In the same way as manual measuring, when inspectors and technical staff of the companies make customers' facility inspections, they can provide information about customers, facilities or problems using comments in natural language. These comments provide additional information about the customers' facilities and habits.

When inspectors find a fraud or an anomaly in the customers' facilities, they will store all information about it in the company databases. They could use pre-formatted information and comments in natural language.

The inspectors have to analyze a great volume of information to determine the problems in customers' facilities. This process can take between 5 and 15 minutes per customer, depending on the quantity of available information about customer.

Solution

The solution proposed to the described problem is a Hybrid Expert System to analyze all the information about customers. Mainly, the Hybrid Expert System architecture is based on:

- The nature of the information to process will determine what type of techniques or technologies are most adapted to analyze it, since the same methods for numeric and alphanumeric information cannot be used directly.
- The way the information is presented to the user. The activities that the employee develops determine which is the most suitable information format.
- The company infrastructure. The system must be measured correctly to allow the implantation in the company infrastructure.

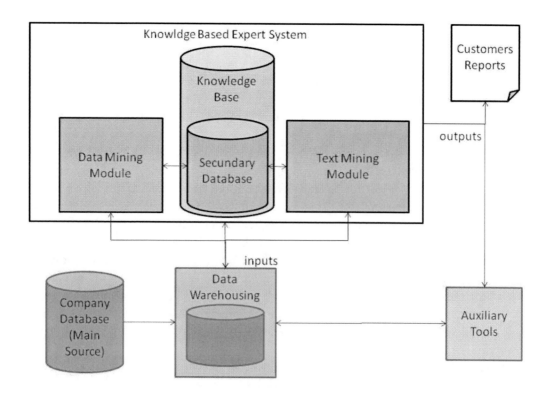

Figure 11. Architecture of the proposed Hybrid Expert System

These conditions are the same for all utility companies, because they use very similar information and volume of clients.

The influence of these three factors is determined by a pre-processing phase of knowledge extraction, selecting the information that can contribute something in the classification and detection process of non-technical losses.

The proposed architecture for Hybrid Expert System, shown in Figure 11, has the following modules:

–   Data Warehousing Module. The company databases have a lot of information about customers: contracts, equipments, locations, customers' information, consumption data, inspectors' comments and documentation, etc. The system cannot directly work with all this information, because the system is busy with other processes (gathering information, registering new clients, etc.). In this way, the information has to be previously extracted from company databases. When the analysis is made on a lot of customers, the volume of information increases considerably. In this case, data warehousing is used to improve the state and quality of information, verifying the coherence, integrity and several kinds of errors (format errors, incorrect values, etc.). In addition, this module provides information to other modules with the correct format. This module provides the inputs for the other modules.

–   Data Mining Module. This technique generates a table of values, which are used to make the utility consumption studies. The trends and ranges of consumption are established by means of statistical techniques. The studies of consumption ranges are carried out through the application of a statistic study which searches normal pattern behavior, but taking into consideration a series of criteria which allow the distinction of one type of consumption from the other. There are a number of key information fields for determining acceptable consumption standard patterns: geographical location, economic activity, billing frequency, time discrimination and contracted power (in other utilities such as gas or water, volume flow). In addition, due to the different patterns that may be found, it may be necessary to establish a temporary division in the information for consumption patterns: absolute, annual, seasonal and monthly. These groups provide with divisions within which are defined normal conditioned patterns by the client characteristics. This technique is used on a great sample to get groups with statistical significance. But it is necessary to pre-process the information: discretization of some values and filter customers with anomalous consumption. Additionally, the table that is obtained by this module allows making reports about general trends and statistics.

–   Text Mining Module. This technique generates a dictionary, which is used to analyze the documentation of inspections made in electrical installation clients. Initially, this module is made based on experience, using concept extraction processes on documentation and inspection comments of customers' facilities. These concepts are organized in several categories that identify several events in customer's facilities. In paper [1] a new method to increase the efficiency of concept classification process is described.

–   Auxiliary Tools Module. This module makes the follow-up of the customers who present certain characteristics in the analysis process.

- Rule-based Expert System Module. This is the main module. This module uses the rules generated by other modules and the expert rules to analyze all information about customers. Additionally, this module coordinates the results of the different modules and takes the decision about the customers' classification. The expert system uses some rule sets classified in seven different groups according to their function. In the power utility case, the system has 135 rules, but client analysis may apply more rules, adding the rules of other modules. There are some rules that have a dynamic antecedent, which is filled with information of the data mining table module and the dictionary of the text mining module. There are a lot of rules because it is necessary to analyze all the information about the customers. In addition, this module gathers all information necessary for inspectors and generates reports showing only the information required for inspections.

Conclusions

The proposed Hybrid Expert System researches focuses in the area of automation of the available information analysis for non-technical losses classifications on utility companies. This system makes following contributions:

- Identification and classification of the necessary knowledge.
- This system reduces the time cost of the analysis. In the performed tests, the system approximately analyzed 14.000 customers in 16 hours.
- This system can be used as a support system for other frameworks. In this way, this system provides a complex filter that removes usually between 20% and 70% of customers who otherwise would be a wasted expenditure, since in most cases they do not have non-technical losses.
- The reports of the Hybrid Expert System provides inspectors and researchers with more information about the client and on the problems presented, as are just and necessary information, using graphic information on a temporary basis. Moreover, in these reports, the reasons why the client has been included in a given category can be found.
- Hybrid Expert System used as a Decision Support System (DSS) for utility companies, using reports and graphics and making the process of selection for inspection easier.
- Testing of the Hybrid Expert System in real cases related with power utility.

REFERENCES

[1]   Liebowitz, J ed. *"The handbook of Applied Expert Systems"*. CRC Press, 1998.

[2]   ITU-T - Recommendation X..711 : *Common Management Information* Service for CCITT applications – 1991.

[3]   Rabinowitz, H. Flamholz, J. Wolin, E., and Eucher, *"J. NYNEX MAX: a telephone trouble screening expert"*. Proceedings of IAAI91, (pp. 217-230). Anaheim, California. 1991.

[4]   Chen, C; Hollidge, T.; and Sharma, D.D. *"Localization of troubles in telephone cable networks"*. *Proceedings of AAAI96/IAA896*, (pp. 1461-1470). Portland, Oregon. 1996.

[5]   Raman, Lakshmi G., "Fundamentals of Telecommunications Network Management," NJ, *IEEE Press*, 1999.

[6]   Liebowitz, J. *"Expert System Applications to Telecommunications"*, John Wiley & Sons, Inc. New York. 1988.

[7]   Ezawa, K; Norton, S., "Constructing Bayesian networks to predict uncollectible telecommunications accounts". *Journal of IEEE Expert, Vol. 11*, No. 5. (pp. 45-51). 1996.

[8]   K. L. Lo, Sabir; S. Ghauri, "Expert System For The Design Of Distribution Networks", *IEEE International Conference on Advances in Power System Control, Operation and Management,* November 1991, Hong Kong.

[9]   Nawal A; El-fishawy, Salah A Khamis, "An Expert System Architecture for the Design of Local Area Networks", Vehicular Technology Conference, 2000. *IEEE VTS-Fall VTC 2000.* 52nd, Volume: 4, 2000.

[10]   Chih-Hung Wu; Shie-Jue Lee, *"An Object-oriented Expert System for Local Area Network Design"*, Computing and Information, 1993. Proceedings ICCI '93., Fifth International Conference, 1993.

[11]   Shurkin J., "Medical Applications. Al moves from the lab to the doctor's office". IEEE Expert 1986: 1. 10-12.

[12]   Kulikowsky C., "Artificial intelligence in medical consultation systems: A review", *IEEE Engineering in Medicine and Biology Magazine* 1988; 7. 34-88.

[13]   Szolovits P, Patil As, Schwartz Wb., "Artificial intelligence in medical diagnosis". *Ann Int Med 1*988; 108: 80-87.

[14]   Kar A, Millea Ge, Shepard Sv. "Pulmonologist: a computer-based diagnosis system for pulmonary diseases", *Int J Bio-Medical Computing* 1987; 21: 223-235.

[15]   C.A.Perry, "Knowledge Bases in Medicine: a Review", *Bull Med Libr Assoc* 78(3) July1992. Pp. 271-282.

[16]   Shortliffe, E.H, "Medical Expert Systems: Knowledge Tools for Physicians", *Western Journal of Medicine*, 145, 1986, 830-839.

[17]   Liu, Chen-Ching, Dillon, Tharam, "State-Of-The-Art Of Expert System Applications To Power Systems", *Electrical Power & Energy Systems Vol. 14* No. 2/3 April/June 1992, Pp. 86-96.

[18]   Germond, A.J., Neibur, D. "Survey Of Knowledge-Based Systems In Power Systems: Europe*", Proceedings Of The Ieee, Vol. 80*, No. 5, May 1992, Pp. 732-744.

[19]   Behera, H.S.; Dash, P.K.; Biswal, B., "Power Quality Time Series Data Mining Using S-Transform And Fuzzy Expert System", *Applied Soft Computing 10* (2010) Pp. 945-955.

[20]   Garcia, Antonio; Biscarri, Félix; León, Carlos; Personal, Enrique, "Estimation Of The Line-To-Line Voltage Phases In Mv Distribution Faults Using Transformer Inrush Currents*", 1010 Ieee Power And Energy Society General Meeting*. 25-29 July 2010, Minneapolis, Mn, Usa, Pp. 1-5.

[21] Sharifian, Hoda; Abayaneh, H. Askarian; Salman, Salman K.; Mohammadi, Reza; Razavi, Farzad, "Determination Of The Minimum Break Point Set Using Expert System And Genetic Algorithm", *Ieee Transactions On Power Delivery*, Vol. 25, No. 3, Pp. 1284-1295, July 2010.

[22] Abdelaziz, A.Y.; Mekhamer, S.F.; Nada, M.H. "A Fuzzy Expert System For Loss Reduction And Voltage Control In Radial Distribution Systems", *Electric Power System Research* 80 (2010), Pp. 893-897.

[23] El-Werfelli, M.; Dunn, Rod; Iravani, Pejman. "Backbone-Network Reconfiguration For Power System Restoration Using Genetic Algorithm And Expert System", *International Conference On Sustainable Power Generation And Supply*, 2009. Supergen'09, Pp. 1-6, 6-7 April 2009.

[24] Burt, G.M.; Mcdonald, J.R.; King, A.G.; Spiller, J.; Brooke, D.; Samwell, R. "Intelligent On-Line Decision Support For Distribution System Control And Operation", *Ieee Transactions On Power Systems, Vol. 10,* No. 4, Pp. 1820-1827. Nov. 1995.

[25] Yujin, Li; Qing, Zhang; Deyi, Zheng; Pengyun, Xu; Baozhong, Wu. "On Operation Ticket Expert System For A Substation Using Object Oriented Technique", *Proceedings Of The 27th Chinese Control Conference*, Pp.2-5. Kunning, Yunnan, China. 16-18 July 2008.

[26] Piga, Erika; Geschiere, Alex. "Self Learning Expert System (Sles) For Power Transformers", *20th International Conference On Electricity Distribution*, Cired, Prague, 8-11 June 2009.

[27] Yu, Xiaodong; Wang, Kui, "Digital System For Detection And Classification Of Power Quality Disturbance", *Power And Energy Engineering Conference, 2009*. Appeec 2009, Pp. 1-4. Asia-Pacific, 27-31 March 2009.

[28] León, C.; Mejías, M.; Luque, J.; Gonzalo, F. "Expert System For The Integrated Management Of A Power Utility's Communication System", *Ieee Transactions On Power Delivery,* Vol. 14, No. 4, Pp. 1208-1212. October 1999.

[29] Luque, Joaquín; Gonzalo, Fernando. "Integrating Power Utility Telecommunication Networks", *Ieee Computer Applications In Power*, Pp. 27-30. April 1996.

[30] Qiu, Wangbiao; Qiu, Zhiyuan. "Design For Symmetrical Management Of Storage Battery Expert System Based On Single Battery", Proceedings Of The 2006 Ieee *International Conference On Mechatronics And Automation*, Pp. 1141-1146, 25-28 June 2006.

[31] Cabral, J.; P. Pinto, J. O.; Gontijo, E.; Reis Filho, J. "Fraud Detection In Electrical Energy Consumers Using Rough Sets", *Ieee International Conference On Systems, Man And Cybernetics*. (2004)

[32] Galván, J. R.; Elices, A.; Muñoz, A.; Czernichow, T.; Sanz-Bobi, M. "A. System For Detection Of Abnormalities And Fraud In Customer Consumption", *12th Conference On The Electric Power Supply Industry*. Pattaya, Thailand. November 2-6, (1998)

[33] Azadeh, A.; Ghaderi, S.F.; Tarverdian, S.; Saberi, M. "Integration Of Artificial Neural Networks And Genetic Algorithm To Predict Electrical Energy Consumption", *Applied Mathematics And Computation* 186 (2007) 1731-1741.

[34] Azadeh, A.; Ghaderi, S.F.; Sohrabkhani, S. "Forecasting Electrical Consumption By Integration Of Neural Network, Time Series And Anova", *Applied Mathematics And Computation* 186 (2007) 1753-1761.

[35] Nagi, J.; Mohammad, A.M.; Yap, K.S.; Tiong, J.K.; Ahmed, S.K. "Non-Technical Loss Analysis For Detection Of Electricity Theft Using Support Vector Machines", *2nd Ieee International Conference On Power And Energy* (Pecon 08), December 1-3, 2008, Johor Bauru, Malaysia.

[36] Nagi, J.; Yap, S,K.; Tiong, S.K.; Ahmed, S.K.; Mohammad, A.M. "Detection Of Abnormalities And Electricity Theft Using Genetic Support Vector Machines", Tencon 2008, *Ieee Region 10 Conference.* 19-21 Nov. 2008, Pp. 1-6.

[37] P. Rohan, *"Introduction to electromagnetic wave propagation"*, Artech House, London, UK, 1991

[38] *National Communications System, Office of Technology and Standards*,701 S. Court House Road Arlington, Virginia 22204-2198, USA, 1996.

[39] R. Adair; D. Peach; D. Bodson, *"The growing family of federal standards for HF Radio Automatic Link Establishment (ALE)"*, QEX July pp.3-8, ARRL, Newington, CT, USA, 1993.

[40] Eric E. Johnson; Robert I. Desordis Jr. et alt. *"Advanced high frequency radio communication"*, Artech House, 685 Canton Street, Norwood, MA 020622, USA, 1997

[41] Radio waves propagation, ITU-R, P *Series Recommendations, Radio communications Assembly,* Geneva, Switzerland, 2010.

[42] W. Stallings, *"SNMP, SNMPv2, and CMIP: the practical guide to network"*, Publication Reading, Mass. Addison-Wesley, 2000.

[43] L. Goleniewski; K.W. Jarrett, *"Telecommunications Essentials, Second Edition: The Complete Global Source"*, Addison Wesley Professional, 2006.

[44] ISO/IEC DIS 10165-4 / ITU-T Recommendation X.722, Information Technology - Open Systems Interconnection - Structure of Management Information - Part 4: *Guidelines for the Definition of Managed Objects (GDMO), International Organization for Standardization and International Electrotechnical Committee*, 1993.

[45] ITU-T, Recommendation M.3400, *TMN Management Functions.* Study Group IV, 1996.

[46] ISO/IEC and ITU-T, Information Processing Systems - Open Systems Interconnection - Systems Management Overview. *Standard 10040-2, Recommendation* X.701, 1998.

[47] N. Hebrawi, *"GDMO, Object modelling and definition for network management"*, Technology appraisals, 1995.

[48] J. Zuidweg, *"Next generation intelligent networks"*, Boston: Artech House, 2002.

[49] J. Giarratano; G.D. Riley, *"Expert Systems: Principles and Programming"*, Book, Brooks/Cole Publishing Co., 2005.

[50] R.J. Brachman; H. J. Levesque, *"Representation and reasoning"*, San Francisco, CA: Elsevier/Morgan Kaufmann, 2004.

[51] C. León; M. Mejias; J. Luque; F. Gonzalo, "Expert System for the Integrated Management of a Power Utility's Communication System", *IEEE Trans on Power Delivery,* Vol. 14, No. 4, 1208-1212, 1999.

[52] S.Ovadia, "Broadband Cable TV Access Networks: From Technologies to Applications", Prentice Hall, 1st. Edition, 2001.

[53] E.Tunmann, *"Hybrid Fiber Optic/Coaxial (HFC) Networks"*, CMP Books, 1st.Edition, 1995.

[54] P. Rigaux, M.O. Scholl, A. Voisard, *"Spatial Databases: With Application to GIS"*, Academic Press, 2002.

[55] R. Sedgewick, *"Algorithms in C++"*. Addison Wesley Iberoamerica, 1992.

[56] F.J. Laso, *"Diagnóstico Diferencial en Medicina Interna"* Harcourt Brace de España, S.A. 1997.

In: Expert System Software
Editors: Jason M. Segura and Albert C. Reiter

ISBN: 978-1-61209-114-3
© 2012 Nova Science Publishers, Inc.

Chapter 10

APPLICATIONS OF FUZZY INFERENCE SYSTEMS IN MINERAL INDUSTRY- OVERVIEW

Michael Galetakis and Anthoula Vasiliou

Technical University of Crete, Department of Mineral Resources Engineering,
University Campus, Chania, Greece

ABSTRACT

This chapter examines Fuzzy Inference Systems (FIS) applications in mining industry using a recent literature review (2000-2010) in engineering and earth science oriented journals. Initially the basic principles of Fuzzy Logic and Fuzzy Inference Systems are presented and an illustrative example of a FIS application, for the evaluation of multiple-layer lignite deposits, is given. FIS applications from the literature review were classified into three main categories corresponding to the major activities of the mineral industry: mineral exploration, mine exploitation and mineral processing. Selected papers from each category are presented and finally, the advantages as well as the trends in future development are discussed.

1. INTRODUCTION

Mineral commodities such as, metals, industrial minerals and fuels are essential for maintaining and improving the standards of living in any modern society. In fact almost everything we use in our society is a product of the mineral industry and agriculture. The life cycle of a typical mineral industry activity starts with the exploration for the discovery and the assessment of a deposit, continues with the extraction and processing of the minerals and ends with the reclamation of the mined area and the post-mining uses. Consequently the major sections of mineral industry are: exploration, mining and mineral processing. Mineral exploration utilizes geological, geophysical and geochemical methods to identify geological structures that may indicate the presence of an ore deposit in subsurface, and drilling techniques for the justification of the previous research results, as well as for the detailed exploration and assessment of the discovered deposit. Mining encompasses all the operations for the extraction of the mineral and the post-mining activities. Finally mineral processing includes crushing, grinding, sizing, sorting as well as separation and beneficiation processes. Exploration, mining and mineral processing are complicated operations which require an interdisciplinary approach presenting unique challenges in their design and implementation.

Most of the problems related with these operations are non-linear and non-random, with large number of interrelated components. Usually the knowledge about mining operations is mainly empirical and it is routinely expressed in natural language. Moreover the study of the geological parameters is based on data collected by means of sampling. Direct sampling of an entire geological formation is prohibitive and consequently the spatial distribution of the studied formation is inferred from the existing samples. This inference is obviously a source of uncertainty. Such complex problems with uncertainty, which are common in mineral industry, cannot be modeled adequately by conventional mathematical and statistical techniques. Recent tremendous progress in information technology in conjunction with developments in artificial intelligence techniques and particularly in fuzzy logic, offer engineers and scientists a new approach in modeling such systems.

Fuzzy logic and fuzzy inference systems (FIS) deal with complex systems, where ambiguous, imprecise or uncertain information is available, or where the real world problems are nonlinear, or where expert knowledge is expressed vaguely in natural language (Hoogendoorn et al., 1999). FIS have provided a new approach to solve many problems that often cannot be dealt with traditional methods. They have the ability to handle imprecise or incomplete or linguistically ambiguous information and to incorporate them into decision-making processes. FIS are computing frameworks, based on the concepts of fuzzy set theory and can be considered as a process for mapping a given input data set to an output set, using fuzzy logic.

The mineral industry has been particularly receptive to FIS since many mining operations and processes are understood and controlled in empirical ways. In addition the orebodies are not uniform nor can be modeled simply. This empirical approach to problem-solving that is based on the existing experiential knowledge can be captured directly into FIS (Meech, 2006).

The remaining of this chapter examines the recent applications of FIS in the mineral industry, the obtained benefits, the emerged difficulties and the future trends. More specifically in section 2 the basic principles of fuzzy logic and fuzzy inference systems are given. FIS development and operation is presented through an illustrative example. This information is essential for understanding the subjects described in the cited papers from the literature review. Section 3 comprises a literature review of FIS application in the mineral industry. This literature review was based on engineering and earth science oriented journals available to Scopus scientific searching platform. The literature was divided into three broader categories corresponding to the major sections of mineral industry (exploration, mining and processing). The list of representative papers described in each category is not exhaustive and consequently the papers cited in each category do not comprise a complete bibliography of the available resources. Section 4 gives the advantages of the application of FIS in the mineral industry, as well as, the trends that seem to have developed over the last ten years across the different areas of mineral industry where fuzzy logic has been applied.

2. FUZZY LOGIC AND FUZZY INFERENCE SYSTEMS

2.1. Basic Principles of Fuzzy Logic and Fuzzy Inference Systems

Fuzzy logic, initiated in 1965 by Zadeh, is a multi-valued logic that allows intermediate values to be defined between conventional evaluations like true/false, yes/no, high/low, etc (Zadeh, 1997). Unlike the classical Boolean set allowing only 0 or 1 value, the fuzzy set is a set with a smooth boundary allowing partial membership. The degree of membership in set is expressed by a number between 0 and 1 with 0 indicating entirely not in the set, 1 indicating completely in the set and a number in between meaning partially in the set.

Fuzzy Inference Systems (FIS) are mainly knowledge-based systems, which uses fuzzy logic, instead of Boolean logic, to reason about data in the inference mechanism. Fuzzy inference systems are also referred as fuzzy logic systems, fuzzy-rule-based systems, fuzzy expert systems, fuzzy modeling, fuzzy controllers and finally simply as fuzzy systems.

In these knowledge-based fuzzy systems, relationships between variables are described by collections of "if-then" rules. These rules attempt to capture the knowledge of a human expert, expressed often in natural language. A simple fuzzy "if–then" rule which relate the input variable x to an output variable y has the form: "If x is A then y is B, where A and B are linguistic values defined by fuzzy sets on the universal sets X and Y, respectively. The "if" part of the rule "x is A" is referred to as the antecedent whereas the "then" part of the rule "y is B" is referred to as the consequent or conclusion (Demico and Klir, 2004).

The basic structure of a FIS, shown in Figure 1, consists of three subsystems: a fuzzifier, a rule base and a defuzzifier. While the fuzzifier and the defuzzifier have the role of converting external information in fuzzy quantities and vice versa, the core of a FIS is its knowledge base, which is expressed in terms of fuzzy rules and allows for approximate reasoning (Czogala and Leski, 2000).

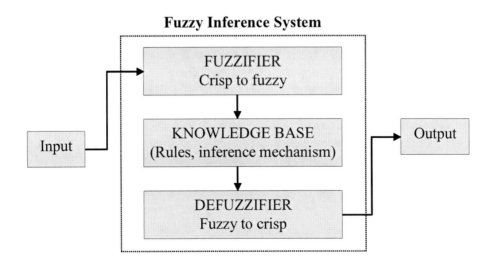

Figure 1. Scheme of a typical Fuzzy Inference System.

Fuzzification refers to the process of taking a crisp input value and transforming it into the degree required by the terms. The fuzzification subsystem measures the values of input variables, performs a scale mapping that transfers the range of values of input variables into corresponding universes of discourses and finally performs the function of fuzzification that converts input data into suitable linguistic values, which may be viewed as labels of fuzzy sets. Such a function is called the membership function and it is determined by the experts.

The knowledge base is consisting of a set of fuzzy "if–then" rules which capture the relation between input and output linguistic variables. From these rules and any fact describing actual states of input variables, the actual states of output variables are derived by an appropriate compositional rule of inference.

The result of each fuzzy inference is a fuzzy set. This set can be converted to crisp number, if needed, by the defuzzification process. The outcome of any defuzzification of a given fuzzy set should be the best representation, in the context of each application, of the elastic constraint imposed on possible values of the output variable by the fuzzy set. Among the various defuzzification methods described in the literature, each of which is based on some rationale, the most frequently used method is called a centroid method. Other available methods are: bisector, middle of maximum (the average of the maximum value of the output set), largest of maximum, and smallest of maximum (Demico and Klir, 2004).

Typically, a FIS can be classified according to two main types of models that are distinguished in the formalization of the fuzzy rules: the Mamdani and the Takagi-Sugeno-Kang models (Castellano et. al., 2002). Mamdani FIS type was proposed as the first attempt to solve control problems, by a set of linguistic rules obtained from experienced human operators. The main feature of such type of FIS is that both the antecedents and the consequents of the rules are expressed as linguistic constraints. As a consequence, a Mamdani FIS can provide a highly intuitive knowledge base that is easy to understand and maintain, though its rule formalization requires a time consuming defuzzification procedure. Mamdani's FIS incorporates the following fuzzy rule schema:

IF x is A then y is B

where, A and B are fuzzy sets defined on the input and output domains, respectively.

The Takagi-Sugeno-Kang (TSK) method of fuzzy inference is similar to the Mamdani method in many respects. The first two parts of the fuzzy inference process, fuzzifying the inputs and applying the fuzzy operator, are exactly the same. The main difference between Mamdani and TSK is that the TSK output membership functions are either linear (first-order) or constant (zero-order). A typical rule for a two input–one output first order TSK fuzzy model has the form (Castellano et. al., 2002):

If Input1=x and Input2=y, then Output is $ax+by+c$

For a zero-order Sugeno model, the output is a constant c since $a=b=0$.

Fuzzy inference systems have been successfully applied in several engineering and scientific fields such as automatic control, data classification, decision analysis, expert systems and many others. According to Hoogendoorn et al., 1999, Sayers et al., 1995 and Sayers et al., 1996, the main advantages of a fuzzy logic approach are:

- Fuzzy systems can fuse quantitative and qualitative information.
- Fuzzy systems can trade off potentially conflicting objectives with the help of expert knowledge.
- Fuzzy control successfully provides a transparent, flexible and adaptable control structure.
- The transparency and intuitive nature of the rule base and input variables adopted in fuzzy logic control system make it relatively easy to develop, test and modify.
- Fuzzy Logic is well suited to deal with nonlinear input/output relationships.
- Fuzzy Logic can handle the model even when the model parameters are not precisely known or when no prior knowledge about the system is present at all. In fact, fuzzy logic techniques use measurement data from the process.

2.2. Application of Mamdani Inference Rules to Selective Mining

Multiple-layered lignite deposits consist of several lignite seams of varying thickness and quality, separated by non-lignite layers referred also as waste layers. One of the most vital considerations in the exploitation of these deposits is the determination of the lignite layers that can be selectively extracted in an economically and technically feasible way. In practice, lignite layers with thickness less than the minimum thickness for selective excavation, or lignite layers with low quality, are not extracted selectively but they are co-excavated with the adjacent non-lignite layers and disposed to waste dump. The minimum thickness for selective excavation and the quality specifications are derived from the limitations of the applied mining procedures and from the consumers' requirements respectively.

The examined lignite deposit is located in the area of Ptolemais in Northern Greece and it is mined with the continuous surface method by using bucket-wheel excavators, conveyor belts and stackers. The deposits consist of many lignite layers with thickness varying from a few centimeters to several meters. The mined lignite feeds a nearby power plant for electricity generation. The determination of exploitable lignite layers is based on the following criteria (Galetakis & Vasiliou, 2010):

- The thickness of the lignite layer. The minimum thickness of a lignite layer for selective mining by bucket-wheel excavator was determined to 0.5m.
- The ash content of the lignite. Ash is the residue of the lignite after its combustion and consequently the higher its ash the lower its quality. The ash content of lignite is the most important quality characteristic for lignite used for power generation. Taking into account the power plant specifications, the maximum allowable ash content of mined lignite layer was set to 50%. Thus the exploitable lignite layers are these with thickness greater than 0.5m and ash content less than 50%.

However, in practice, the decision for excavating selectively a lignite layer is based on subjective and interrelated criteria. For example, relative thin lignite layers with low ash content are more favourable for selective mining, compared to ones with the same thickness but with higher ash content. The decision for selective mining is also affected by other parameters, such as the working conditions in the bench, the demand for lignite and the experience of the excavator's operator. Although these additional parameters can not be modeled easily and thus, it is difficult to be encompassed into the existing methodology for the determination of the selectively exploitable lignite layers. Advances in Fuzzy Inference Systems (FIS) provide a new approach for solving such problems. FIS have the ability to handle imprecise or incomplete or linguistically ambiguous information and to incorporate them into decision-making processes.

A Mamdani type FIS, based on the knowledge of an expert (mining engineer) was developed and validated. New linguistic variables, concerning with working conditions, operators' experience and the required production rate (demand for lignite) were added. The inputs of the developed FIS were considered the thickness of lignite layer, the ash content, the experience of the excavator's operator, the working conditions in the bench and the required production rate. A single output was selected for the FIS, the exploitation index. Exploitation index varies between 0 and 1 and indicates the degree that a given lignite layer is favorable for selective mining. The value of 0 is assessed to non-selectively mined lignite layers, while the value of 1 is assessed to a selective mined layers. Values of exploitation index between 0 and 1 indicate that lignite layers could selectively mined occasionally, under specific conditions. A value closer to 1 indicates that the lignite layer is more favorable for selective excavation. Therefore, exploitation index determines the possibility for selectively mining a lignite layer with a specific thickness and ash content, under certain operational conditions. The knowledge base of the developed FIS consists of 13 rules. Such a typical rule, in verbose format, is shown below:

IF lignite layer is thin AND its ash is low AND operator's experience is high AND required production rate is low AND working conditions is normal THEN exploitation index is average

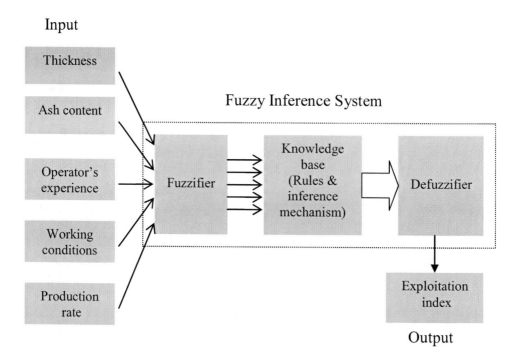

Figure 2. Structure of the developed FIS.

The structure of the developed FIS is shown in Figure 2. The optimal values of membership parameters were determined during training. Typical selective mining cases, representing different operational conditions, were given to FIS as input data and the obtained results were compared to that evaluated by an experienced mining engineer. Based on comparison results FIS parameters (membership functions and rules) were tuned. For the development of the above described FIS the Mathworks Fuzzy Logic Toolbox was used.

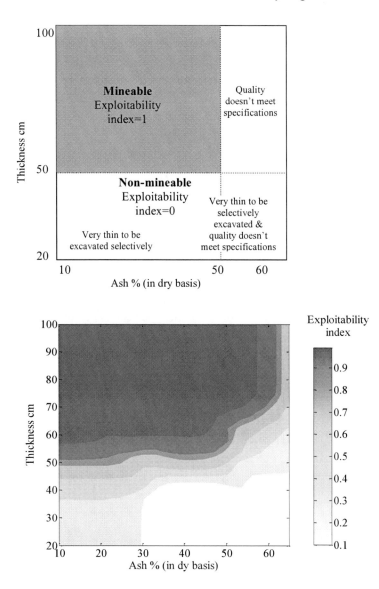

Figure 3. Classification of the lignite layers to mineable and non-mineable by using the conventional methodology (above) and the developed fuzzy inference system (below). For the estimation of the exploitation index by FIS, the operating conditions were considered difficult.

The exploitability indices of lignite layers of the examined deposit were evaluated by the conventional way and by the developed FIS. Three different cases, related to expected exploitation conditions were examined via the FIS evaluation methodology. In the first case the exploitation conditions were considered as ideal, in the second as normal and in the third as difficult. Results indicate that for thick and medium thickness lignite layers with low to medium ash content, FIS and conventional methodology produce similar results for all cases. More specifically for thick lignite layers (thickness> 60cm) the computed difference is negligible. However for thin and medium thickness lignite layers with medium to high ash content, the results are different, especially when normal and difficult exploitation conditions were assumed (Figure 3). Since thin and medium thickness lignite layers (thickness<60cm) may represent a significant portion of a lignite deposit, the accurate evaluation of the selectively mineable lignite layers is of high importance. In the case of the examined lignite deposit in the area of Ptolemais (Greece), thin lignite layers (thickness< 60cm) represent 15% of the total lignite reserves (Galetakis and Kavouridis, 1998). Changing operating conditions (experience of the excavator's operator, working conditions in the bench and required production rate) from "ideal" to "difficult", result in a decrease of ~18% in the mineable reserves. Taking into consideration that mines are dynamic workplaces, where working conditions change considerably, FIS enables mining engineers to estimate the mineable reserves in a realistic way.

3. APPLICATIONS OF FUZZY INFERENCE SYSTEMS IN MINERAL INDUSTRY-A LITERATURE REVIEW

In mineral industry sector, as already discussed, many processes are described and controlled in an empirical way. Because of this empirical culture of mining, fuzzy logic was able to proliferate quickly once a formal scientific basis was given by Zadeh in 1965. Application of this fuzzy theory established a rationale for relative weights of importance used to evaluate deposits, to characterize rock masses, to select mining methods and excavation equipment, to design excavations, to control mineral processing operations and many others (Meech, 2006). Thus it is not surprising that mineral processing engineering and other closely related areas have seen early and extensive use of fuzzy logic.

After the first successful application of fuzzy logic occurred in the field of process control with Mamdani's famous paper on the control of a laboratory-scale steam engine in 1975, a Danish cement industry applied the technique developed by Mamdani to control a cement kiln. This was considered the first successful application in industrial scale. Today almost all cement kilns in the world use fuzzy logic-based control system. In mining the most successful early applications of fuzzy logic were also developed for the control of the crushing plants (Harris and Meech, 1987). Since then many novel application based on fuzzy logic have been developed and applied with success in mining, mineral processing, mineral exploration and other fields of mineral industry.

This review about the recent application of fuzzy- based systems in the mineral industry was based on a literature survey covering the last decade, 2000-2010 (October). Initially all engineering and earth science oriented journals, available to Scopus scientific searching platform, was used. The search terms included the words "fuzzy" and "mining industry". Then the results were refined and divided into three broader categories corresponding to the major sections of mineral industry (exploration, mining and processing). The analysis results are shown schematically in Figures 4 and 5. Figure 4 indicates the total number of the related articles as well as the articles published per year from 2000 to 2010 (October). The rate of published articles shows clearly a significant increasing trend. The percentage of published articles in each category is given in Figure 5. The majority of FIS applications are related to mineral exploration and processing while those related to mining are fewer.

After this literature survey, representative articles from each category were selected and are presented below briefly. The list of representative papers described in each category is not exhaustive and consequently the papers presented in each category do not comprise a complete bibliography of the available resources.

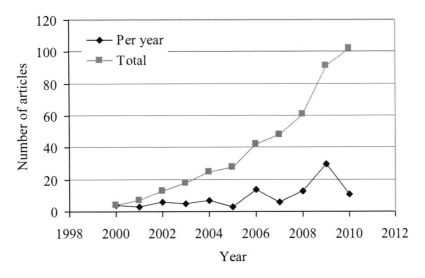

Figure 4. Number of articles published in engineering and earth science oriented journal in the fields crossing the "fuzzy" and the "mining industry".

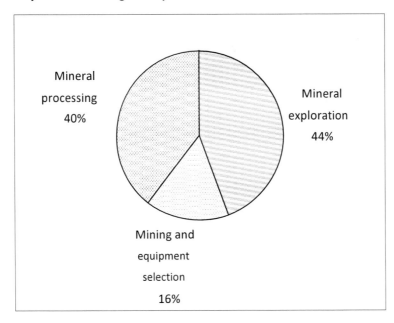

Figure 5. Number of articles published in three categories representing the main mineral's industry activities.

3.1. Applications of Fuzzy Inference Systems in Mineral Exploration and in Reserves and Grade Estimation

Tangestani and Moore, 2003, in their article: "Mapping porphyry copper potential with a fuzzy model, northern Shahr-e-Babak, Iran", applied fuzzy set theory to prospecting the porphyry copper deposits in the north of Shahr-e-Babak, Iran. The geological layers incorporated into the porphyry copper model include: geochemical and geophysical anomalies, bedrock geology, proximity to east-west lineaments, proximity to granitic and intermediate intrusive bodies and proximity to alteration haloes. These data were processed in a raster GIS and fuzzy membership functions were evaluated for each data layer. Areas with high to moderate favourableness encompass well-known porphyry copper deposits, namely Meiduk and Sara. Areas with low to moderate favorableness are justified for further exploration investigations.

Luo and Dimitrakopoulos, 2003, in their article: "Data-driven fuzzy analysis in quantitative mineral resource assessment", developed a novel, data-driven formulation for calculating mineral favorability indexes based on fuzzy logic. Different geo-variables are considered fuzzy sets and their appropriate membership functions are defined and modeled.

Bardos and Fodor, 2006, in their article: "Application of fuzzy arithmetic and prior information to the assessment of the completeness of a mineral exploration program: A case study", discuss the completeness of an exploration project, that is of crucial importance for making a decision to start or to give up a mining investment, or to continue the exploration to get complementary information. The authors discuss this problem on the example of the Halimba bauxite deposit, Hungary. The authors found that there is no single "overall" value to express the completeness of a mineral exploration program, but the main geological, mining, and economic factors must be evaluated separately. The reliability of the results can be quantified by the application of new "uncertainty-oriented" mathematical methods.

Zou et al., 2006, in their article: "Software realization and application of the Fuzzy Comprehensive Adjudgment (FCA) model in the expert-assisted mineral exploration system: A case study of the prognosis of concealed orebodies in the Huize Pb-Zn deposit, Yunnan, China ", take the Huize Pb-Zn deposit for example, are-controlling strata, structures and lithologies are selected as the fuzzy evaluation factor set to construct a FCA model, and its software realization is done through the computer programming. Based on experiments of adjudging the tectono-geochemical data, the prognosis of concealed orebodies has been made. The results show that the mineralization anomalies controlled by multiple factors are in accord with what drilling has revealed. The FCA model has common significance, and it can be used to evaluate events controlled by multiple factors in different fields of: geology, ecology, environment, meteorology, agriculture and economy.

Cheng et al., 2007, in their article: "Application of fuzzy weights of evidence method in mineral resource assessment for gold in Zhenyuan district, Yunnan province, China", implemented fuzzy weights of evidence method in GeoDAS GIS and applied to delineate targets for exploration of gold mineral deposits in Zhenyuan mineral district, Yunnan Province, southwestern China. According to the mineral deposit model compiled by USGS, the mineral deposit type discovered in the area is determined as mesothermal gold deposit. The mineralization associated elements are determined, which include Au, As, Hg, Ag, Sb, Pb, and Cd. The singularity method and S-A methods provided in GeoDAS GIS were applied to delineate the weak anomalies and mixing anomalies related to gold mineral deposits. The detailed comparison of fuzzy weights of evidence method with the ordinary weights of evidence method shows that the former can produce better results during construction of discrete evidential layers.

Li et al., 2007, in their article: "Optimization of the grade index of magnetite ore in Baiyunebo Iron Mine in China", deal with the ore grade index of Baiyunebo Iron Mine in China. The ore grade index was optimized by constructing three system models, including ore reserves model, mineral processing model and technological economic analysis model, and by adopting fuzzy comprehensive evaluation. The results showed that the cut-off grade of magnetite ore in Baiyunebo Iron Mine should be readjusted from 20% to 15%.

Tutmez et al., 2007, in their article: "Fuzzy Modeling for Reserve Estimation Based on Spatial Variability", present a new reserve estimation method which uses fuzzy modeling algorithms and estimates the reserve parameters based on spatial variability. The performance evaluation indicated that the new methodology can be applied in reserve estimation and similar modeling problems. Also Tutmez, 2007, in his article: "An uncertainty oriented fuzzy methodology for grade estimation", presents a new uncertainty oriented methodology for global grade estimation. The proposed method uses a series of fuzzy algorithms and estimates the ore grades based on fuzzy interval arithmetic.

3.2. Applications of Fuzzy Inference Systems in Mining, Rock Mechanics and Equipment Selection and Utilization

Kesimal and Bascetin, 2002, in their article: "Application of fuzzy multiple attribute decision making in mining operations", have discussed decision making in a fuzzy environment for solving multiple attribute problems of optimum equipment selection in surface mining and optimum underground mining method selection. Fuzzy multiple attribute decision making can result in final design that is more practical and financially efficient than conventional approaches.

Karakus and Tutmez, 2006, in their article: "Fuzzy and Multiple Regression Modeling for Evaluation of Intact Rock Strength Based on Point Load, Schmidt Hammer and Sonic Velocity", present a fuzzy model based on Schmidt Hammer Hardness test (SHR) and Sonic velocity (Vp) test have been carried out on nine different rock types yielding to 305 tested specimens in total. Comparison proved that the best model predictions have been achieved by fuzzy modeling in contrast to multi-linear statistical modeling. As a result, the developed fuzzy model based on point load, Schmidt hammer and sonic velocity can be used as a tool to predict the unconfined compressive strength of intact rocks.

Tutmez and Tercan, 2007, in their article: "Spatial estimation of some mechanical properties of rocks by fuzzy modeling", compares the performances of two fuzzy modeling approaches such as Mamdani model and Takagi–Sugeno model in spatial interpolation of mechanical properties of rocks. The results indicate that prediction performance of the Takagi-Sugeno fuzzy modeling approach is higher than that of the Mamdani model. Analyzing the rock properties by standard laboratory tests is sometimes too difficult. Fuzzy approaches provide a promising tool for modeling these structures.

Bascetin, 2009, in the article: "The study of decision making tools for equipment selection in mining engineering operations", has been directed to the research of an optimal loading-hauling system to a power station to be established in an open pit coal mine located

Orhaneli, west of Turkey. Within this paper, the Analytical Hierarchy Process (AHP, non-fuzzy method) and different fuzzy methods are presented as an innovative tool for criteria aggregation in mining decision problems.

Bazzazi et al., 2009, in their article: "Optimal open pit mining equipment selection using fuzzy multiple attribute decision making approach", deal with select optimal loading-haulage equipment in Sungun open pit mine of Iran. Combination of Analytical Hierarchy Process (AHP) and entropy method applied to calculate global weights of the attributes. The weights then passed to the Technique for Order Preference Similarity to Ideal Solution (TOPSIS) method that the most efficient mining equipment alternative(s) could be appointed through distance measurement, so that the best alternative has the nearest (distance) to the ideal solution and farthest from the negative-ideal solution in fuzzy environment.

Li Wen-Xiu and Li Hai-Ning, 2009, in their article: "Fuzzy system models (FSMs) for analysis of rock mass displacement caused by underground mining in soft rock strata" developed a fuzzy system model for the movement and deformation of rock mass on the basis of the assumption that the displacement and deformation of rock mass is a fuzzy event, and from this model theoretical formulas are derived for calculating the rock mass displacement due to underground excavation. The agreement of the theoretical results with the field measurements shows that fuzzy model is satisfactory and the formulae obtained are valid and thus can be effectively used for predicting the displacements and deformations due to underground mining in soft rock strata and the safety evaluation of the buildings on the ground surface.

Cao et al., 2010, in their article: "Fuzzy evaluation on the safety of coal gas station based on a new algorithm of membership degree transformation", built a new algorithm of membership degree transformation and applied it in fuzzy evaluation on the safety of coal gas station. Results show that the new algorithm can be used to evaluate the safety of coal gas station more accurately, rather than with existing membership degree transformation methods.

3.3. Applications of Fuzzy Inference Systems in Mineral Processing

Torres et al., 2000, in their article: "Intelligold – An expert system for gold plant process design", present an expert system for project development teams to use at the preliminary evaluation and conceptual project stages. Information and knowledge from geology/mineralogy, processing, and economics are organized, and recommendations on process options and estimated costs and revenue are given. Success in building this system suggests application to other ores, such as copper and complex base metals.

Wei, Wang and Zhou, 2003, in their article: "Study on the fuzzy ranking of granite sawability", a new method by fuzzy mathematics was developed to establish the dependence function and fuzzy relationship between the quartz content, quartz grain size, hardness, compressive strength and abrasiveness of granite with sawing force as well as tool wear. The sawability of several types of granite was evaluated and classified by this method. With the fuzzy ranking system established and the sawability classification, it is very convenient to evaluate the sawability and select a suitable saw blade and the proper sawing parameters for a new granite type by only the petrographic analysis and mechanical properties testing.

Zhou et al., 2009, in their article: "Intelligent optimal-setting control for grinding circuits of mineral processing process", deal with the operation of a grinding circuit. In this paper, an Intelligent Optimal-Setting Control (IOSC) approach is developed for a typical two-stage Grinding Circuit (GC) so as to optimize the production indices by auto-adjusting on line the setpoints of the control loops in response to the changes in boundary conditions. Both industrial experiments and applications show the validity and effectiveness of the proposed IOSC approach and its bright application foreground in industrial processes with similar features.

Abou and Dao, 2010, in their article: "Association rules mining approach to mineral processing control", deal with analogous questions for nonlinear systems with application to mineral processing. In this paper, a method that can control and provide accurate prediction of optimum milling condition and power consumption, water and chemical additive requirement is developed for mineral plants operation. A fuzzy mining algorithm is proposed for extracting implicit generalized knowledge on grading process performance as qualitative values. Using a generalized similarity transformation for the error dynamics, simulation results show that under boundedness conditions the proposed approach guarantees the global exponential convergence of the error estimation.

4. CONCLUSIONS - FUTURE DEVELOPMENTS

Recent advances in FIS have provided a new approach in solving many problems related to mineral industry, a traditional economic activity which is heavily based on the experiential knowledge. The success of FIS is mainly due to their similarity to human perception and reasoning, and their intuitive handling and simplicity, which are important factors for the acceptance and usability of the mining systems. FIS have the ability to handle imprecise or incomplete information and to incorporate them into decision–making processes, based on the knowledge of an expert. The literature review of the recently published related articles indicates that there is an increasing number of FIS applications in almost all fields of mineral industry.

More specifically, in the area of mineral exploration the main advantages of the application of the FIS are:

- FIS can easily and effectively capture the geologic knowledge that is usually expressed in natural language. FIS also offer a much more convenient way to describe geological variables.
- FIS in conjunction with Geographic Information Systems provide a convenient framework to combine and analyze both qualitative and quantitative data of diverse nature from multiple sources (remote sensing, geological, geochemical, geophysical, borehole data etc). Thus the integration of geological and other information, obtained during exploration, can be achieved.
- FIS can handle effectively the geological uncertainty that is related to the sampling of the geological formations.

In the fields of mining and mineral processing main benefits of FIS applications are:

- FIS can be applied to study and solve extremely complex and intricate problems concerning with issues such as the selection of mining methods or the control of a mineral processing plant. FIS superiority over conventional systems is based on their capability to acquire knowledge from mining engineers, geologists, operators, and other experts and to represent and manipulate it in expert systems in a human-like manner.

- The transparency, intuitive nature, flexibility, and short response time of FIS, make them unique for controlling processes such crushing or froth flotation. Moreover fuzzy logic-based controllers are suitable for on-line monitoring systems (assaying from mineral streams) and for fault detection.

From the literature review it is clear to be a major trend in the use of fuzzy logic in the fields of mineral exploration, mining and mineral processing. Initially, fuzzy-based systems were used to capture the experiential knowledge and to handle the geological uncertainty. Many fuzzy-based systems were also used in combination with the previous developed deterministic models. These hybrid fuzzy systems are combinations of knowledge-based and model-based fuzzy systems. At this time knowledge-based fuzzy systems are more developed than model-based or hybrid fuzzy systems. Another interesting approach that is growing rapidly with remarkable potential for applications in mineral industry is the fusion of fuzzy systems, artificial neural networks and genetic algorithms.

REFERENCES

[1]   Abou, S.C. and Dao, T-M., 2010. Association rules mining approach to mineral processing control. *Engineering Letters*, 18(2).

[2]   Bardos, G. and Fodor, J., 2006. Application of fuzzy arithmetic and prior information to the assessment of the completeness of a mineral exploration program: A case study. *Special paper of the geological society of America*, (397), 217-224.

[3]   Bascetin, A., 2009. The study of decision making tools for equipment selection in mining engineering operations. *Mineral Resources Management*, 25(3), 37-56.

[4]   Bazzazi, A.A., Osanloo, M. and Karimi, B., 2009. Optimal open pit mining equipment selection using fuzzy multiple attribute decision making approach. *Archives of Mining Sciences*, 54(2), 301-320.

[5]   Cao, Q-K., Ruan, J-H. and Liu, K-D., 2010. Fuzzy evaluation on the safety of coal gas station based on a new algorithm of membership degree transformation. *Journal of the China Coal Society*, 35(3), 467-471.

[6]   Castellano, G., Fanelli, A.M. and Mencar, C., 2002. Generation of interpretable fuzzy granules by a double-clustering technique. *Archives of Control Sciences: Special issue on Granular Computing*, 12(4), 397-410.

[7]   Cheng, Q., Chen, M. and Khaled, Z.J., 2007. Application of fuzzy weights of evidence method in mineran resource assessment for gold in Zhenyuan district, Yunnan province, China. *Journal of China University of Geosciences*, 32(2), 175-184.

[8]   Czogala, E. and Leski, J., 2000. *Fuzzy and Neuro-Fuzzy Intelligent Systems*. Physica-Verlag.

[9]   Demicco, R. and Klir, G., (editors), 2004. *Fuzzy Logic in Geology*. Academic Press-Elsevier Science (USA).

[10] Galetakis, M. and Kavouridis, K., 1998. Quality control of lignite produced by continuous surface mining, using statistical methods. *Scientific Journal of the TCG (V)* 1-2, 49-61.

[11] Galetakis, M. and Vasiliou, A., 2010. Selective mining of multiple-layer lignite deposits. A fuzzy approach. *Expert Systems with Applications*, 37, 4266–4275.

[12] Harris, C.A. and Meech, J., 1987. Fuzzy Logic: A Potential Control Technique for Mineral Processing. *CIM Bulletin*, 80(905), 51-59.

[13] Hoogendoorn, S., Hoogendoorn-Lanser, S. and Schuurman, H., 1999. Fuzzy perspectives in traffic engineering. *Workshop on Intelligent Traffic Management Models, Delft.*

[14] Karakus, M. and Tutmez, B., 2006. Fuzzy and Multiple Regression Modeling for Evaluation of Intact Rock Strength Based on Point Load, Schmidt Hammer and Sonic Velocity. *Rock Mech. Rock Engng.*, 39(1), 45–57.

[15] Kesimal, A. and Bascetin, A., 2002. Application of Fuzzy Multiple Attribute Decision Making in Mining Operations. *Mineral Resources Engineering*, 11(1), 59-72.

[16] Li, K., Niu, J., Yuan, H. and Liu, B., 2007. Optimization of the grade index of magnetite ore in Baiyunebo Iron Mine in China. *Journal of University of Science and Technology Beijing*, 29(3), 334-337.

[17] Li, Wen-Xiu and Li, Hai-Ning, 2009. Fuzzy system models (FSMs) for analysis of rock mass displacement caused by underground mining in soft rock strata. *Expert Systems with Applications*, 36, 4637–4645.

[18] Luo and Dimitrakopoulos, X. R., 2003. Data-driven fuzzy analysis in quantitative mineral resource assessment. *Computers & Geosciences*, 29, 3–13.

[19] Mamdami, E.H. and S. Assilina, 1975. An experiment in linguistic synthesis with a fuzzy logic controller. *International Journal of Man-Machine Studies*, 7(1), 1-13.

[20] Mathworks Inc, 1999. *Fuzzy Logic Toolbox for use with Matlab*. User's Guide version 2.

[21] Meech, J., 2006. *The evolution of intelligent systems in the mining industry*. In Proceedings of the international conference on mineral process modeling, simulation and control, Laurentian University, Sudbury, Ontario, June 5–7, 1–30.

[22] Sayers, T M., Bell, M G H., Mieden, Th. and Busch, F., 1995. Improving the traffic responsiveness of signal controllers using fuzzy logic. *IEE Colloquium on Urban Congestion Management*, 207, 6/1-6/4.

[23] Sayers, T M., Bell, M G H., Mieden, Th. and Busch, F., 1996. Traffic responsive signal control using fuzzy logic—a practical modular approach. *Proceedings of the 1996 IEE Colloquium on Fuzzy Logic Controllers In Practice*, 200, 5/1-5/4.

[24] Tangestani, M.H. and Moore, F., 2003. Mapping porphyry copper potential with a fuzzy model, northern Shahr-e-Babak, Iran. *Australian Journal of Earth Sciences*, 50 (3), 311-317.

[25] Torres, V.M., Chaves, A. and Meech, J.A., 2000. Intelligold - an Expert System for Gold Plant Process Design. *Cybernetics and Systems*, 31(5), 591-610.

[26] Tutmez, B., Tercan, E. and Kaymak, U., 2007. Fuzzy Modeling for Reserve Estimation Based on Spatial Variability. *Mathematical Geology*, 39(1), 87-111.

[27] Tutmez, B. and Tercan, E., 2007. Spatial estimation of some mechanical properties of rocks by fuzzy modeling. *Computers and Geotechnics*, 34, 10–18.

[28] Wei, X., Wang, C.Y. and Zhou, Z.H., 2003. Study on the Fuzzy Ranking of Granite Sawability. *Journal of Materials Processing Technology,* 139, 277-280.

[29] Zadeh, L.A., 1997. Toward a theory of fuzzy information granulation and its centrality in human reasoning and fuzzy logic. *Fuzzy Sets and Systems*, 90, 111-117.

[30] Zhou, P., Chai, T. and Wang, H., 2009. Intelligent optimal-setting control for grinding circuits of mineral processing process. *IEEE Transactions on Automation Science and Engineering*, 6(4), 730-743.

[31] Zou, H., Han, R-S., Fang, W., Liu M-L. and Dang, L-C., 2006. Software realization and application of the Fuzzy Comprehensive Adjustment (FCA) model in the expert-assisted mineral exploration system: A case study of the prognosis of concealed orebodies in the Huize Pb-Zn deposit, Yunnan, China. *Geological Bulletin of China*, 25(4), 521-527.

[32] Zou, H., Han, R-S., Fang, W., Liu M-L. and Dang, L-C., 2006. *Geological Bulletin of China,* 25(4), 521-527.

INDEX

D

T

U